D0490348

X400 000018 6038

Neil
high
year
who
retu
righ
fron
tran
into
war
cou
inha
min
in a

he
ve
ble
0s
he
ng
ow
ty
of
es
ho
a-
ife

| 1 | 41 | 81 | 121 | 161 | 201 | 241 | 281 | 321 | 361 | 401 |
|---|----|----|-----|-----|-----|-----|-----|-----|-----|-----|
| 2 | 42 | 82 | 122 | 162 | 202 | 242 | 282 | 322 | 362 | 402 |
| 3 | 43 | 83 | 123 | 163 | 203 | 243 | 283 | 323 | 363 | 403 |
| 4 | 44 | 84 | 124 | 164 | 204 | 244 | 284 | 324 | 364 | 404 |
| 5 | 45 | 85 | 125 | 165 | 205 | 245 | 285 | 325 | 365 | 405 |
| 6 | 46 | 86 | 126 | 166 | 206 | 246 | 286 | 326 | 366 | 406 |
| 7 | 47 | 87 | 127 | 167 | 207 | 247 | 287 | 327 | 367 | 407 |
| 8 | 48 | 88 | 128 | 168 | 208 | 248 | 288 | 328 | 368 | 408 |
| 9 | 49 | 89 | 129 | 169 | 209 | 249 | 289 | 329 | 369 | 409 |
| 10 | 50 | 90 | 130 | 170 | 210 | 250 | 290 | 330 | 370 | 410 |
| 11 | 51 | 91 | 131 | 171 | 211 | 251 | 291 | 331 | 371 | 411 |
| 12 | 52 | 92 | 132 | 172 | 212 | 252 | 292 | 332 | 372 | 412 |
| 13 | 53 | 93 | 133 | 173 | 213 | 253 | 293 | 333 | 373 | 413 |
| 14 | 54 | 94 | 134 | 174 | 214 | 254 | 294 | 334 | 374 | 414 |
| 15 | 55 | 95 | 135 | 175 | 215 | 255 | 295 | 335 | 375 | 415 |
| 16 | 56 | 96 | 136 | 176 | 216 | 256 | 296 | 336 | 376 | 416 |
| 17 | 57 | 97 | 137 | 177 | 217 | 257 | 297 | 337 | 377 | 417 |
| 18 | 58 | 98 | 138 | 178 | 218 | 258 | 298 | 338 | 378 | 418 |
| 19 | 59 | 99 | 139 | 179 | 219 | 259 | 299 | 339 | 379 | 419 |
| 20 | 60 | 100 | 140 | 180 | 220 | 260 | 300 | 340 | 380 | 420 |
| 21 | 61 | 101 | 141 | 181 | 221 | 261 | 301 | 341 | 381 | 421 |
| 22 | 62 | 102 | 142 | 182 | 222 | 262 | 302 | 342 | 382 | 422 |
| 23 | 63 | 103 | 143 | 183 | 223 | 263 | 303 | 343 | 383 | 423 |
| 24 | 64 | 104 | 144 | 184 | 224 | 264 | 304 | 344 | 384 | 424 |
| 25 | 65 | 105 | 145 | 185 | 225 | 265 | 305 | 345 | 385 | 425 |
| 26 | 66 | 106 | 146 | 186 | 226 | 266 | 306 | 346 | 386 | 426 |
| 27 | 67 | 107 | 147 | 187 | 227 | 267 | 307 | 347 | 387 | 427 |
| 28 | 68 | 108 | 148 | 188 | 228 | 268 | 308 | 348 | 388 | 428 |
| 29 | 69 | 109 | 149 | 189 | 229 | 269 | 309 | 349 | 389 | 429 |
| 30 | 70 | 110 | 150 | 190 | 230 | 270 | 310 | 350 | 390 | 430 |
| 31 | 71 | 111 | 151 | 191 | 231 | 271 | 311 | 351 | 391 | 431 |
| 32 | 72 | 112 | 152 | 192 | 232 | 272 | 312 | 352 | 392 | 432 |
| 33 | 73 | 113 | 153 | 193 | 233 | 273 | 313 | 353 | 293 | 433 |
| 34 | 74 | 114 | 154 | 194 | 234 | 274 | 314 | 354 | 394 | 434 |
| 35 | 75 | 115 | 155 | 195 | 235 | 275 | 315 | 355 | 395 | 435 |
| 36 | 76 | 116 | 156 | 196 | 236 | 276 | 316 | 356 | 396 | 436 |
| 37 | 77 | 117 | 157 | 197 | 237 | 277 | 317 | 357 | 397 | 437 |
| 38 | 78 | 118 | 158 | 198 | 238 | 278 | 318 | 358 | 398 | 438 |
| 39 | 79 | 119 | 159 | 199 | 239 | 279 | 319 | 359 | 399 | 439 |
| 40 | 80 | 120 | 160 | 200 | 240 | 280 | 320 | 360 | 400 | 440 |

# PIGS MIGHT FLY

# PIGS MIGHT FLY

*by*

Neil Hanson

**Magna Large Print Books**
Long Preston, North Yorkshire,
BD23 4ND, England.

British Library Cataloguing in Publication Data.

A catalogue record of this book is
available from the British Library

ISBN   978-0-7505-4305-7

First published in Great Britain in 2015 by Dale Publishing

Published in Large Print 2017 by arrangement with
Dale Publishing

Magna Large Print is an imprint of Library Magna Books Ltd.

Printed and bound in Great Britain by
T.J. (International) Ltd., Cornwall, PL28 8RW

In memory of 'Uncle Olaf',
aka Eric Torsten Bailey,
1920–2014

# Contents

# Foreword

My last book, *The Inn at the Top* told the tale of a year in the dim and distant era of the late 1970s, when I and my wife worked as managers of the most wild, woolly and generally god-forsaken inn in the country, in a far corner of the Yorkshire Dales.

Perched on top of the Pennines, four miles from its next door neighbour, with only sheep, grouse and other moorland birds for company, it was the highest inn in Great Britain. That was both its raison d'être and its curse, for while its fame – or notoriety – as the highest inn brought most of its paying customers to the door, its altitude also meant that it was exposed to some of the most extreme weather to be found anywhere on the British mainland.

We had experienced the full brunt of that during our year there, but we were now moving on, not so much because of that, but because we had also experienced the full brunt of the people we had been working for, the inn's unscrupulous owners. However, we left with a pledge to our friends and regulars at the inn that we would try to return one day, should the owners ever put the inn up for sale.

A heartening number of people contacted me

in the wake of the publication of *The Inn at the Top*, both to tell me that they had enjoyed the book and, I suspect more importantly, to try to discover if we had indeed ever returned to the inn, as we had pledged. So to satisfy their curiosity, and to make sure that I have scratched every part of the personal itch that is the story of my time at *The Inn at the Top*, here is the next and perhaps the final instalment of the tale: *Pigs Might Fly.*

However, before reading on, one note of explanation is required. Several people have queried why I chose to call the inn by the *nom de plume* of The Inn At The Top and never used its real name in the book, when anyone who knows the Yorkshire Dales or, indeed has read any of the reviews or articles about it, will recognise it at once.

The reason is that, at the time I was writing the book, my Baldrick-style cunning plan was not to identify the inn in the hope of generating a bit of 'buzz' among readers speculating about its identity and wondering if their favourite Dales pub could be the one featured. This still seems to me to have been a reasonable plan and indeed, *The Dalesman* reported a bit of exactly that sort of buzz from readers, when the serialisation began in that magazine.

However, the publishers of the first book felt that there was greater publicity mileage to be gained from identifying it as the highest inn in Britain, and since they were paying the piper, it seemed only fair to let them call the tune. So that's what we did and the sales figures suggest they may well been right, but I still wanted to make its readers do a bit of detective work so, rather than the inn's real name, I left it as The Inn At The Top.

The second often-voiced query was why – present company excepted – none of the characters in the book were identified by their real names. A few people have suggested it was to dodge potential libel writs but, while that's always a potential concern among nervous writers, my principal reason was to protect the privacy of those I was writing about. Many are now dead, of course – the first book was about the inn in the late 1970s and the second covers the period up to the mid-1980s – but many others are still alive and many of those who have died had children who are still living in the area. It did not seem fair to me to subject them to potential intrusions into their lives by well-meaning but not necessarily welcome outsiders. If they recognise themselves and want to identify themselves, they can of course do so, but that will be by their choice, not mine.

For similar reasons, none of the locations were identified by name. It doesn't take a genius to work out the name of a small Cumbrian town with an annual horse fair, but once you start naming names, they lead on to others, and some of the places are so small that to name the village or hamlet would render pointless any attempt to disguise the identity of the individuals living there. So, with apologies to those who had already been driven to distraction by it in *The Inn at the Top*, the characters and places have been similarly disguised in *Pigs Might Fly*. I hope it doesn't spoil your enjoyment!

**Neil Hanson, May 2015**

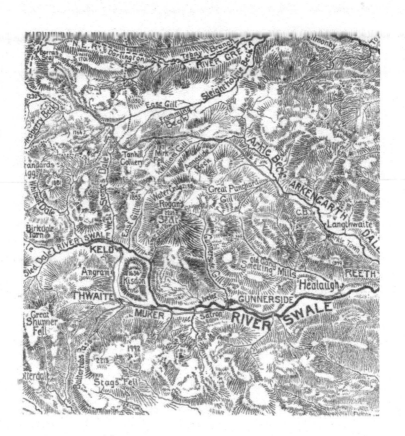

# CHAPTER 1

## The Del Boy Trotters of the North-East

On the last day of April 1979 we drove away from the Inn at the Top for what might well have proved to be the very last time. For a year we had been living and working at the highest inn in Great Britain, set in an ocean of bleak moorland at the northern end of the Yorkshire Dales. It had been our job, our home and our life, and it was heart-breaking to leave it behind. However, while we loved the place and the people who were our locals and regulars, we had nothing but hatred for the owners, Stan and Neville, the pair of Geordie wide boys for whom we'd been working. Sly, crooked and penny-pinching, they had left us to endure one of the harshest winters of the entire century without heat, light or water other than melted snow, and their negligence had contributed to a fall I took down the stone stairs that could easily have resulted in a much more serious injury than the concussion I sustained.

The result of all that was that it was inconceivable that we would ever be willing to work for them again, but we had vowed to ourselves and to our friends and locals that if Stan and Neville ever grew tired of running the inn into the ground and put it up for sale, we would do everything in our power to buy it. Sadly we could do nothing to influence the timing of that – if it ever happened – we could only hope that their patience would run out sooner rather than later. Meanwhile we had to turn our backs on the inn and its surrounding moorland kingdom that we'd come to see as our own, and try to pick up the threads of our former lives. That would be much easier said than done, because we had no home, no jobs and precious little money on which to restart a normal – or relatively normal – life.

Many of our friends and regulars at the inn had turned out to see us off and, after we had said all our tearful goodbyes, they all stood, handkerchiefs at the ready, to wave us off. There was just one small technical hitch: not for the first time that winter, the wind had driven snow in through every chink in the engine compartment of the car – through the radiator, under the edges of the bonnet, and up through the chassis and wheel arches, so that every nook and cranny beneath the bonnet was full of tight-packed and now hard-frozen snow. Having laboriously cleared all that out and checked that the anti-freeze in the radiator had really lived up to its name despite temperatures that had dropped below minus 20° Celsius at times, I found that the spark plugs and distributor-cap – remember those items from the golden age of old-fashioned motoring? – were too damp for the engine to fire. So I had to take out the plugs, disconnect the distributor cap, and then unlock the door of the inn again and go back in one last time. The ashes of the previous night's fire were still glowing, so I raked them back into life and then arranged the spark plugs and distributor cap

18

around the fire for ten minutes to dry them out in its warmth.

Second time around, our battered Morris 1000 coughed and spluttered into life and, after exchanging yet another round of farewells, we set off with the wheels spraying up jets of snow as we skidded across the car park and swung out onto the road. We'd had two bags of coal in the boot all winter, so that the weight over the rear wheels would give us extra grip on the snow, but they had now been jettisoned and replaced with the boxes containing our meagre possessions. Before moving to the inn as managers twelve months before, we had sold or given way almost everything we owned, so we had precious little left now; our entire worldly goods were contained within our car.

The back seat was piled high, leaving just enough room to squeeze in our dog Gnasher – my parents had banned me from reading the *Beano* when I was a kid so I had made up for lost time by becoming a fully paid-up member of the Dennis the Menace fan club and naming our dog after his pet. The slightly fearsome name belied her nature; half-Airedale terrier with an unknown controlling interest, possibly a wolfhound, she was one of the softest and gentlest dogs you could ever meet. Far from having to keep an eye on our dog in case she was out worrying the sheep, our principal concern had been that the sheep might have been worrying our dog.

Both of us had lumps in our throats as we turned the corner on to the road leading down into the Dale and watched the familiar shape of the inn, outlined on the horizon against the grey scudding clouds, dwindle in the rear-view mirror and then disappear from sight altogether as the road dipped. The evidence of the bitter winter of 1978–79 – right up there with 1947 and 1963 as one of the worst of the entire century – was all around us. It had left snowdrifts twenty and thirty feet deep in places and even here, where the wind tended to scour the exposed areas of the moor clear of snow, at every dip in the road, we found ourselves driving past walls of snow that were piled up head-high on either side of us. Only the tops of the ten-foot snow poles stood out above the snow. Even when snowdrifts had buried every other feature of the landscape, leaving it a wilderness of white, the snow poles, banded with hoops of black and red, marked the line of the road for the drivers of the snow-ploughs and snow-blowers. However, after months of blizzards, high winds and savage frosts, the snow had been so hard frozen and compacted that neither snow-ploughs nor snow-blowers could make any impression on it and in the end, the council workers had been forced to use JCBs to cut through the drifts, piling up the snow at the side of the road one block at a time.

Since the road had been re-opened, wherever rising ground gave a little shelter, the wind had dumped low drifts of fresh snow across the road and we had to keep up enough speed to plough through them and reach the next stretch where the wind had blown the snow off the road instead, leaving the tarmac exposed. We were very aware that we were lucky to be getting out when we did. After over three months in which we had been cut off by snowdrifts for all but a handful of days, including one continuous spell of eleven weeks, a thaw had then proved to be just another false dawn and yet another ferocious blizzard had once more cut off the inn for a couple of weeks until the snow-blowers carved a way through to us once more. In that dismal spring of 1979 it would have been no surprise to find the roads being blocked by yet another snowstorm even in May, so we kept a wary eye on the grey clouds overhead as we drove on.

At Level Hill, a stream tumbled down the hillside, its waters stained orange by the rusting iron from the long-abandoned mine workings that gave the hill its name – a level being a tunnel driven into the hillside to provide access to, or drainage from the coalface. Looking up to our left towards the top of the moor, on the skyline above us we could see the silhouettes of the day's first Pennine Way walkers trudging towards the inn through the snow covering the fells. They were in for a disappointment because, despite having given them more than a month's notice that we would be leaving, and that was a lot more courtesy than they deserved, the inn's dodgy owners, Neville and Stan – the Del Boy Trotters of the North-East, but without the charm – had not yet got around to appointing new managers, so the doors of the inn would be remaining closed for the time being.

We crossed the bleak plateau below the moor-top, where the dun-coloured fells surrounding the road were dotted with the peat-stained, off-white fleeces of the sheep. They were browsing among the remaining snowdrifts in a probably forlorn search for the first growth of new grass – the 'early bite' as the farmers called it – the dense grey-green tufts of sheep's fescue that thrived on these barren, acid moorlands where other grasses would simply have withered and died.

At the far side of the plateau we crested another hill and passed down the other side through the tiny hamlet of half a dozen houses – our long-range next-door neighbours – where we stopped to say another sad farewell, this time to the farmer's wife who lived in one of them. On several occasions during the months when we were snowed in, she had baked a cake or some scones for us, parcelled them up and given them to her son to deliver to us while he was out foddering his sheep high on the fells. He would leave them for us at the outlying barn where he stored a few bales of hay and I would then trek down through the snow to pick them up and take them back to the inn. They were invariably eaten within twenty-four hours and the knowledge that we were not forgotten was almost as good for our morale as the taste of those delicious cakes and scones.

After a last word with her and a promise 'not to be strangers', we then drove on down the preci-pitous, one in four hill at the far end of the ham-let. The corkscrewing double bend in the middle of it caused many of the summer visitors palpi-tations and prevented anything bigger than a farm wagon from reaching the inn from that direction. At the foot of the hill we crossed the river for the last time. In the heat of high summer we had sometimes swum in one of its deep pools at the foot of a waterfall that churned the water like a natural Jacuzzi, but now its brown, peaty waters were ice-cold, swollen with snow-melt, and surging angrily over the falls that punctuated its course.

We turned down the road that ran the length of the Dale and followed it alongside the river for another few miles, exchanging a wave with one of our regulars who was out foddering his sheep in a field at the side of the road. Then we turned south and began climbing out of the 'Beautiful Dale', as it was christened in the song that was the local anthem. It had been sung by an inebriated 'choir' of our regulars on many Sunday nights, when the farmers came to the inn from as much as thirty miles away to talk, drink and argue about tups and yows until the sheep came home.

As we rounded a bend near the top of the climb, we had our last sight of the Dale – and who knew how long it would be before we'd see that beautiful prospect again? It was one of the finest views in Britain, with the wild moorland suddenly opening onto the narrow, almost hidden dale, with its patchwork of jewel-like hay meadows, neat dry stone walls and stone field barns, and the river's sinuous course – silvered by that cold Northern light – winding among them like a stream of mercury.

We drove on, reaching the summit of the pass, a moorland watershed that was almost as high and barren as that surrounding the Inn at the Top, and dropped down onto the broad valley floor of the neighbouring dale. Whereas our Dale was narrow, dramatic and closed off from the outside world by its high walls, this one, carved into a broad U-shape by the Ice Age glacier that had gouged its way through it, always seemed – admittedly on the basis of no hard evidence whatsoever – a gentler place where life might be a little easier and farming, if no less hard work, could also be a more financially rewarding occupation.

We drove up the narrow cobbled street of the small market town, past the shops where we used to buy most of our supplies for the inn: the baker where we had bought our bread and pies, the old-fashioned grocer who supplied our cheese and the chemist where, strangely enough, we had bought our wines and spirits. At the top of the main street we turned off past the factory where they made the cheese that Wallace and Gromit would one day make world famous, and passed through the tiny hamlet where that fine travel writer Geoffrey Moorhouse lived, a man who had forever en-deared himself to me by naming a pair of curlews as his luxury on Desert Island Discs, so that wherever in the world he might be, he had only to hear the cry of the curlew to be transported in his mind back to the Yorkshire Dales. We shared a love of rugby league as well as the Dales and had become friends, but this was not the day for a social call. Instead we began the long climb up a road that clung dizzyingly to the side of a steep escarpment below the fell-top. The rising air cur-rents that were always sweeping up the face of the cliff at the top of the climb normally made it a magnet for hang-gliders, but none were airborne this early on a frigid, grey spring morning.

We passed over the Roman road running arrow-straight along the summit ridge and crossed the

24

narrow plateau separating us from the next in the series of dales we had to cross. As a rule we would have paused to enjoy the stunning views in all directions, including the familiar, distinctive profile of Yorkshire's highest mountain that overlooked my eccentric Uncle Olaf's country estate. However on this sad day we had little appetite for sightseeing and we at once began the plunge down through a tiny side-dale. At its heart was a hamlet with a beautiful old hall where Charles I was said to have once stayed, and a stone chapel in Venetian style that had been designed by John Ruskin. We emerged from that little side-valley near the head of the second most beautiful of all the dales and followed the river down dale.

Running alongside the road, the river was at first little more than a mountain stream, splashing over the flat slabs of rock that formed the riverbed but, fed by hundreds of moorland streams, it swelled rapidly in size. The numerous pools and small waterfalls and the easy access to the river from the grassy banks made this stretch a popular picnic spot in summer and in a few weeks time, there would be the sound of children's laughter as they splashed in the water, while their parents watched indulgently from the banks, but in this cold spring there was still a chill in the air, and the fast-rushing river and the road that ran alongside it were deserted.

We passed through a hamlet with a fine old pub – such a favourite spot of the great Yorkshire writer, J. B. Priestley, that he left instructions that his ashes were to be buried in the graveyard of the twelfth century church across the river. By ancient tradition, reportedly dating back to the days when the pub served as the vicarage for the church and a lit candle showed that the vicar was in, whenever the pub was open, a lighted candle was still placed in the window.

We drove on along the winding, often single-tracked road into a dale that was bursting into spring. Up at the Inn at the Top it was still winter – spring was always a month later, and autumn a month earlier on those cold, windswept 'tops' than in the dales below. One visitor in late September reported 'a warm summer like day in the valley below' but when he reached the inn 'found water frozen here and the ground white as winter with hoar frost'. The Honourable John Byng, touring through the area in the late eighteenth century, wrote that even in June, 'In such a distant quarter of the Metropolis as this is, only visited by some (foolish, romantic) tourists, or shooters; else they are shut up in winter, or in snow, for the snow was not wasted till a month ago and since that, the ground has been covered by hailstones!' Like many upper-crust travellers of that era, Byng found the Northern moors and fells not at all to his taste. 'Now gentle reader,' he wrote. 'If thou hast only travelled to Hackney or Clapham, you can form but little idea of the country I have traversed, or of the roads I have trodden today; the one, all black, miserable moor, and the other sharp pavement, which if quitted, you plunge into a bog.'

Not much had changed in the intervening centuries and snow had even been recorded at the Inn at the Top in the first week of August. However in the gentler spring climate of this dale, violets and primroses were already studding the grassy banks alongside the road, bluebells were painting the floor of the still-shadowed woods on the lower slopes and the leaves of every tree were bursting into life, opening in a multitude of different vivid shades of green.

That air of rebirth and renewal helped to lift our spirits a little as we drove on, and we began to turn our thoughts to the urgent topic of what would come next for us. We had made a few tentative enquiries before we left the inn, but with the radio telephone still not working – its aerial had been encased in a sheath of ice all winter, and when the generator failed, the batteries that powered the telephone had gone flat – it had proved difficult to do much more than post out our CV's and send a few speculative letters.

We'd arranged to stay with my mother for a couple of weeks while we found our feet and planned our next move – with no home, no job and precious little money, we had nowhere else to go. She lived on the fringes of Saltaire, a model village clustered around a huge textile mill, three miles outside the 'woolopolis' of Bradford, a city built on the wool textile trade and once one of the richest cities in Britain. Bradfordians used to say with characteristic Yorkshire pride that shaded into braggadocio, 'There are more Rolls Royces on the streets of Bradford than there are on the streets of London'.

That might well once have been true. I can still vividly remember the Rolls-Royce owning parents of one friend of mine. His father – I never discovered his christian name, since even his wife

27

never used it, preferring to refer to him only by his surname, but let's call him 'Clough' – was a mill owner, but it was a small mill by Bradford standards and he was by no means among the wealthiest of his peer group. However, he was certainly rich enough to afford a Rolls and the lifestyle to go with it, albeit one with a characteristically Yorkshire flavour. Three or four nights a week, the chauffeur would be summoned to bring the Rolls-Royce round to the front door of their mansion, which was flanked by mock-Corinthian columns. Mr and Mrs Clough would then emerge, Mr Clough dressed in evening suit, including cummerbund and spats, and his wife dripping with diamonds and wearing a mink coat.

'All right love?' Mrs Clough used to say to me. 'Me and Clough are just off to Harry's, aren't we, love?'

And they would climb into the back of the Roller and sally forth to Harry Ramsden's famous fish and chip emporium at White Cross, on the outskirts of Bradford and Leeds. There, beneath the chandeliers in the cafe, Clough and Mrs Clough would dine out in style on best haddock and chips, fried in beef dripping – no ketchup of course, just salt and vinegar – with bread-and-butter and a cup of tea on the side, and the chauffeur would then drive them home again.

I still saw them occasionally driving around in their now ageing Rolls-Royce, but Roller-driving Bradford woolmen were a dying breed. If that Bradfordian boast had ever been true, it now no longer held water. Bradford was a city in decline, its textile mills closing down one by one, while others burned down in mysterious fires that, if the rumour mill around the city was to be believed, left at least some of their owners shedding a few crocodile tears for the television cameras before hurrying off to collect their insurance money.

I had an emotional reunion with my mother. I had barely seen her in the course of the year since we moved to the inn and not at all since her last visit there the previous September, and I was shocked at how much she seemed to have changed and aged in that time. The straight-backed, well-upholstered figure that she had cut throughout my life was now visibly diminished, her hair chalk-white and thinning, her shoulders a little hunched and her features more angular, the skin stretched tauter over her cheekbones. However, her smile was as warm and open as ever, and she dismissed any questions about her health with a chuckle. So I hid my concerns from her, and we settled in, caught up on each other's news and then Sue and I began to give serious thought to what our next step should be.

For a year we had been living almost as insular and isolated an existence as if we had been marooned on a desert island – albeit one with a very large number of day-trippers constantly dropping in. In that pre-satellite television era, there was no TV reception on our bleak mountain top, and in any case, in an inn that was perman-ently busy whenever the roads weren't blocked by snow, we'd have had no time to watch it, even if we could have got a signal. We had no radio either and though the postman delivered a daily newspaper along with the mail – or at least he had done so until the snow began to fall and he stopped calling – the only people with enough time to read it were the customers.

From Christmas onwards, the weather had closed in, the postman no longer included us on his round and the vast majority of would-be customers gave up on any attempt to reach us. Apart from a handful of brave or foolhardy customers who had battled their way up through the snowdrifts and as a result usually became snowed in with us for anything from a few days to a few weeks for their pains, and one solitary farmer who had trekked up through the snowdrifts to buy cigarettes because he'd run out of them, and had also drunk the last bottle of beer in the entire place while he was at it – we'd seen no one at all. Our only contact with the outside world, the radio telephone, had ceased to work and since the snow began to fall, we had been almost permanently cut off by snowdrifts. Already without any newspapers or mail, we were unable even to catch up with the news of the outside world through conversations with our regulars and visitors, since there were virtually none of either of those. Had the Martians invaded Earth during those frigid weeks and months, we would probably only have found out about it if one of them had popped in to the inn for a drink.

We were now back in the real world again but, if still uninvaded by Martians, the mainland Britain we had rejoined had nonetheless undergone some profound changes during our twelve month absence from it; nothing was ever going to be quite the same again. While we had been battling for our survival, buried in the snowdrifts at the Inn at the Top, the rest of Britain had been enduring a winter that was almost as miserable, albeit for rather different reasons. Although nowhere near as extreme, the winter weather in the lowlands had been no joke either, but the discomforts from the cold, snow and ice had been made far worse by what the tabloid newspapers, with unusually Shakespearian overtones, had christened 'The Winter of Discontent'.

The then Labour Prime Minister, James Callaghan's avuncular, 'Farmer Jim' act and his promise to 'sort all this out with the unions with a chat over a pint and a few sandwiches', had been wearing more than a little thin as strike succeeded strike all through that winter. It was pure karma for Callaghan, who had been one of the prime movers in torpedoing his Labour colleague Barbara Castle's 'In Place of Strife' union legislation which, had it been passed into law by Parliament, would have made most of the industrial actions that winter illegal. Now he was paying the price. Inflation was out of control and workers in a score of key industries: car workers, hospital porters, dustbin men, power workers, lorry-, train-, petrol tanker- and ambulance-drivers, and even grave-diggers – had been and in many, cases still were out on strike in support of their demands for substantial pay rises. Depending on your political point of view, they were either taking totally justifiable action to defend their living standards at a time of wage freezes and rapidly rising inflation, or were simply 'holding the country to ransom'.

Three days after we left the inn, the 1979

General Election was held – the news that an election was pending had also passed us by up there – and it resulted in a comprehensive defeat for Jim Callaghan and a victory for the Conservative 'new broom' Margaret Thatcher that was attributed by most political commentators to the after-effects of the Winter of Discontent and her pledge to get tough with the unions. The 'Loadsamoney' era was now beginning ... though not for us, since we didn't have any, nor much prospect of earning any.

Apart from the Winter of Discontent, one other factor was increasing the general feeling of doom and despair in Britain. Despite an unprecedented police manhunt, the Yorkshire Ripper was still at large. If that both horrified and fascinated the rest of the country in apparently equal measure, in the North and especially in Yorkshire, where the majority of his killings had taken place, the knowledge that a psychotic killer was still on the loose was tainting almost every aspect of daily life. Even up at the inn we had not been immune to the fear that was gripping the country and a combination of our own paranoid imaginations and a touch of cabin fever had even convinced us that one of the two people snowed in with us for several weeks actually was the Yorkshire Ripper. To say that our sleep was troubled by that thought was the understatement of the century. As an engineer with a Tyne- or Wear-side accent – as a Yorkshireman with a Welsh wife, I didn't feel qualified to differentiate between the two – who regularly travelled all over the North, he fitted the profile that the police had publicised just before we lost touch with the world, and there was certainly something a little odd about him. However, after a couple of weeks of paralysing fear about having the Yorkshire Ripper under our roof, the object of our paranoid suspicions of course turned out to be a perfectly harmless individual.

The Ripper had killed his tenth victim in April 1979, just three weeks before we arrived to stay with my mother, and I had the proof of just how all-pervasive the fear he engendered had become when I took our dog for a walk on the first evening that we were staying with her. She lived in a small semi-detached house in a perfectly ordinary suburb of Bradford – exactly the sort of suburb where the Ripper turned out to have been living all the time, of course, though no one knew that until he was finally caught, two years later, in 1981. However, even after dark, there was nothing in the well-lit, suburban streets lined with houses with neatly tended gardens that surrounded my mother's home to cause anyone the slightest feeling of concern in normal times, but then, these were very definitely not normal times.

With the dog padding faithfully along at my heels, I turned the corner at the bottom of my mother's street and began to walk along the road. I had gone a short distance when I saw a woman turn the corner at the far end, about 100 yards away, and begin walking towards me. She had only gone a few strides when she caught sight of me as I entered the glow of one of the street lamps. Her footsteps faltered and she froze, staring towards me. I guessed at once what she must have been thinking: Is it the Ripper?

I tried to reassure her by calling out 'It's all right, I'm just walking my dog,' and turned to point to the dog, only to discover that she had chosen that precise moment to disappear up the grassy track leading to the local tennis courts in pursuit of an enticing smell, and was now nowhere to be seen. By the time I looked round again, the woman had turned on her heel and, with an occasional fearful glance back over her shoulder, was hurrying back the way she had come. From then on, whenever I was walking anywhere after dark I deliberately crossed to the other side of the street if I saw a woman on the same side as me, but in truth, there were very few women venturing out alone after dark anyway.

In their desperation to catch the Ripper, at times the West Yorkshire police had been reduced to what appeared to be clutching at straws, and they were also evidently turning a blind eye to various crimes and misdemeanours that would normally have guaranteed a trip to the nick. Just days after we had left the inn, my brother and his wife had arrived from New Zealand for a long-planned return visit to the old country – he's never forgiven me for giving up the inn before he had had time to turn up and down a few free pints there! We hadn't seen each other in five years and in celebration of our brotherly reunion we went on a pub crawl around Bradford with a couple of old friends. As we drove back, with my brother already dozing on the back-seat – he claimed it was just the effects of jet lag but I have my doubts – and with the designated driver having had at least two more pints of beer than was either sensible or, come to that, legal, we were pulled over by a police patrol. 'Well, there goes my licence,' our friend said, with a heavy sigh.

However, when he wound down the window and prepared to meet his fate, the policeman who approached the car merely said 'It's all right, lads, relax. I'm not bothered about anything you might have been up to tonight, nor how much you've been drinking, I just want to see your teeth.'

Exchanging baffled looks with each other, we all – including my brother, once he'd been roused from his slumbers – bared our teeth at the policeman, who then shrugged and said 'All right, lads, off you go, then. Drive carefully.'

No explanation for that strange behaviour was offered at the time, but I later discovered through a chat with a journalist who was cultivating one of the police in the 'Ripper Squad', that a bite mark on one of the bodies of his victims had shown them that the Yorkshire Ripper had a gap between his front teeth, and that was what our policeman had been looking for. When Peter Sutcliffe was finally arrested, sure enough, he had such a gap between his teeth but I shudder to think how many innocent male citizens of Bradford and elsewhere had been hauled in for the third degree on no more solid grounds than that they had a similar gap in their front teeth.

# CHAPTER 2

## Flogging A Dead Horse

Apart from dark circles under our eyes, a tiredness that took weeks to lift and my broken and capped teeth – lost up at the inn that previous winter in a collision between my mouth and the steel casing of the stand-by generator – it was frozen to the ground and when I tried to move it, my feet proved to be the only movable objects – we had little to show for our twelve months as managers of the highest inn in Great Britain. We certainly hadn't taken a pot of gold away with us, so finding paid work was now an urgent necessity.

My early career, such as it was, had included a bewildering variety of short-term jobs; they weren't necessarily intended to be that way, but that was how it had often panned out. They in-cluded spells as a plasterer's mate: too gruelling; an ice-cream salesman: too seasonal; a holiday camp redcoat: too libidinous and again too seasonal; and a door-to-door salesman of, in rapid succession, 'velvet pictures' – actually flock paper – encyclopaedias and solar panels. The latter was clearly an idea at least twenty years ahead of its time, but like the other direct sales jobs I had tried, trying to flog things which were not worth the money being asked to people who would only be interested if they were sufficiently naive and credulous to believe the spiel the salesmen had to learn by rote before being unleashed on them, was much too dispiriting, immoral and dishonest to appeal to anyone other than the terminally cynical and corrupt, or the truly desperate. For a while I'd certainly felt desperate enough to overcome my moral scruples, but in every case, a week or so of cold calling, knocking on doors and telling what were at best half-truths to un-deserving householders, was enough to make me quit.

I'd then finally found what passed for a proper job compared to everything that had gone before, working in a series of art galleries, and eventually rising through the ranks to the dizzy heights of a temporary exhibition organiser – and for once in my life, it was the exhibitions that were temporary rather than the nature of the employment – before moving on to work simultaneously as an art critic and a rugby league reporter. On the face of it, this was not the most logical combination, since the two jobs were just about as far apart on the employment spectrum as it was possible to get, but anyone who had ever experienced the chiaroscuro of the 'scratching shed' during a Bailey versus Dewsbury 'Heavy Woollen derby' match at the inaccurately named Mount Pleasant ground in the dog days of a cold and foggy mid-winter afternoon would have got the connection straight away.

I had then gone on to work as a freelance journalist and apprentice author, which was the start of my actual career as a writer, though I didn't know that at the time. Now however, desperate for an income, I had made up my mind to revisit the art game and with great good fortune, I found a job almost at once, back in my old trade as an exhibition organiser, after taking up the offer of a roving commission from the Arts Council of Great Britain. They wanted me to attempt to increase appreciation of the contemporary visual arts in an area of the country – a grimy northern industrial town – previously noted mainly for its implacable hostility to such things, and were paying the whole of my salary for the first year in an attempt to convince the local council of the wisdom of picking up my tab after that. My own enthusiasm for the job increased dramatically when I discovered that the art gallery in which I was to be based was just across the corridor from a council-run, fully-licensed bar.

Having stayed with my mother for three weeks, we were now ready to boldly go once more to yet another new location. We had been together for less than ten years but had already lived in five different places and, picking up the pace, would add another five to the tally over the next few. What little money we'd managed to accumulate up at the inn was now almost gone and though we had been planning to rent a house, we found that the available options were distinctly unpromising. We could not afford the more upmarket semis and detached houses on the newer estates surrounding the town where I would be working, and the only houses we could find that we could afford seemed to be dank and damp terraces in streets where at least half the houses were derelict or boarded-up, and neither of us fancied that very much.

Then a friend had an inspiration. 'Why don't you rent a narrow-boat?' she said. 'My brother-in-law has a boatyard on the canal. You can rent a narrow-boat from him, have a little holiday trip in it over the Pennines, then find a nice berth on the tow-path just outside the town and you'll have the best of both worlds: country living and a cheap place to live as well!'

It sounded like a splendid idea; what could possibly go wrong? We negotiated a deal with the boatyard owner, with a substantial reduction in the price out of the tourist season, and the narrow boat then trundled majestically along the canal at a steady walking pace of four miles an hour, taking a 'staircase' of locks and the long tunnel through the Pennines in its stride. We arrived in the town where I would be working and berthed the narrow-boat about half a mile from the town centre, a few yards from a road bridge, near which we could park the car.

The canal was not exactly a limpid, babbling brook. It was impossible to see what was concealed in the murky depths, but in various places along the edge of the canal we could see rusting bicycle wheels and supermarket trolleys poking above the surface of the water. A regular stream of flotsam, jetsam and just plain rubbish drifted by and one of the first things we saw while gazing idly out of the window at the canal as it flowed past was a dead guinea pig – presumably someone's discarded pet – that came floating slowly by on the current, performed a pirouette in an eddy and then disappeared downstream at the same stately pace, heading for the Irish Sea.

I watched it pass with equanimity for it was nothing to what I had discovered early one morning a couple of years before, when I was working in an art gallery that had been set up, for no obvious reason, in part of a former wool mill on the outskirts of Bradford. It was not the most bijou of areas and on the corner of the road that led to the gallery there was a patch of what an unscrupulous estate agent would probably have described as 'a garden area' or at worst 'rough grazing', but which would much more accurately have been labelled 'derelict land'. As I set off for home one evening, I noticed that someone – either a passing gypsy or one of the local rag and bone men – had driven a steel stake into the ground and left his piebald horse to graze the weeds there. Whether the diet did not agree with him, or old age had finally caught up with him, or an assassination had been carried out during the night, I'm not sure, but when I arrived for work the next morning, I discovered that the horse was now lying, stone dead, in the middle of the patch of waste ground.

Disposing of deceased horses did not appear anywhere in my job description so, like a bad samaritan, I passed by on the other side, and went to work, though I kept a close eye on subsequent proceedings from the gallery window. A short while later one of the local 'knacker-men' appeared – the men who collected the bodies of dead livestock and sold them on. Provided it was not too ripe, the carcass would go to a pet food manufacturer, the hide to one of the local tanneries, and the bones to a glue manufacturer. He pulled up in his battered, stinking truck, whereupon what was presumably the horse's owner appeared from somewhere and began negotiations. Whatever the knacker-man was offering was clearly not enough for the owner, but after the former shrugged his shoulders and made to get back into the cab of his truck, the owner, with a face like thunder, accepted the presumably modest price and the knacker-man then winched the horse's carcass onto his truck and drove off in the direction of the glue factory, while the disconsolate horse-owner trudged away in the opposite direction, perhaps heading for the only equine companion still available to him: the Bay Horse. I at least had the consolation of knowing that having tried and failed to interest the local populace in contemporary art, I hadn't been the only person trying to flog a dead horse around there.

The place where I was now working, bisected by the canal along which the dead guinea pig had been floating, was a declining textile town with a high unemployment rate and a couple of 'sink estates' on its outskirts. We only discovered that we had berthed within comfortable range of one of those, when we returned to the narrow-boat to discover that one of the windows had been kicked in and our radio, Sue's bag and a suitcase containing some of our clothes had been stolen. Wondering quite how good an idea a narrow-boat had been after all, we boarded up the broken window and set sail once more, retracing our steps until we reached open country.

We chose to berth the narrow-boat at a place where the canal ran in an embankment raised above the level of the surrounding land, making it clearly visible for some distance, in the hope that its visibility would be a deterrent to further burglaries, though of course it could equally well have been a prominent advertisement to any passing thieves instead. It was now a three mile walk, car or bus-journey into town for me to go to work, but that was a small price to pay for the pleasure of not having our windows kicked in, and there was also a nice pub a mere 400 yards away across the fields, where Sue soon found work.

We had no more problems with burglaries after that but, as summer turned to autumn and then winter, we discovered another problem that, if less serious, was far more persistent. Narrow-boats are made of steel – or that one was anyway – and when condensation meets cold steel it turns to water. This elementary science lesson was relevant only because, as we soon discovered when the temperatures started to fall, while we slept every night, our breath would be condensing on the cold steel roof above our heads. When I woke in the morning and opened an eye, the first sight that now invariably greeted me was a roof-full of drops of ice-cold water, like a forest of stalactites, directly over our heads.

Had we been living in a nice stable house – or even a nice stable – with or without a steel roof, this would not have been a problem for I could simply have slipped out of bed and tiptoed away without disturbing the water-drops. However, this was not a house and it was definitely not stable. Any movement in the boat set it rocking gently on the waters of the canal and, however carefully I tried to ease my way out of bed, the slightest motion was enough to start the boat rocking. That in turn induced a short, sharp shower of ice cold water to fall off the roof and on to us. I'd never been a huge fan of a cold shower first thing in the morning, least of all while I was still in bed, but that now became a regular part of our daily routine.

A Calor gas fire that was our only form of heating and the Calor gas stove we used for cooking merely added to the condensation problem. We stuck it out as long as we could and then, tiring of early-morning cold showers, no matter how invigorating they might be, we at last admitted defeat, returned the narrow-boat to its owner and, digging deep into our threadbare bank account, we set up home in a property made of bricks and mortar rather than steel, and sited in a back-street of the town a safe distance from the canal.

Apart from our stolen property, I was to suffer one other serious loss in my first few days in the town. In need of a haircut, I called in at a barber with the winning business name of 'Jessie the Cropper'. His shop window was like an Olde Curiosity Shoppe, with dust-covered jars of Brylcreem flanked by fiendish looking trusses – surgical supports – and bits of second hand merchandise that his regular customers had apparently given him to sell on their behalf. Clearly this was not a Vidal Sassoon style salon, but time was pressing, so I went inside anyway.

Jessie turned out to be a venerable and slightly tetchy gentleman of a certain age, with a short back and sides 'bowl cut' hairstyle that had clearly been formulated in the nit-infested days

43

of the 1930s and had never been altered since. A couple of his regulars – men of similar vintage and hairstyle – were sitting on the benches but Jessie waved me into the barber's chair, and as I settled myself, I saw the regulars exchange a knowing look. This was still the 1970s – just – and, old hippie that I was, I had still kept my hair on the long side.

I started to say 'Just tidy it up, please. I lik–' but the rest of my words were lost in the whining noise as he revved up his electric clippers. Before I knew what was happening, Jessie had mown a swathe right up and over the top of my head, leaving only a quarter inch of stubble in the wake of the clippers. By the time I'd found my voice, he'd added another one, and by then, with the damage done, there was no option but to allow him to complete the carnage. He swept up the mounds of severed hair and then charged me 'five bob' (25p) for the cut; decimal currency had been introduced eight years earlier, in 1971, but Jessie was clearly having no more truck with that than he was with men's long hair, which had been around even longer.

'Do you ever listen to what your customers ask for?' I said, as I reluctantly paid him.

'No I don't,' he said. 'Do you ever read the sign in the window before you go into a barber's?'

'What?'

He opened the door and steered me outside. Hanging in a corner of the window was a small piece of brown cardboard torn from a box, on which he had added the hand-lettered inscription 'Long Hair Cut Down To Nowt – Five Bob.' I could still hear his regulars cackling as I walked away up the street. It turned out that Jessie was a celebrated local character who was long past retirement age but kept going to work as much for his own amusement as from any financial need and, as his cardboard sign indicated, he loved nothing better than shaving the head of some 'long-haired hippie' who had innocently strayed into his lair. It was not a mistake I was ever likely to repeat in the future.

If the town itself – never a beauty spot even in its heyday as a mill town – had now seen better days, we found that the people who lived there were as warm as welcoming as all the Northern clichés would suggest. Having grown up in Yorkshire, I was used to such friendliness, even from strangers, but some of my friends and acquaintances who had spent their lives in the rather less spontaneous Home Counties could find it a trifle unsettling. One woman acquaintance, an assistant at a Bond Street Art Gallery, whose Hampstead and girls' public school background had evidently not ade-quately prepared her for encounters with those of less gilded origins, arrived to supervise the de-livery of some artworks to the gallery. Having done so, she took a stroll around the town and when she returned, she announced to me in tones of horror that, as she was looking at something in a shop window display, an old woman had plucked at her sleeve and said 'Don't buy that here, love, you can get it ten bob cheaper at the store round the cor-ner.' She fled back to Bond Street soon afterwards but unlike her, even if we still found the town something of an acquired taste, we really liked the people – yes, even Jessie the Cropper – and we enjoyed our time there, and made some good friends.

The art gallery where I was working was on the first floor of a brutalist concrete building that also housed the public library. The gallery was a fine space to exhibit contemporary art, a white-walled, high-roofed, open space unbroken by any windows and entirely lit by artificial light. In between exhibitions, it made an even finer indoor cricket pitch where I and the gallery attendants used a tennis ball and an old cricket bat to practice our leg-breaks and flashing cover drives, though we had to be careful with lofted shots or top-edges which risked dislodging the spotlights from the tracks set into the ceiling. I'm not sure if the Arts Council would have approved, but we enjoyed it enormously.

At the end of my working day, I would often pop in for a quick after-work drink at the bar across the hall – support your local industries has always been my watchword – but on several occasions I also had the chance to watch the rather unedifying spectacle of the local councillors assembling for one of the regular 'free bars' that they voted themselves out of the council funds collected from their hard-pressed ratepayers.

On such nights the councillors' noses were usually pressed to the glass of the door, puppies-in-a-pet-shop-style, long before the scheduled opening time, and as soon as the doors swung open, they would burst into the bar and begin machine-gunning orders for gin, whisky, vodka, brandy, rum and coke, Tia Maria, Pernod, and every other drink known to mankind, all of them doubles or trebles. The inevitable results could be seen in the Gents an hour or two later, when one or two of our distinguished local elected representatives could invariably be spotted, violently throwing up in the cubicles. Undaunted, all would be back in their customary positions when the next free bar or 'Mayor making' ceremony came round again.

Such gross behaviour was by no means confined to the councillors, for some of the council employees – present company excepted, of course – could be just as bad. A stately home, left to the town by a nineteenth century industrial baron, had been converted into a banqueting venue and country park that was the jewel in the crown of the borough. The industrial baron had also left a large collection of valuable paintings to the town but they must have been pinched and flogged off by someone, possibly a council employee, in the post-war years, because when I went up there to try and make an inventory of them, I discovered that all that remained of the collection was a series of very large and very empty gilded frames, all bearing identification numbers, but with no trace whatsoever either of the paintings that had once filled them, or the catalogue to which the numbers must have referred and which would have identified the missing paintings.

The council had sustained other grievous losses over the years including the occasion in the 1930s when the local private coal mining company had extracted a substantial sum from the council in compensation for their pledge not to mine any of the coal directly under the town hall. The councillors were even conducted to the bottom of the pit on a fact-finding mission and led through the mine-workings to the blank wall of coal and rock where, or so they were assured, a few hundred feet above them, the grounds surrounding the town hall began. Only in the late 1940s, after the coal industry had been taken into public ownership, did a survey of the newly-nationalised mine reveal that, having trousered the council's cash, the coal company had then gone ahead and extracted all the coal under the town hall anyway. They had then given the councillors a guided tour of a coal face that was nowhere near the true location of the town hall. Only by good fortune had it not fallen victim to subsidence and disappeared into a hole in the ground.

One of the attractions of the country park on the town outskirts was a small zoo, at which the local ratepayers and their kids could get up close and personal with a modest assortment of animals. Among them was a herd of deer, which after a few torrid rutting seasons, had grown to such a size that a cull was necessary. Over a beer in the pub one night, the director of the relevant department had promptly offered the job to a drinking crony of his, a full-time butcher and part-time hunter. The resultant venison was to be added to the menu of the banqueting suite. Clad in camouflage gear and toting a rifle, the crony had driven up to the zoo the next day, and taken up his stance, standing on a bench outside the deer compound. He then began loosing off pot-shots with his rifle, but he fired with such inaccuracy that he wounded as many deer as he killed. Even worse, all this took place under the horrified gaze of some visitors and their children. After one of them, in tears, phoned the local newspaper and reporters began asking questions, a form of council *omerta* was practised and any council employee who talked to the press about it was threatened with instant dismissal. That did not apply to the director of the department responsible for the horror show, who remained in his post until his retirement many years later. The incident is still vividly remembered by older residents of the town to this day.

It would be fair to say that my attempts to interest the borough's ratepayers in contemporary art were not much more popular than the director's cull of the country park deer. One exhibition of conceptual art not only stretched the imagination of the viewing public, but also taxed the patience of my political masters, who found themselves struggling to explain to the reporter on the local newspaper exactly how exhibits including a glass of water entitled 'An Oak Tree' or a wooden table-top bearing four steel pails of water that, by an ingenious arrangement of ropes and pulleys, was not only standing on the table-top but also supporting it, could be said to be art.

They would probably have been equally baffled by the gallery owner with whom I had arranged the show. One of the most kind and charming men I've ever met, he had been an officer in one of the Guards regiments before resigning his commission to set up one of the most avant-garde commercial art galleries in London. To say the least, Army officers and cutting edge contemporary art were not the most obvious of bedfellows, but as a man who had combined art criticism with rugby league commentary, I was hardly well-placed to challenge him about it.

The gallery director had largely kept his interest in contemporary visual art to himself while he was in the army, but he also had another secret life as well. When in London, he was every inch the model of an urbane, charming, pinstripe-suited gallery director, and a very generous host, never more than a few yards away from a corkscrew and a bottle of Chablis, but when at his country residence – a venerable stately home in the shires – although an equally generous host there, he preferred a rather different dress style. Those who received a coveted invitation to stay for the weekend would arrive to be greeted by the very same gallery director, though this time, resplendent in a glittering evening gown and a long blond wig. Throwing the doors wide open, he would exclaim 'Call me Gloria!' as he ushered his sometimes shell-shocked guests inside. One artist, a Northern lad who the gallery represented, had had a sheltered upbringing, and was reportedly so startled by the director's transformation that he turned on his heel and disappeared back down the drive without ever crossing the threshold at all.

In my all too brief career in the grimy industrial town's art gallery, the nadir – at least as far as the councillors and probably the ratepayers too were concerned – was reached with an exhibition involving a collaboration between two celebrated artists. One was British, Richard Hamilton, whose collage 'Just what is it that makes today's homes so different, so appealing?' had made him one of the founding fathers of British pop art. The other artist was a German painter called Dieter Roth.

After much earnest discussion, the format for the exhibition was established. Hamilton had produced a series of collages and screenprints which were to be hung at eye-level around the walls of the art gallery. Roth's contribution was a series of small oil paintings of sausages which, as directed by him, I hung six inches above the skirting-board. The idea was that the local dog-owners could call in at the gallery while out for a stroll with their pets, and while the owners pondered the meaning of the images hung at their eye-level, the dogs could get to grips with the sausages hung at theirs.

I thought it was a splendid idea, a bit of harmless fun with some decent art thrown in as well – what was not to like? – though in that, as in so much else in life, I proved to be sadly mistaken. All might have been well had someone not made an anonymous phone call to the *Daily Mirror,* complaining about the exhibition – well, I had to do something to boost the pitiful attendance figures... At the time, the Mirror was deep into one of those periods when it could always be roused to paroxysms of synthetic indignation by 'a shocking waste of public money on so-called modern art'. The spittle-flecked fury induced in the tabloid hacks by the Tate Gallery's purchase of Carl André's infamous 'Equivalent VIII' – also known as 'the pile of bricks' had barely died down when this fresh affront to public decency came into view and, predictably enough, a furious 'modern art-bashing' piece duly appeared in the *Daily Mirror* the next day, accompanied by pictures of a suitably baffled-looking dog, under the headline 'Hot Dog – It's Art!'.

The article included a number of quotes from the hapless and quite unprepared chairman of the relevant council committee, who probably didn't even know the exhibition was taking place and on previous form, was unlikely to have been able to spell contemporary art, never mind begun to justify it. At half past eleven that night, I was just about to get into bed when the phone rang and I found myself taking a call from the irate and by now extremely inebriated wife of the unfortunate committee chairman. 'Why are you trying to ruin my husband's career?' she sobbed. 'He's standing for re-election next month.'

'Never mind,' I said, trying to look on the bright side. 'At least the dog-owners will vote for him.'

He did manage to get himself re-elected, albeit by a wafer-thin majority – good thing for him the dog-owners turned out – but strangely enough, when my contract came up for renewal, the council committee he chaired decided not to renew it. However, those who fail to learn from their mistakes are doomed to repeat them, and the Arts Council then offered me a similar contract at another gallery, though this time in the outer reaches of the North, not too far from the Inn at the Top. With another round of sad farewells to the friends we had made while we were there – it was becoming something of a habit – coupled with a few sighs of relief from me that I would no longer

have to deal with that particular council committee, feelings that the committee would have
echoed in spades, Sue and I uprooted ourselves
once more.

# CHAPTER 3

## An Earthly Paradise

We packed, moved house and then unpacked our
worldly goods again for what seemed like the
hundredth time in recent years, and then spent a
few weeks living in a house provided by the council which was employing me until we could find a
home of our own. We looked around the area,
found a place we liked a few miles outside of town
and then took the plunge and, using my salary as
security, we bought ourselves a cottage. It was half
a mile up a country lane from a small village a few
miles south of the town where I was working. The
middle one of a row of five cottages situated on a
sharp bend, it was an unusual wedge shape with
only a tiny courtyard at the back as outdoor space,
but it was still a nice house in a lovely and very
quiet setting ... or at least it was at weekends
which, as it turned out, by no coincidence whatsoever, was the only time that the vendor was
available to show purchasers around it. We saw it,
loved it, had an offer accepted and a few weeks
later, we moved in one bright Saturday morning.

We spent a peaceful weekend unpacking boxes

and settling ourselves in, and then, bright and early on the Monday morning, we were woken by the teeth-rattling din of a lorry grinding up the lane and swerving around the bend, passing within a handful of inches of the house walls as it did so. There was then a squealing sound as the driver locked up his brakes and juddered to a halt, just managing to dodge a lorry thundering along in the opposite direction. For the rest of the working day, that scenario was repeated with monotonous regularity and the only surprise was that – up to that point at least – none of the procession of lorries had cut the corner enough to come straight through our living room wall instead of just shaving it. Now we knew why the previous owner had only been available for viewings at weekends, because during the week our quiet country lane was transformed into a hyper-busy 'rat-run' for lorries grinding their way down the valley from the quarries a couple of miles up in the hills, and heading for the motorway a few miles away.

We stuck it out for twelve months, then put the house back on the market – funnily enough, we were also only available to host viewings at weekends – and having sold the house almost at once, we tiptoed guiltily away, leaving the new owners to make the same unsettling discovery on their first Monday morning.

The place we had found to move to was an earthly paradise a couple of miles further up the road that led to the fells. It was a rented farmhouse in a beautiful setting, nestling in a hollow two hundred yards down its own winding, private drive from a quiet country lane that in turn led off another quiet country lane, and this time it really was quiet seven days a week – believe me, we checked. The white-washed, double-fronted house was south-facing and had a cottage garden at the front, full of old fashioned plants like hollyhocks and delphiniums that were protected from marauding livestock by a low wall capped by wrought iron railings.

At the back of the farmhouse was a field that, as well as providing grazing for the farm's cows, also contained an old orchard. Beyond that was a steep bank of oak and beech woodland that gave shelter from the north and east winds. To either side of the house were a byre and a hay-barn to which the swallows returned every spring and they had also colonised the long disused watermill across the farmyard. It had something of the air of the Marie Celeste about it; beneath a thick layer of dust, all the equipment, including the millstones, was still in place and it felt as if the miller had popped out for a few minutes fifty years ago and never come back. Outside, the water wheel was still there as well, but long out of use, and what had once been the mill race was now a silted up and overgrown ditch. At the front of the house, across the bridge over the old mill race, a meadow led to the banks of the river winding its way through the lush pastureland.

We had only been able to rent the farmhouse because of a happy coincidence. The owner, a farmer, was keeping the house for his son to live in when he grew up, but meanwhile he was willing to rent it, providing a suitable tenant could be found.

However, he didn't want any 'off-comers' or other strangers renting it, and definitely no tourists, so it was not being advertised anywhere. Luckily our next-door neighbour at our previous house, a retired farmer himself, was a friend of the owner and, knowing we were looking for somewhere to live, he first of all recommended the house to us, and then vouched for us to the owner.

Our new home had great charm and a location to die for. It was unmodernised and with solid floors, metal-framed windows, no damp proof course, no insulation and no central heating, winters there were likely to be an ordeal, but in summer it was the nearest thing to heaven we were likely to find this side of the pearly gates. For the ridiculously modest rent of £10 a week – even at early 1980s prices that still represented an absolute bargain – we were now the proud possessors of a five-bedroomed farmhouse surrounded by woods and open fields and with fishing rights on the trout-rich waters of the river within fifty yards of our front door. It would have been worth at least ten or twenty times as much on the open market and we had to pinch ourselves a few times to make sure we weren't dreaming.

It was one of those farmhouses that seemed to have grown organically, with newer extensions built on to the original house at either end and at the front of it as well. The oldest part, now disused, and reached through a door opening off the tiny, cobbled yard at the back of the house, probably dated back to the seventeenth or even the sixteenth century. We explored it after we moved in and the struggle to open the door and the inches-deep dust covering the stone-flagged floor showed we were the first to have done so in years and maybe in decades. Among the dust-covered kitchen utensils and bits of equipment, all so old they would have qualified as antiques had they not been so corroded by rust or infested with wood-worm, we found some curious stones hanging on strings from the ceiling. They were rounded, water-worn pebbles from the river, but had been pierced through with holes. What their purpose was we could not guess, but when I asked our old neighbour he told me 'Oh, those would be witch-stones. Farmers used to hang them in their houses and byres to protect themselves and their livestock from witches and evil spirits. I think the idea was that the witches and evil spirits would be unable to resist trying to find out what was hidden inside the stones and then would be trapped and unable to find their way out again.'

'Farmers back then didn't have a very high opinion of the intelligence of witches, did they?' I said.

He laughed. 'I don't suppose the witches had a very high opinion of the farmers' intelligence either!'

The bedroom next to the bathroom in the main part of the house was the site of a potentially more alarming phenomenon. We didn't use it, even as a spare room, because the floorboards were too rotten to make that a good idea, so we kept it closed. However ... and here is the strange thing ... there was no lock on the door but there was a handle with a catch that definitely functioned. When you closed the door, however hard you pushed against it, it wouldn't open until you turned the handle. We always kept the door shut and yet when we got up to go to the bathroom first thing in the morning, we would often find that the door of the bedroom next to it was wide open. It could not have been the wind, because the door had been firmly shut and could only be opened with the handle, and there was no one else in the house but us and we certainly hadn't opened it. Yet there it was: almost every morning we would find the door open. It didn't frighten us; there had not been a break-in and we had never felt any threatening presence, normal or paranormal, in the house at all, but it remained inexplicable. Some time later I mentioned it to the farmer's son while he was down there mucking out the stalls in the byre where they kept a few heifers in winter. He gave me a curious, guarded look.

'What is it?' I said.

He hesitated for a few moments and then shrugged. 'Many years ago, my aunt hung herself from the hook on the back of that door,' he said.

'Blimey, so do you think the place is haunted by her?'

He shook his head. 'I'm not saying that at all. I'm a farmer, not some hippy mystic. I don't believe in ghosts. But it is curious, right enough.'

He could say that again! A more imaginative couple might have bolted at that point and never slept under that roof again, but since we'd never felt remotely threatened by the ghost, if that's what it was, we continued to live there quite happily; with four spare bedrooms, there was plenty of room for his sadly deceased aunt if she wanted to keep an eye on the place from beyond the grave, without disturbing us.

Despite the presence of spirits, real or imagined, in summer, as we'd hoped, the house was an absolute delight to live in. It was sun drenched from dawn to dusk and surrounded by fields full of wildflowers. The hedgerows at the side of the lane were a mass of dog-roses and brambles, and delicious wild strawberries grew on the steep banks underneath them. At weekends we strolled with the dog for miles through the fields and woods that surrounded us or had a barbecue on the rocky island in the middle of the river. That involved a couple of hours hard work, piling up the driftwood washed down by the river during the winter floods, and then innumerable trips to and fro across the field and splashing through the shallows to reach the island, carrying food, wine, rugs and cushions.

Once settled as comfortably as possible on the mounds of rocks and pebbles, I would then invariably have to go back to the house at least three times to collect the things we'd forgotten: usually a box of matches to light the fire, the corkscrew to open the wine and the insect repellent which the clouds of midges filling the air around us, drawn by the fresh meat reclining on the island, made essential. Finally we could then relax, on our own or with friends, watching the smoke from the fire rising into the air and the river drifting by, as the sun sank lower in the sky; and we often stayed there until well after dark. If we wanted to socialise with other friends and neighbours, there was also a very nice pub, run by a retired Irish National

Hunt jockey, at the crossroads a mile from our house. What more could we possibly want?

However, as we had feared when we moved in, when the temperatures began to fall in winter, our paradise became a little less idyllic. Concrete floors and thin, damp walls were not conducive to comfort when the temperature was well below zero and our first winter in the farmhouse was a real tester. Although nowhere near as prolonged as the winter that we had endured at the Inn at the Top, the icy spell beginning in December 1981 was even more intense; it proved to be the coldest December since the nineteenth century. The severe weather began in the first week of December and lasted through to Christmas. On the night of the twelfth to the thirteenth of December, the temperature in parts of England fell below -25°C and it certainly felt every bit as cold as that in our rented farmhouse. Just as heat rises, so cold also sinks, and the position of the house, in a natural bowl at the foot of the slopes leading up to the high fells, meant we were in a 'frost pocket'; and as the temperature fell, the cold air rolled down the slopes and settled around us like the snow.

We had no heating other than the open fire in the kitchen and, with no insulation and only single-glazed, steel-framed windows, the inside of the house felt almost as cold as the outside. Our breath fogged in the air, sometimes even in the kitchen where the fire was always kept burning, and the only way to get from there to the bedroom and back again in the morning was to sprint. Once in bed, even with every blanket we possessed piled on top of us, it was still almost too cold to sleep.

Nonetheless, we fared better than one of our poor, deep-frozen bantams. Bantams are pretty free range creatures at the best of times and having acquired a few soon after moving in there, under our regime of benign neglect they had become semi-feral. They ate the food we gave them as a supplement to the seeds, insects and grubs they found for themselves in the fields and hedgerows, they roosted in a tree in the field next to the farm-house, and laid eggs in spring and summer that – when we could actually find them – were as deli-cious and deep-yolked as any I've ever eaten. The places they laid them varied from inaccessible to absolutely bloody impossible, usually in the heart of the deepest, darkest, densest patch of nettles they could find. Every two or three days, like kids at Easter, we had an egg-hunt and came up with at least half a dozen, but many more went undis-covered until long past their sell by date, and there are probably some still out there somewhere that have never been discovered at all.

Using china decoy eggs sometimes worked be-cause, like hens, bantams will usually react to the sight of an egg or two by laying their own egg on top of them to add to the clutch. The trick was to prevent the clutch of eggs from reaching critical mass, at which point any bantam coming across it would stop laying and start brooding instead. If we found them in time, we could extract the eggs from beneath the irate bantam, earning a few pecks on the backs of our hands for our pains, and the bantam would then go off and within a few days began laying again. If we didn't find them, we would only know that one of our bantams had disappeared without trace. We usually assumed it had been taken by a fox, only for it to reappear two or three weeks later, leading a brood of tiny bantam chicks to add to our ever growing flock.

Our motley crew of bantams included a couple of Marans – larger birds that were closer in size to hens and which laid the most delicious eggs of all – and a few smaller ones of various assorted breeds, that were the generous donation of my eccentric Uncle Olaf from the flock he kept at his country cottage elsewhere in the Dales. We also had two cockerels, one large and macho with a proud scarlet comb, who for obvious reasons we christened Butch, and the other fey, weak and spindly, who for reasons that were equally obvious, to us at least, and with apologies to all the Kevins out there, we unkindly named Kevin.

For a few months, poor Kevin pecked forlornly in the dirt around the fringes of the flock, while Butch quite literally ruled the roost, dominating the hens and driving off Kevin whenever he tried to sneak past him to attempt a discreet liaison with one of the hens. Then one evening, perhaps lingering for a few moments too long before flying up to his roost as the shadows lengthened, Butch disappeared, leaving only a pile of blood-stained feathers as testament to the unequal struggle with the fox that had claimed him. Almost overnight, Kevin was transformed. Now the ruler of the roost himself, his previously pale and flaccid coxcomb became erect and bright crimson, he grew to what seemed to be twice his previous size, and strutted his stuff around the farmyard to such effect that we were soon almost knee-deep in bantam chicks.

We gave as many away as we could and the foxes, stoats and birds of prey also helped to keep a lid on the numbers by claiming a few more, with the result that, by winter, we were once more down to a hard core of Kevin and his harem of half a dozen bantam hens.

They roosted every night in the same tree by the gate leading to the field behind the farmhouse, perching on a stout branch a few feet above the ground, where they were safe from marauding foxes. As the cold spell persisted, I would come out of the house first thing every morning to feed the bantams and put a bowl of warm water down for them, replacing the deep frozen stuff from the day before, and I would find them huddled together on the branch of the tree, their feathers completely covered in frost. Nonetheless, the air trapped by their feathers seemed to provide good enough insulation for them to revive rapidly at the sight of food to eat and water to drink. They would flutter down from the tree and after a few minutes of stiff-legged walking around the yard, they were almost back to normal.

However, one morning, about a week into the great frost, with Radio 4's cheerful news that the overnight temperature throughout the country had fallen close to -20°C, and an RAF base in Shropshire had recorded -25°C ringing in my ears, I came out of the house as usual to feed the bantams. I was shivering in the savage cold, despite the several layers of clothing I was wearing, but as usual, most of the bantams stirred themselves at the sight of food, shook the frost from their feathers and fluttered down to begin rather arthritically pecking at the corn I'd scattered for them.

However, one bantam hen remained frost-covered and motionless where it was perched on the branch of the tree. It was out of reach above my head and though I clapped my hands and whistled, it failed to move. I wasn't sure if it was dead, or simply refusing to move until the air temperature rose. It remained there throughout the morning as the sun climbed higher in the sky and the temperature lifted a little, and finally, about eleven o'clock that morning, it suddenly toppled from its perch and fell to the ground with a thud, stone dead. It must have frozen to death during the night, but had remained iced to its perch until the sun's rays had warmed it enough to melt the ice holding its feet to the branch. Even though the temperatures remained at record low levels for another week and then again fell so low in January that the temperature at Braemar in Scotland reached -27.2°C, the lowest temperature ever recorded in the UK, like us, Kevin and his remaining bantams somehow survived until the arrival of spring promised easier times for everyone.

Spring also brought us an unexpected, but very welcome, financial windfall. As part of my Arts Council-funded post in the museum and art gallery where I worked, it was my job, whether they liked it or not, to keep the local population abreast of current developments in contemporary art. Video installations were all the rage among contemporary artists, or at least those artists funded by the Arts Council, at the time, and I had arranged a temporary exhibition by one of the more celebrated practitioners. A video recorder connected to a television set allowed visitors to stay for as long as they wished, staring at the flickering images on the screen, although to be honest, most did not linger long.

The whole piece took about an hour to run through and frankly, even to someone being paid to promote it, one viewing was probably enough, and two at least one too many. Thus it was that on a quiet winter afternoon, after a shifty look around to make sure there were no art-loving visitors within range, I and the two gallery attendants had disconnected the video recorder and instead spent half an hour watching the National Hunt racing that was being televised. As I watched the feature race, a steeplechase with a modest field, I saw one horse clearing every fence with feet to spare, before going on to win at a canter.

At the end of the race the commentator noted that the horse, named Aldaniti, was entered for the 1981 Grand National. The horse was only just recovering from an injury that had threatened to signal the end of his racing career and, such were the doubts about his future prospects that, before the race I had just watched, he had been on offer at the generous odds of 200 to 1 for the Grand National. His victory had now seen his odds for the big race sharply reduced to 50 to 1, but that still seemed generous odds to me for a horse that had such good stamina and was such an effortless jumper of big fences. Before the end of the afternoon I had slipped out of the gallery, gone down to the nearest bookmakers and put

£20 on the horse for the National. It should have been more but it was as much spare money as I had at the time.

A few months later, in April 1981, I watched with bated breath as Aldaniti and the rest of the field lined up for the start of the Grand National. It turned out that not only was the horse recovering from a career-threatening injury, the latest in a string of injuries that had repeatedly disrupted its career, but the jockey, Bob Champion, was in remission from life-threatening cancer and had only recently returned to the saddle after enduring six months of chemotherapy and radiation treatment. The story of this ill-starred partnership battling against the odds had warmed the hearts of so many Britons that, by the time the race started, Aldaniti had been backed down to ten to one second favourite. As I had hoped, the horse jumped like a stag all the way round and took the last fence well clear of the field but, visibly tiring on the long run to the finish, he then only just managed to hold off the fast finishing favourite, Spartan Missile. Had that horse's amateur jockey, who was also its owner, not lost his stirrups as he tried to drive his horse on to the line, the result might well have been different, but Aldaniti had done enough and hung on to win the Grand National by four lengths. As well as winning his owner a first prize of £50,000, he also earned me a rather less handsome but still very welcome £1000 return on my £20 stake. I owed it all to my unauthorised use of the television set in the video installation at the art gallery, and whatever the town's ratepayers might have thought of video art, I was now a huge fan.

When at work, I shared an office with the museum and art gallery's resident archaeologist and we spent our entire time there in a state of mutual incomprehension about the work the other did. Like the majority of the British public at the time – and probably ever since – the archaeologist could make no sense whatsoever of contemporary visual art and, while I understood the purpose and value of archaeology, I was hard-pressed to see the point of much of the work he actually did. I was all in favour of conserving the artefacts from the past for present and future study, but I was equally convinced that there came a point where diminishing returns started to operate.

The museum's store shelves and cellars were already groaning under the weight of literally tens of thousands of shards of Roman pottery, the vast majority small, undistinguished and, to my admittedly jaundiced eye, indistinguishable fragments of plain, dull-looking earthenware. Teams of archaeologists were continually adding to that number, burrowing like moles into every building site in the town before construction was allowed to begin, and working at various 'digs' in the open country around the town as well.

With every passing hour, the resident archaeologist was adding a few more bits of pottery to the mountains already stored at the museum. At either side of his desk there were two large brown, conservation quality, cardboard boxes. The one on his left would be empty at the start of the working day, while the one on his right was full of yet more fragments of Roman pottery excavated from in and around the town. He picked up each small, near-identical fragment in turn, wrote an accession number several digits long on it in microscopic script, using a special fine-pointed pen, and entered the details into his ledger.

He then made a painstaking drawing of it – when I helpfully suggested that taking photographs would produce quicker and probably more accurate reproductions, I received a withering, silent glance – and finally placed the fragment in the box on his left. After watching his performance for some time, I made what I thought was another helpful suggestion. 'Rather than writing a number on each piece of pottery,' I said. 'Why don't you just write one number on the cardboard box and put all the bits of pottery into it? Think of the time you'll save.'

He was only just beginning a lengthy explanation when he spotted the smile I was trying to hide and with a sigh of exasperation and a pitying look in my direction, he went back to his interminable task.

# CHAPTER 4

## An Overweight Actor With
## A Lot Of Ham In Him

Back at the farmhouse, we were making preparations to welcome a new arrival. At the side of the old water mill there were a series of stone pig-sties where pigs used to be fattened on the farm's waste crops and the spent grain from the mill. Into one of these abandoned sties, one sunny spring morning, we introduced our new pet, who had just arrived, *porcus ex machina,* in our lives. The theatrical metaphor is entirely appropriate, for the small, but perfectly-formed piglet who emerged blinking into the bright sunlight from the back seat of a friend's car, was a seasoned thespian. He was fresh from trotting the boards in a two week engagement of a mock-Jacobean production, chillingly and, given the presence of a porcine star, rather insensitively entitled *'Blood Pudding'*, that had been put on at the ICA in London by the Lumiere and Son Theatre Company.

The piglet, the runt of a litter and originally christened Martin, was cast by the play's director after a successful audition for the role and a financial transaction with the pig-breeder, the sordid details of which need not detain us here. As a result, Martin duly left his childhood home for the bright lights of the theatre and a trot-on part at the end of Blood Pudding. If not exactly a leading role, it was nonetheless a good test of temperament for a young pig with thespian inclinations.

After intensive rehearsals, Martin made his stage debut on the opening night. Much to the delight of the audience, who didn't have much else to entertain them during the grim, blood-spattered production, Martin was released in the wings at stage left and the sight of a handful of food waved at him from the opposite side of the stage was enough to induce him to tread the boards, scampering right across the apron of the stage before exiting stage right. That was his only moment of glory during the play itself, though he reappeared at the end of the play to take a solo curtain call.

Unfortunately the production appeared to have had more affinities with a turkey than a pig and although Martin was an instant hit, according to the critics he was a solitary silk purse in a company of sows' ears. He was the only member of the cast to draw a good review from the *Guardian*'s then theatre critic Nicholas de Jongh, who barbecued the rest of the company, calling the play 'a single shapeless mass, heavily flavoured with a surfeit of pretensions, but still leaving the blandest of tastes in the mouth... A small piglet, who performs briefly during the evening, is the only creature allowed a curtain-call. And sadly this seemed the wisest decision of the night.'

Despite the presence of a pig, *Hamlet* it clearly was not, and unsurprisingly after that review, the show did not transfer to the West End. Throughout the rehearsals and performances, Martin had been sharing the director's London flat – apparently not an unusual arrangement, because I had only recently been reading a newspaper article about one man who had been keeping his pet pig in a flat on the fourteenth floor of a tower block in Birmingham, until complaints from the neighbours about the noise and the smell led the council to intervene. However, when the play closed, Martin became homeless and, despite his rave reviews, like so many thespians he found himself 'resting' between parts. The future theatrical plans of his owner/director included no room for such an easily typecast star and Martin was facing a one-way ticket to oblivion of a far more than theatrical kind until, moved by the pleas of a friend of ours – one of the actors whose reviews had been rather less complimentary than Martin's – we offered to rescue him, adding him to a fast-expanding menagerie that already contained a dog, a cat and our half-dozen bantams.

While Martin had been happily flat-sharing up to now, we felt that our mutual happiness, not to mention the fragrance of our own quarters, might be best served by letting him occupy a separate bachelor apartment of his own, rather than sharing our house. On the day before his arrival, we therefore cleaned and scrubbed out one of the old pig sties, repaired its venerable wooden gate (for what was to prove to be the first of many, many times), and installed a wooden sleeping platform to keep him out of the draught, for pigs are as susceptible to draughts as humans and can easily get chills. We found him bowls for his food and water, and scattered plenty of fresh straw both to serve as his bedding and as a light, roughage-laden, between-meals snack, and then, as a finishing touch, we hung a gold star on the door to make our retired actor feel at home.

The next morning Martin arrived by limousine ... all right, it was actually in a Ford Escort, the back-seat of which had been liberally covered with old newspapers in an only partially success-ful attempt to preserve the upholstery. We settled him into his new home under the watchful and rather tearful gaze of his previous owner, who bade him a sad farewell and then drove off up the lane. Martin was about to begin a new life with us and we decided that he would also be doing so under a new name. His previous one did not seem to us to do full justice to the gravitas and character of this seasoned thespian, and after much thought we settled on 'Marlon' instead. It was not so different from his previous handle that he would have problems with recognising it as his name and anyway, as an overweight actor with a lot of ham in him, his new name practically chose itself!

Although a rural pig-sty was obviously a long way from the chic sophistication of his previous apartment, he hid his disappointment like a trooper and inspected his new quarters with a tolerable show of enthusiasm. He obviously expected to be speedily rescued from his bucolic obscurity with the offer of a really meaty part in some new production, and for the first couple of weeks he just sat idly turning the pages of his copy of Variety with his snout and waiting for his agent to phone. When the call never came, however, he bade a regretful farewell to thoughts of stardom, put the stage behind him and settled with increasing contentment into the life of a country squire.

Marlon's bachelor pad seemed to suit him well. His split-level living and sleeping quarters opened onto a stone-flagged yard where he could take the air or, when the need arose, utilise the discreet corner complete with stone drain. His wooden front gate led onto the farmyard, including a 'midden' – a steaming heap of gently rotting cow poo, dug out of the cowsheds during the winter and now maturing nicely before being spread on the fields in the autumn. I could never pass it without thinking of the old joke about the inhabitants of a mental hospital calling out to a farmer driving past with a cart load of steaming manure: 'Where are you going with that manure, farmer?'

'I'm going to put it on my strawberries.'

'And they call us mad...'

The midden also yielded us a good crop of courgettes that summer, or at least it did until Marlon discovered them on one of his first un-authorised excursions outside his sty. Once in the farmyard, having helped himself to a few courgette plants, only a five-barred gate stood between him and the field containing the old orchard, full of apple and pear trees, and gooseberry and currant bushes. For the most part, the vicious thorns on the gooseberry bushes kept both Marlon and the livestock at bay, but all he had to do was bide his time and he could snuffle up the ripe fruits when they fell to the ground.

Flanking the field was the wood that cloaked the slopes of the ridge and shielded the farm-house from the north wind. Long-established, the wood was rich in mature oak and beech trees, providing further delicious windfalls of acorns and beech-mast for a foraging pig. To the front of the house, he could also cross the bridge over the old mill race and make for the banks of the river, a favourite place for us to walk the dog, soon to be equally popular with Marlon.

He grew rapidly, as pigs are wont to do, and his pleasure in human company, not to mention the delights of the riverbank and the orchard, led him to make frequent unscheduled excursions from his sty. He was given at least two daily con-stitutionals, together with a large amount of unsupervised recreation time in the orchard, but when returned to his quarters, the wooden gate on his yard chafed his free spirit. A little surreptitious work with his nose, followed by a full-blooded shoulder charge was usually enough to burst open his gate and send him charging out, chortling his delight at his freedom.

This was a potential source of problems: *The Animals Act, 1971,* made it an offence to allow animals to stray onto the public highway. As his owners, we would also have been responsible for any damage to property or injury to people caused by our rambling pet. So I regularly patched up his gate, but he just as frequently broke it down again. I could simply have bought a new gate, of course, but I was a firm adherent to the belief that there is no problem in life so intractable that it cannot be solved by a bit of scrap wood, a hammer and a few six-inch nails, so I continued to patch or, if you will, botch up the gate, and Marlon continued to break it down.

A pig's nose is a truly remarkable organ, soft and delicate enough to locate the scent of truffles hidden beneath the soil, or a toffee in someone's pocket, yet strong enough to plough a furrow through grassland and uproot some major obstacles including, as we rapidly discovered, five-barred gates. Once in the farmyard, a flick of Marlon's nose would send the gate to the field at the back cartwheeling off its hinges, and while the farm heifers emerged to sample the delights of the yard, Marlon was free to resume his perusal of the day's windfalls from the fruit trees and bushes. After a fresh fruit entrée, he then moved on to the acorns and beech-mast in the wood for his main course and had been known to travel even farther afield in search of dessert, at which point his occasional attempts to ingratiate himself with the neighbours proved to be a major stumbling block to our own.

We were just sitting down to supper one summer evening when the phone began to ring. 'Excuse me,' a frightfully refined voice said when I picked up the phone. 'Have you by any chance lost a pig, because we seem to have found one? It's in our vegetable patch, so I'd be grateful if you could come and get it sooner rather than later.'

Given the carnage that Marlon could wreak on a field, let alone a vegetable patch in a couple of minutes, I thought the owner of the voice was showing commendable restraint. We duly sprinted up the lane to retrieve our errant pig and I left a case of wine for the owners of the vegetable patch the next day, by way of a peace offering and some compensation for the devastation that he had left behind.

Marlon also displayed a pig's considerable intelligence as well as his strength. His great delight was to burst into the house and raid the kitchen, where he could be sure of a bowl of dog food and a supply of fresh vegetables, kept in a floor-level rack in the corner. Knowing that a frontal assault would lead to instant eviction before he could eat his fill, however, he would first of all stage a diversionary attack at the front of the house, where he would rattle the iron garden gate with his nose until he heard us coming through from the kitchen to see what was going on. Marlon would meanwhile be sprinting round the side of the house, and he would then shoulder charge his way in through the back door and gleefully inhale as much of the dog-food, vegetables and anything else he could reach in the thirty seconds before we ran back in and expelled him.

As well as his accommodation, there were two other absolute essentials for Marlon's happiness and well-being. One was a plentiful supply of clean drinking water, for pigs drink a lot, especially in hot weather. He was also a fervent consumer of other drinks, particularly tea, and he shared with most pigs a fondness for beer; if he drank less than us, that was only because we never took him to the pub with us. Fearing the consequences in the confined space of our local if he took a fancy to a pint of beer or a bag of crisps at the other end of the room, we preferred to do our drinking only in the company of those who could stand upright when entering the pub if not always when leaving it – and also buy their round without having to borrow the money from us.

The other necessity for a happy Marlon was a constant supply of tasty meals and snacks. He was a pleasure to cook for; whatever we provided was rapidly consumed with evident relish, and as we opened the door to take out his bowl of food every morning and evening (and most times in-between), we always had the pleasure of hearing him singing lustily for his supper.

Marlon was a creature of habit and we soon devised a regular daily routine to help him through the day. As a service to those who may be tempted to follow our example and acquire a porcine pet, I append the following helpful schedule.

**Daily Routine**

**7.59 am** – reveille
**8.00 am (prompt)** – breakfast – a light breakfast of tea, toast and swill – all served together to save time – is acceptable. The morning newspaper should also be provided for roughage.
**8.01 am** – breakfast complete, clear away dishes.
**9.00 am** – second breakfast (For obvious reasons, a traditional full English breakfast is definitely not acceptable, try and tempt his appetite with a café complet – a few croissants, brioches and petit pains with unsalted butter, preserves and a cafetiére of freshly ground coffee).
**9.01 am** – second breakfast complete, clear away dishes and prepare the bath (asses milk or mud as preferred).
**10.00 am** – third breakfast. A repetition of either (or preferably both) of the first two will be quite adequate.
**10.01 am** – third breakfast complete, clear away dishes.
**10.02 am** – morning constitutional – a stroll through the fields, ideally taking in an orchard for apples, pears, plums, etc., and a deciduous wood for beech-mast and acorns. Be sure to take along a few biscuits and chocolate bars for the journey. Return in time for...
**11.00 am** – elevenses.
**11.01 am** – elevenses complete, clear away dishes.
**11.02 am** – morning nap.
**12 noon** – first sitting of lunch.

**1.00 pm** – second sitting of lunch.

**2.00 pm** – third sitting of lunch (N.B. your pig will normally wish to attend all three sittings).

**2.01 pm** – lunch complete, clear away dishes.

**2.02 pm** – post-prandial nap.

**3.00 pm** – afternoon snack.

**3.01 pm** – snack complete, clear away dishes.

**3.02 pm** – afternoon constitutional (see morning constitutional for preferred route). Return in time for...

**4.00 pm** – afternoon tea.

**4.01 pm** – afternoon tea complete, clear away dishes.

**5.00 pm** – high tea.

**5.01 pm** – high tea complete, clear away dishes.

**6.00 pm** – first sitting of dinner.

**7.00 pm** – second sitting of dinner.

**8.00 pm** – third sitting of dinner (see lunch for useful comments).

**8.01 pm** – dinner complete, clear away dishes.

**9.00 pm** – coffee and after-dinner mints.

**10.00 pm** – mid-evening snack.

**10.01 pm** – snack complete, clear away dishes.

**11.00 pm** – bedtime snack: cocoa, biscuits, etc.

**11.01 pm** – bedtime snack complete, clear away dishes and settle him down with his personal stereo, TV, or books and magazines.

**11.30 pm** – relax, enjoy yourself, the rest of the day is yours to do with as you please, except for...

**12 midnight** – feast in the dormitory – sandwiches, fruitcake (homemade, of course), apples, biscuits, chocolate, lemonade, etc., etc.

**12.01 am** – midnight feast complete, clear away dishes.

**12.02 am** – lights out.

The normal domestic chores: making his bed, cleaning, dusting, polishing and hoovering his quarters, could be fitted in whenever convenient (to him). Silk sheets were optional, but clean, fresh straw was required at least once a week. Having removed the old straw from his quarters – mixed with his dung, it made very good compost – swept out his sty and put in a bale of new straw, we re-admitted Marlon, who then spent a blissful few minutes, rolling in the straw, strewing it around and then pushing it into a heap with his nose until his bedding was arranged just the way he wanted it.

No doubt he would also have liked an occasional holiday or weekend break, but we had to draw the line somewhere. He would certainly have enjoyed a walking tour of the beech woods of the Chilterns, the orchards of Kent or Herefordshire and Worcestershire, or the vegetable fields of East Anglia, and suitable activity holidays might also have included a course of flying lessons or a teach-yourself truffle-hunting holiday. Even a 'get away from it all' break overseas might have been popular with Marlon, providing the destination was chosen with care; Israel would have been an excellent choice, but Denmark best avoided.

However, if planning to take your pig travelling in a hot country – or even if he's doing some sun-bathing on a hot summer's day at home – it is important to ensure that he packs his sunglasses, sunscreen and parasol, for a pig's skin (note the correct spelling, 'pigskin' is both incorrect and insensitive to your pet's finer feelings) is as susceptible to sunburn as our own. Holiday reading can also prove a thorny problem. *'Animal Farm'* contains a quite unjustified slur on pigkind and may upset your pet, while *'Playboar'* is an offensive publication – sexism, anthropomorphism and porkism all in one. Try to persuade your pig that this kind of publication is really unworthy of him.

As well as the essential food and drink, Marlon liked a few toys and luxury items to keep him amused and entertained. A set of stereo headphones and a bottle of Dior's *Eau de Porc Sauvage* would perhaps have been high on his own personal Christmas list, but he had to make do with less exotic items, including a branch or two on which he could chew. Hardwoods such as oak, apple and pear lasted longer and also minimised the risk of him hurting his mouth on splinters from wood that split too easily. He also formed an attachment to a deflated red plastic football that came second only to his love of his food bowl, a recycled plastic washing-up bowl, which he used to drag off to bed with him every night.

Marlon also enjoyed the luxury of a morning bath. His particular favourite place was the patch of ground by the cattle trough, which wet weather and the feet of the farm heifers would soon convert into a dark brown morass. He liked nothing better than to roll over and over in the mud, emerging smothered from head to foot in mud, like a chocolate-covered pork surprise.

His other favourite place was down by the river, where he would spend half an hour rubbing himself luxuriously against the trunk of a tree that had been left high and dry by the winter floods. He had been subjected to the unkindest cut of all while in the possession of his previous owner, but nonetheless appeared to derive considerable pleasure from rubbing his underparts against the trunk. We thought it best to pretend we hadn't noticed and leave him to carry on. Unfortunately our attempts to teach him to swim were as unsuccessful as his flying lessons, for while rolling about in ecstasy in a patch of mud on the riverbank one day, he overbalanced and toppled into the river with a squeal of fright. He emerged from the water like a bullet from a gun and so great had been the shock to his system that he could never be induced to get more than his trotters wet from then on.

His spells down by the riverside were an important part of his daily routine, which also included a couple of walks with ourselves and the dog. While he didn't always walk to heel, he would come when called and in dire emergencies, the sight or sound of his food bowl being rattled was enough to bring him scampering from whatever corner he had disappeared to. If he stopped for a mouthful of food, which he did constantly, he would charge after us to catch up like a demented pot roast with his ears flapping in the breeze. It was a sight that reduced us to fits of laughter, but put the wind up more than one visitor strolling innocently down the public footpath that ran alongside the river, who looked up to see about a quarter of a ton of grunting pig bearing down on him at high speed.

Despite a pig's lifelong love affair with his

81

stomach, it was perfectly possible to feed Marlon without suffering undue assault and battery, but it was useful, bordering on absolutely vital, to get his food down in front of him as quickly as possible. In his headlong enthusiasm to get stuck into his rations, he would often send bowl and food flying in all directions with effects on the bearer of the glad tidings that can easily be imagined by anyone who has seen a pebble-dashed house.

Though he would eat anything and everything, we tried to feed him a balanced diet with plenty of roughage, something fortunately provided in ample quantities by his extra-mural snacks in the fields and orchard – fortunately, because pigs are as prone to constipation as humans. The only differences are that they can't reach for the milk of magnesia when constipation strikes and that a full grown pig is bad news when constipated and a walking disaster area when the siege is finally lifted.

After dogs and cats, the British like pigs more than any other animals. That news may surprise those whose only acquaintance with the *genus porcus* is at the breakfast table, but it must be true – I read it in *The Sun* – and Marlon's story may make you think about sampling the delights of a pet pig for yourself. Succumb to the temptation. On rare occasions pigs may be just as moody, argumentative and downright cantankerous as their human owners, but their needs are simple and their demands are few; and providing the rations are regular and substantial, a pig-pal can make your days seem like one long, contented wallow in the manure heap of life.

First catch your pig, as Mrs Beaton probably didn't say. Assuming that you are as inexperienced at pig-keeping as we were, you would probably be best to start off with a weaner (a pig about eight weeks old which has just been weaned from its mother's milk). Boars, sows or gilts (not gilts as in safe investments, but as in female pigs which have not yet had a litter of piglets) are best left to more experienced pig-keepers. It is also advisable, bordering on essential, that your weaner has been gelded; uncastrated boars are definitely not recommended for inexperienced pig-keepers.

Assuming that you are just going to keep your pig as a pet, choose one whose jib you like the cut of, always bearing in mind the need to choose a breed with a good temperament and one that is hardy enough to survive and thrive in your local weather conditions. There are a score of different pig breeds from which you can choose, including exotics like Vietnamese pot-bellied pigs, but if you're planning to keep yours outside, choose one of the hardier breeds like Berkshires, Hampshires, Gloucester Old Spots, Saddlebacks or Tamworths.

The Berkshire is black with a white mark on its face, white feet and a white-tipped tail. The sows make very good mothers and it is also a very hardy breed, thriving on rough land and wintering outside without needing much in the way of shelter. The Hampshire – originally not from the English county but from New Hampshire in the United States – has stocky legs and a narrow band or 'saddle' of white around its middle. The sows are docile and they also thrive indoors and out.

The Saddleback has drooping ears and a black head and body with a white saddle around the middle, front shoulders and legs. They have a docile temperament, make good mothers and thrive even in hard Northern winters, though not perhaps in those as hard as the ones at the Inn at the Top.

The Gloucester Old Spot – my personal favourite – is white and hairy with a number of irregular black patches on its body. It has long, drooping ears and a permanently suspicious expression which always makes me smile. The Old Spot thrives in cold climates, and once more has an excellent, docile temperament.

Finally, originally native to the Birmingham area, though fortunately – as far as I could tell – without the 'Brummagem' accent, the Tamworth is red and hairy, with sharp pointed ears and a long snout that it uses to forage for windfall fruits, acorns and beech-mast. Its thick coat helps it to survive and thrive outdoors in all but the very coldest British climates.

Having chosen your pig, if you are not fortunate enough to have a disused watermill to hand, you can house your pet in any suitable outbuilding, or in a proprietary or custom-built 'ark', which you can then move from time to time to a fresh patch of ground. You could also improvise a shelter from bales of straw, roofed with a couple of old doors or a sheet of corrugated iron, but make sure that the entrance is pointing away from the prevailing wind direction. Just like humans, pigs prefer a south-facing site, but if there are no trees to provide shade, you will also need to provide some shelter for him from the fierce heat of the summer sun.

You will have to be willing to clean out his quarters regularly – all the more important if you have neighbours nearby – and if there is a bad smell coming from your pig's quarters, it is your fault as much as your pet's because, contrary to their 'happy as a pig in s**t' image, pigs are very clean animals and in fact are even easier to house train than dogs or cats.

At one time, you could feed your pig on household scraps or swill – waste food, vegetable peelings, etc – collected from friendly neighbourhood pubs, cafes and restaurants. It is now the law that all swill must be boiled for two hours before it is fed to a pig to avoid him suffering everything from a minor stomach complaint to swine vesicular disease. A poorly pig is a tragedy – *Hamlet* on trotters – and if your pet turns into a boar with a sore head, the most likely causes are either his food or his accommodation. Bacterial infections may cause problems; treat your pig's food and his food bowl as if it were your own china plate and gourmet dinner for one, and there should be no problems. But if, despite all your best efforts, your pig does get an infection, the fastest cure is to move him to different, temporary housing, while you clean and disinfect his quarters, and then allow them to dry before putting him back. Keep him warm and dry, buy sacks of pig food from a farm supplier, mix in some fresh greens for roughage and, together with whatever grubs, roots and windfalls he finds for himself, he will have a healthy, balanced diet and you will have a happy pet pig.

Pigs are not only admirable companions and pets, they also have a multitude of other uses, apart from the obvious one. A pig is a waste disposal system that never needs a plumber and he is also the gardener's friend. A pig without a ring in his nose is an all-purpose rotovator, who will get rid of stubborn weeds and pests, turn over the soil, manure it and leave it in perfect heart for cultivating prize-winning vegetables (N.B. it is advisable to remove the pig before attempting the latter or he will certainly wish to claim his share of the prizes). With a ring fitted – and it is allegedly no more distressing for the pig than having an ear pierced is for us and essential if you want to prevent him from rooting up his patch of ground – he will graze happily on grass, keeping your lawns exquisitely manicured and providing useful practice for amateur golfers – a seven iron is ideal for chipping the droppings off the grass and into the decent obscurity of the shrubbery. If you prefer, leave him unadorned with facial jewellery, but be prepared for the consequences to your turf.

One other use for pigs was discovered by the Mafia, who, when they tired of dumping the corpses of their victims in vats of sulphuric acid or burying them in the concrete foundations of buildings and highway fly-overs, chopped them up and fed them to pigs instead. This behaviour is not recommended; quite apart from its illegality, pigs do not thrive on excessive amounts of protein and besides, they tend to hurt their teeth on the machine gun bullets.

We were fortunate to have had all the essential ingredients for true porcine pleasure at our fingertips, but anyone can form a meaningful relation-ship with a pig. The most basic facilities will please him: a shelter, a warm dry sleeping area and plenty to eat and drink – though not necessarily in that order. Choose your pig with care, spend time with him, look after him tenderly, feed him, water him, get him a few toys, take him for walks, discuss the affairs of state with him, but, above all, keep the food flowing, and you will have a devoted friend and companion for life. As long as the trough is topped-up, your pig will listen patiently and sym-pathetically to all your problems, while never being so crass as to suggest any solutions or ven-ture any opinions of his own. Pigs are so intel-ligent, affectionate and loveable that you may end up by missing out on your home-fed bacon, because you have grown too fond of him to see him end his days in your freezer, but if so, you will be amply compensated by the devotion and the eternal gratitude of the perfect pet – the pig.

We had befriended one of nature's gentlemen, who turned his back on a distinguished theatrical career and spent the rest of his days in the coun-tryside. In return for some care and attention, and several hundredweight of assorted foodstuffs, he became a cheerful, uncomplicated, loyal and caring friend; a bon viveur, raconteur and boon companion along life's highways and byways. And although he never appeared in any of the great Shakespearian roles, in his brief life he did manage to play everything from contemporary theatre to Bacon.

# CHAPTER 5

## The Clause Thirteen Club

At the end of my contract at the museum and art gallery, we moved again, to another old farmhouse, but this time in a little hamlet at the foot of one of the hills leading up to the Inn at the Top. All the time we'd been away, we had received regular bulletins from our friends and former customers about the events and comings and goings, not to mention the sackings, at the Inn at the Top. It was sheer schadenfreude for us, but we tried to hide our glee at hearing reports from our former locals that none of our successors had been as successful or popular as we had, and it was also distressing to hear how the pub was deteriorating. It was once more being closed and boarded up every winter, and as a result was becoming steadily ever more damp, dirty and decrepit.

The house we had moved to was another lovely old building in a beautiful setting. The house dated from the seventeenth century and there were two venerable oak court cupboards on either side of the living room door. One end of the house was dug into the slope of the hill on which the house stood and the ground floor room at that end, which I used as an office, was damp as a result. When we bought the house, that room came complete with four old carpets laid one on top of each other. Although there was no smell of mildew and no mushrooms growing out of it, the top carpet felt a little damp and I wasn't anxious to find out what the ones underneath were like but, although damp, they appeared to be no worse than the top one, so I replaced them all and got on with my work. When we sold the house and moved on, we left the carpets in situ and they may even have remained there, untouched to this day.

There was one major change from our previous house. This time as it lacked sufficient land and outbuildings, our house had to be a pig-free zone and that meant saying a sad farewell to Marlon, who had spent two years with us before setting off on his journey to the great sty in the sky. Inevitably it was a very tearful parting. The deed was done while Sue was at work one day – she couldn't bear the thought of being there as he was driven away and I had to supervise the loading of Marlon into the van that was to take him to the auction mart. The lorry pulled up outside the farmhouse and with the skill born of two years practice, I led Marlon up to the tailgate of the truck, luring him on with his beloved food bowl and a couple of treats. Unfortunately a small calf was already in residence in the truck and Marlon took one look at the calf and then, either not liking the look of his potential companion on the journey, or else remembering that he had not paid a visit to the orchard that morning, he turned on his heel and stalked off back the way he had come.

The driver of the truck and I then had to turn Marlon around, and turning round an unwilling pig weighing in at the best part of 200 kilograms is about as slow and ponderous as making a three-point turn in a super-tanker. We then began 'boarding' him back to the truck – steering him by holding a wooden board alongside his head to encourage him to turn the way we wanted. Even then, it took a couple of extra special treats to lure him up the ramp and into the wagon. I avoided Marlon's eye as the driver closed the tailgate of the truck and, feeling rather like Judas Iscariot at the Last Supper, I watched it drive slowly off up the lane while the sound of Marlon singing lustily for his own last supper could still be heard above the sound of the engine.

One of the farmers we knew from the Inn at the Top was at the auction mart that day and phoned me later on to say he'd seen Marlon trotting through the sale ring. 'By, he was a size and a half, wasn't he? He seemed quite happy as he was going through the ring,' he said, though whether that was true or just an attempt to soothe our feelings, I'm not sure. History did not relate who had bought him and, though I tried to convince myself and Sue that someone might have bought him as a pet, her expression showed that I had failed to convince her, or myself, for that matter.

We'd kept in close touch with our friends from the Inn at the Top while we'd been away from the area and we had made a particular point of coming back for the annual sheep show, the Swaledale sheep world championship, held at the inn every year on the last Thursday in May. By then lambing was over, hay-time had yet to begin, and the farmers' prize young tups and yows – rams and ewes – had had enough time and good grazing to recover from the rigours of winter and regain peak condition.

We still knew next to nothing about the local breed of sheep, other than the obvious fact that they were off-white with black faces and white noses, but it was a great chance to catch up with all of our friends and former regulars in one fell swoop, because only terminal illness would have kept any of them away from the inn on show day. We stifled any resentment we felt inside at the sight of someone else behind the bar – this was our pub, what were they doing there? – and tried to enjoy the day for what it was: 'a reet grand day out'.

It was another sign of our acceptance into the wider community of the Dale that we had a coveted invitation to tea at one of the neighbouring farms. Our invitation came from the farmer's wife who, during our winter at the inn, had often baked treats for us and sent her son up the hill with them. The sheep show attracted people from far and wide and every farmer's circle of friends and large extended family put great pressure on space at the tea-table of the handful of farms within a reasonable distance of the inn, so we were favoured indeed to be invited.

It was an old-fashioned 'High Tea', served on a spotless linen cloth decorated with posies of wild violets and primroses and the table was groaning under an accumulation of food that would no doubt have had Enid Blyton's characters in the

Famous Five adventures enthusing about 'sandwiches and pies and sausage rolls and scones and biscuits and cakes and lashings and lashings of ginger pop'. There were home-made pork pies, the meat coming from the farm's own pigs, home-cured ham and sausage rolls from the same source, hard-boiled eggs with yolks as dark and rich as the ones from our own bantams, courtesy of the hens that free-ranged over the fields behind the farm. There were mountains of sandwiches – even the bread was home-baked – and plate upon plate of home-made cakes, biscuits, tarts and pastries, with strawberries and thick double cream for those who still had room. In deference to the chapel folk among us, there was no alcohol, just cups of industrial strength tea, and home-made lemonade or ginger beer for the kids.

After an hour or so on the sofa to recover, we all headed back up to the inn in time for the silver band's traditional impromptu concert and the judging of the yows and tups, including the crowning of the supreme champion. Tradition required that the owner of the champion should then fill the silver cup with whisky and pass it round for all to drink his health and that was the prelude to a long, raucous night in the pub with most of the unsuccessful exhibitors busily explaining to anyone within earshot why the judges had got it so hopelessly wrong.

Having turned my back on the art game for what I hoped would be the last time, I was now working from home as a freelance journalist, book editor and author. In that sense I had come full circle, for it was now six years since I had abandoned that career (if that isn't too strong a word for my ramshackle progression from odd job to odd job), for the dubious delights of managing the Inn at the Top. Sue had meanwhile again found work as a care assistant in a nearby market town. We were back within range of our old locals from the inn, and were neighbours with some of them, and we were living only a fifteen minute drive from the Inn at the Top itself. So we were right on the spot should the inn's owners, Stan and Neville, finally decide to throw in the towel and sell it. Whether we had anywhere near enough money to buy it was another question, but we had a house that, courtesy of the mid-1980s housing boom, we could hope to sell at a profit, and with a few quid in our bank account, plus the aid of a hoped for loan from a bank, another from a brewer, and, with luck, an investment from a sleeping partner, we thought we might just be able to scrape together sufficient cash.

Our friends continued to regale us with a regular flow of gossip about the inn and we continued to try to disguise our pleasure at their stories of the endless procession of temporary managers who were coming and going with ever-increasing frequency, including one who lasted precisely two weeks before deciding the inn's bleakness and loneliness were more than he could cope with. However, as one newspaper correspondent observed at the time, 'the rapid turnover of staff has given rise to speculation that it is not the seclusion which has caused it, but the brisk style of management. The last couple to run the gaunt, unassuming white-washed building lasted only a few months and left, according to the owners 'because we felt they were not suitable for the job'. Their predecessors, Neil and Sue Hanson,' the newspaper added, 'who ran it from March 1978 until April 1979, eventually left, disillusioned not with the isolation but by the management.'

That we were not alone in our opinion of them was confirmed for me recently in a letter sent to me by a man who had just finished reading *The Inn at the Top* and who recalled his own narrow escape from managing the inn for the same dodgy duo. 'In 1978 I was working for Ever Ready Batteries at their Newburn Factory,' he wrote, 'and my first wife and I fancied a complete change when we read an advert in the *Newcastle Evening Chronicle:* 'Ever Thought About Joining The Licensed Trade – Ever Thought About Moving To The Home Counties?' At the time I wasn't even sure who or what the Home Counties were, but nevertheless we applied to a company called St Georges Taverns, a trading arm of Chef & Brewer. We were interviewed in a hotel in the Newcastle Area and we were offered the job of Trainee Managers.

'While waiting for our start date and training programme the management position at what you call The Inn at the Top was advertised so, thinking it would be closer to home, we applied. We had an interview by the two guys you refer to as Neville and Stan, I couldn't remember their names to save my life but you describe them extremely well. The interview took place at a table in a room full of people in a bar in Jesmond; not at all very professional and I was old and wise enough to realise that these two were not going to be good employers, so we stuck to our original guns and went off to the Home Counties a few weeks later.

'Obviously I wanted to visit the pub to see it with my own eyes so we took my Mam and Dad to see exactly where the pub was located. I actually loved what I saw and always promised to go back to see how it was going, but because of constraints of distance and time it has taken me a further thirty-six years for my second visit. Your book made me doubly glad I never actually got offered the inn as I feel I would not have had your appetite for the extremely hard life style of living on the top of one of the windiest and coldest hills in the UK, topped with having two unscrupulous Geordie Wide Boys as my employers, and having to run a successful public house as the icing on the cake. You should have been awarded a medal the size of a frying pan for what you and Sue went through.'

Whatever schadenfreude we might have felt in reading about the Geordie Wide Boys' troubles and the rapid turnover of staff, we had only sympathy for one unfortunate manager. He had been sleeping in front of the fire – presumably Stan and Neville had once more taken a crucial part of the central heating boiler away 'for repairs', just as they had in the grim winter that we had spent up there to stop us 'wasting money' by running the central heating – when an aerosol can of air freshener that he had left too close to the fire exploded, badly injuring him.

The inn was once more being closed and

boarded up throughout the winter, but in the six months that it was open for business each year, Stan and Neville had managed to work their way through an average of two managers a year and in the previous season had excelled themselves by getting through no less than three ... as Lady Bracknell might have said, to lose one might be regarded as a misfortune; to lose three smacked of carelessness.

While awaiting developments, we threw ourselves into community life, which in my case required my participation in the annual football cup competition that was fought out – and I mean that literally – among the villages and hamlets of the upper Dale every autumn. I was soon introduced to its bruising brutality. Finesse and football skill are all very well, but the Cup also required a Passchendaele-like willingness to go over the top, whatever the cost in lives or limbs. Such was the clumsiness and ferocity of the tackling that it was an unusual year in which one or two legs were not broken along the way.

I was almost entirely bereft of footballing skill, but I launched myself at the opposition with such gusto that I was threatened with post-match violence by no fewer than three of them. Had a football manager been watching, my wholehearted commitment would certainly have had him reaching deep into his store of clichés. I put my body on the line, gave 110 per cent, and would have run through a brick wall for my teammates, and at the end of the day, that's what the game's all about. However, no gain without pain, and after our derby match against our hated rivals from the next hamlet, I could scarcely walk for two days. Even so, I was in better shape than one of our neighbours, who was so stiff that he had to be lifted bodily into his tractor seat the next morning to do his daily work around the farm.

I had also offered to help out a couple of the local farmers either at hay-time or whenever a helping hand was needed, and one of our near neighbours, Kenny, a chicken farmer who had a contract with a large egg-producer to rear day-old chicks until they reached point-of-lay, duly asked me to help him load his latest consignment of chickens aboard the truck that had come to transport them. I'd smelled the aroma wafting over the fields from his farm buildings whenever the wind was in the right – or do I mean wrong? – direction, but until I entered the rearing sheds I had never experienced the full, ammonia-laden stench of hundreds of chickens at close quarters. I now understood why Kenny had no sense of smell – the stink of his chickens had completely burned out his nasal passages.

However, a promise was a promise, so with a scarf wrapped around my face in a futile attempt to minimise the smell, I followed Kenny's example and began scooping up chickens and loading them into crates that there were then stacked, several-deep, in tiers on the back of the truck. It didn't seem an ideal way to travel, but I was assured that the chickens would be none the worse for their journey. 'It's in my interest to make sure they arrive in good condition,' Kenny said. 'If I lose too many or they don't lay, I won't get any more contracts to rear them.'

Despite our friendship with many of the locals, we still had much to absorb about life in these remote and long-established rural communities. They had their own way of doing things and some of their customs and practices were completely alien to anything we had ever previously experienced. That was vividly demonstrated one weekend when I decided to fell the old and creaking ash-tree at the bottom of our garden. I picked up a hired chainsaw from the local dealer one Saturday morning, and though it rained all that day, Sunday dawned bright and clear. After a leisurely morning, that afternoon I revved up the chainsaw and with a due application of science, cut a notch on the side I wanted the tree to fall. I then began a cut to meet it from the other side of the trunk. All was going well until the chainsaw coughed once, like an undertaker clearing his throat, and then died on me. My increasingly frenzied attempts to re-start it proved useless.

I couldn't leave the tree half-sawed, teetering on the brink, but the dealer was closed for the weekend and none of our friends had a chainsaw that I could borrow. However, there were three farms in the hamlet and we knew the farmers slightly – enough to nod and say 'Good morning' to them at least. Since all farmers tended to have a chainsaw somewhere about the place, I was still relatively relaxed as I downed tools and, with an anxious look over my shoulder at the ash-tree and a futile request to Sue to 'Keep an eye on it for me' – quite what I thought she was going to do if it started to topple, I have no idea – I set off at top speed to borrow a chainsaw.

What I had not factored into my calculations was that it was a Sunday and all three farmers were staunch and very strict Methodist 'chapel folk'. On Sundays, as I now discovered, it was their custom to attend chapel in the morning, then return home, draw their curtains and remain in quiet prayer and contemplation in their parlours for the rest of the day... Or at least, that was the theory. For all I know they may actually have been mixing cocktails, watching TV, dancing the fandango or playing strip poker. However their strict observance of their religion permitted them to do no work on the Sabbath, and their definition of that was evidently sufficiently rigorous to embrace a refusal to answer the telephone or reply to knocks at the door, no matter how persistent. I knew they were there – I could see them moving around through the chinks in their curtains and at one point a shadowy figure emerged from his living room to peer at me from the recesses of one of their darkened halls – but not one of them could be persuaded to open their door or even acknowledge my presence in any way. I even tried lifting the flap of the letterbox of one house and shouting 'Hello! This is an emergency! Do you have a chainsaw I could borrow?' But still I received no reply, no acknowledgement, and definitely no chainsaw.

It was now late in the afternoon and dusk was fast approaching. I went back to the house and in sheer desperation, I picked up the steel wedges that I was going to use to split the logs once the tree had been felled and cut up, and instead drove them into the saw-cut with a sledgehammer. The cut wasn't deep enough for the wedges to complete the job of felling the tree, but they were at least pressed into emergency use as chocks to stop the tree rocking backwards and forwards on the cut that I'd made.

'It should be fine,' I said nervously to Sue, 'there's hardly any breeze.' During the course of that evening the wind steadily strengthened and, unable to sleep, I lay awake all night, listening to the progressively louder creaks and groans from the ash-tree towering above the house like the Sword of Damocles. When the chainsaw dealer arrived for work early the following morning, he found me already pacing up and down on his doorstep. I screeched back home with a replacement chainsaw, knocked out the wedges, and had barely begun cutting before the tree started to topple. It was down in less than a minute but mercifully it fell the way it was intended to drop and not back onto the house.

I was clearly not cut out for a career as a lumberjack but, after another series of improbable changes of career direction, and by a route which, even now, I have difficulty in understanding myself, let alone explaining to anybody else, I had now started a new job as editor of the Campaign for Real Ale's annual boozer's bible, *The Good Beer Guide*. I did have one faint qualification in that I had just finished editing a directory of all the temporary exhibition spaces in Great Britain, from public art galleries to the windows of building societies, where artists could display their work. In a poor light, if you kept your eyes half-closed, you could just about mistake it for a similar volume to the *Good Beer Guide.*

I was also an avid consumer of CAMRA's favourite product and, carried away with my enthusiasm for it, I had even joined the organisation, though my Groucho Marx-like refusal to be part of any club that would have me as a member meant that I never went to any meetings. Nonetheless, in company with my friend Pete, I had devoted countless evenings to a restless, relentless quest for the perfect pint of beer. No part of the North of England was too obscure, no taproom too dingy, provided there was the prospect of a decent pint. However, like the quest for the Holy Grail, the search for the quintessential pint of amber nectar was as much about travelling hopefully as actually arriving and even when we found a pint that was as near perfect as makes no difference, we had barely wiped the froth from our lips before we were abandoning that pub and setting off to try out the next one on our list.

So I did have some relevant experience and qualifications when I applied for the job – by no means always the case in previous job applications. The CAMRA Company Secretary later revealed to me that one of the people who had drawn up the shortlist of candidates had given me a slightly ambivalent commendation: 'Could be perfect for the job, providing he doesn't turn out to be a complete bull-shitter.' I'd like to think that I was not a complete bull-shitter, just a partial one, and therefore eminently acceptable. However, it was still almost as much a surprise to me as it probably was to the panel of CAMRA's great and good who had interviewed me, when after due deliberation and – inevitably – much stroking of beards, they offered me the job.

It turned out to be a job that required not only editorial skills but also the ability to sink copious pints of the Campaigns' preferred product. Indeed it was the only job I'd had where it was practically a sacking offence NOT to go to the pub at lunchtime. I hasten to add that things are very different at the Campaign for Real Ale these days, but back in my day, the ability to stand your round and sink your pint often seemed to be almost as important as the need to possess some competence in the work you were doing ... which of course may help to explain how I managed to get the job in the first place!

On my first day there, I was summoned from my desk at ten-thirty in the morning by one of my senior colleagues. 'Time to get to work,' he said. 'There are seventy-two pubs in St Albans and the record for the fastest time to drink a pint in each of them is just over a week. I hold it and now you're going to beat it.' We left at once for 'lunch' and after a brief respite during the afternoon, which I spent head down on my desk, he frog-marched me back to the next pub on our itinerary, prompt at the evening opening time of five-thirty. By the time I phoned Sue that night to let her know how I'd got on during my first day, I was so drunk and incoherent that she couldn't understand a word I said. To my eternal shame, I didn't quite manage to break the record, even though I damn near perished in the attempt.

That set a pattern for my employment: a little light editing in the morning, and possibly the

102

afternoon, punctuated by incessant 'working lunches', 'early-doors' and 'lock-ins' and, indeed, the champagne breakfasts, cocktail parties and other festivities with which the staff – and I confess, I was one of the ringleaders in this – enlivened the occasional interludes of office-work and campaigning. Some of these forms of harmless light entertainment also earned us the stern disapproval of some of the Campaign's more unbending members, who, whatever their own nightly beery excesses, had only loathing and contempt for those who indulged in 'ladies' drinks' like champagne, wine, cocktails or gin and tonics.

Excessive consumption proved to be the rule, not the exception, among many of the CAMRA employees who, contrary to the snide remarks from some sections of the licensed trade, proved perfectly capable of running a booze-up in a brewery, and pretty well anywhere else, come to that. The Campaign's offices were then sited in a Victorian house in St Albans that had been so minimally converted to office use that it still had an intact and fully functioning kitchen and bathroom. That and the stiff price of accommodation in St Albans made it not merely a splendid party venue, but a desirable residence for itinerant, part-time employees like me, and also for a number of casual visitors. On one famous occasion the eleven members of the cricket team formed by one of the Northern CAMRA branches bedded down for the night in the offices after a hardfought match against the South Hertfordshire branch that was followed by an even more hardfought drinking bout.

The use of the office as overnight accommodation was one of a multitude of things that were banned by the catch-all Clause Thirteen of CAMRA's lease, which among other things also forbade the use of the premises for music, dancing, the consumption of alcohol or drugs, and a multitude of other lewd, immoral, depraved or licentious purposes. This blanket prohibition was routinely ignored by some staff members whenever – and it was often – the post-work drinks extended well into or even throughout the evening. A select few staff members, including myself, had a sleeping bag secreted somewhere around their office and so many of us broke the Thirteenth Commandment that the Company Secretary even established a 'Clause Thirteen Club', complete with its own tie, with membership open only to those who had broken almost every single one of Clause Thirteen's numerous sub-clauses. The only restriction imposed by Clause Thirteen that none of us ever got round to breaking was the prohibition on charging people to watch 'cinematographic performances'. As CAMRA's legendary Company Secretary at the time remarked to me: 'Gambling? Sale of alcohol? Sundry activities that might offend a Puritan? Yes! Yes! And Yes! But charging people to watch a film? Never!'

There was a strict vetting procedure for those wishing to be elected to club membership, as we were reminded in a memo from the Company Secretary: 'Those wishing to be considered for membership of the Clause Thirteen Club should submit details of the event(s) and/or occasion(s) arising from which membership of the Club is being claimed. Stringent proof will be required (in most cases). Indicate also under which category (or categories) your membership application is to be considered.' It was a proud moment when I joined that august gathering, but the fact that there were more than a dozen other members tells its own debauched tale.

I slept on the floor of my office three or four nights a week, six months a year, for the entire five years I worked for the Campaign, but one of the full-time staff members claimed to hold the UK all-comers record, having lived there continuously, seven days a week for the first two years of his full-time employment, including the Christmas holidays, while existing – or so he insisted – on a diet solely comprising of beer and Pot Noodles. The fact that he then underwent an operation for what his doctor allegedly referred to as 'the worst case of piles I have ever seen', lent some credibility to a claim that might otherwise have been dismissed as ludicrous.

By the time I joined the organisation, his diet had at least been expanded to include a regular curry at the end of his evening's beer-related activities. He tended to save half of it and eat it stone cold for breakfast while opening the mail the next morning, a disconcerting sight to be greeted with first thing in the morning, and one made worse by his habit of keeping a couple of 'Bombay Ducks' – the quite extraordinarily pungent dried, salted and fried lizardfish served in most Indian restaurants at the time – in his breast-pocket. While fumbling in his pocket for a pen, he would chance upon one of these stinking fish instead, and eat it with evident relish, while the rest of us shuddered, averted our eyes and covered our noses. When I reminded him of this recently he added that a neatly folded chapati could also be used to fill the breast-pocket in place of the more traditional folded handkerchief!

A majority of the Great British Public, if they'd heard of CAMRA at all, probably tended to regard it – not always, it must be conceded, entirely without some accuracy – as the social club of a bunch of beer-sodden piss-artists. The Campaign devoted much attention to this image problem and one of the more pleasing ironies of the job was the chance to eavesdrop on the endless earnest debates and furious tirades about the need to improve the Campaign's public image, often delivered by bearded, stringy-haired and clinically obese men who lived with their mothers and wore supersize jeans and tee-shirts still bearing ample traces of last night's beer and curry spills.

For special occasions, like beer festivals, some of them favoured kaftans made from the drip towels that pub landlords put on the bar to soak up the spilt beer – I kid you not, it really was something of a fashion statement among a certain coterie of CAMRA members at the time. One of the more memorable sights I have encountered in my life, I still wake screaming in the night at the mere thought of it, was that of a bearded, pot-bellied, twenty-stone CAMRA member I saw at the campaign's Annual General Meeting. The AGM was held in a different venue every year and this one was at the Brighton Metropole, a conference centre accessed by way of an escalator from the ground floor lobby.

The portly CAMRA member had evidently indulged in copious refreshment during the lunch interval and was now returning, revitalised, if somewhat unsteady, to the fray. However as he began ascending the escalator in his flowing robes, I saw his eyes widen in terror as the hem of his drip-towel kaftan became entangled in the metal teeth of the escalator he was riding. While he heaved unavailingly at the kaftan, it was relentlessly shredded by the moving escalator until he eventually stood before us in all his naked glory, saving only a pair of very grey and grubby looking Y-fronts, plus a small frayed circlet of his garment still hanging around his neck like a tattered necklace. As my old Aunt Betty used to say: 'The things you see when you haven't got your gun!'

The determined efforts to improve CAMRA's public image were never more evident than at the Campaign's annual shop-window: the Great British Beer Festival, a gigantic drinkathon that involved hiring some aircraft hangar-sized building, filling it to the rafters with barrels of beer and then unleashing the CAMRA membership and any interested members of the general public upon it. A couple of years before I joined the staff, the chosen venue was the Alexandra Palace in London, which unfortunately burned down about a month before the event, though as far as I know the two things were not connected. It was too late to advertise a change of venue – all the posters and publicity material had already gone out – so the decision was taken to go ahead with the Festival in a series of giant marquees erected in the grounds of the smouldering 'Ally Pally', and in such an insecure venue, a number of burly CAMRA members had to be recruited to act as night security guards.

According to a much loved part of the CAMRA apocrypha – its actual protagonist insists the story is the merest hear-say – two of the security guards were on patrol at three in the morning on the first night of the Festival, well after the official closing time, when they heard a noise from one of the tents. When they went inside, they found a ginger-haired, extravagantly moustachioed, and quite spectacularly sozzled Irishman helping himself from one of the barrels. They grabbed hold of him, dragged him outside, gave him a stern lecture about being 'the sort of drunken swine that gives the Campaign For Real Ale a bad name', and then threw him out and he stumbled off into the night.

The next morning one of them was idly leafing through the latest edition of the Campaign's newspaper, *What's Brewing*, when he came across a photograph of the latest addition to CAMRA's roster of paid employees ... a curiously familiar ginger-haired and extravagantly moustachioed Irishman. However in his defence I have to say that, with the exception of that inauspicious start and the later unfortunate occasion when he left the company chequebook on the bar of a dingy taproom in Belfast, he proved to be an extremely competent and skilful member of staff, who rescued the organisation's tangled administration from its previous barely disguised chaos, and turned it into a picture of logic and order ... while still managing to prove a lively and very entertaining companion on our innumerable liquid evenings out.

Unusually for a seasoned administrator, he had a cavalier attitude to the paperwork which swamped his desk, a large, double-sided partners' desk that was almost completely covered with a mound of papers and correspondence. He claimed that it was just his own idiosyncratic filing system and that he knew the whereabouts of every piece of paper on it, but the occasional emergence of unanswered and sometimes even unopened letters including one memorable occasion when one turned up after being buried under his paper mountain for over two years, suggested that the system was not entirely without its flaws.

While editing the *Good Beer Guide* I was also operating as European correspondent for a chain of New Zealand radio stations, which often required me to manage the miraculous feat of apparently being in two different places at the same time – ah, the magic of radio... On one occasion, the morning of the wedding of Prince Charles and Princess Diana, I was woken from a deep sleep at two in the morning – and as usual I was sleeping on the floor of my office – by a call from Auckland. 'Morning Neil,' an unfeasibly cheerful Kiwi voice said. 'Sorry to wake you up, but I wonder if you'd mind giving us a quick colour piece live into the lunchtime news. You know, set the scene on the royal wedding route – that sort of thing?'

'Well, I could with pleasure,' I said, except that it's the middle of the night and I'm in St Albans which is about twenty-five miles away from the wedding route.'

There was a brief pause. 'Well ... can't you busk it?'

Thus it was that radio listeners in New Zealand were treated to a lavish, OTT description of the royal wedding route as dawn was about to break over London on this day of days, complete with people sitting in deck-chairs or curled up in sleeping-bags staking their claim to prime positions, street vendors arriving to begin hawking paper union jacks, plastic periscopes and other souvenir royal tat, and Police, Bomb Squad and Royalty Protection Group teams checking manhole covers and towing away parked cars, while black-clad police snipers took their places on rooftops overlooking the route. As far as I know, it was all absolute cobblers, but in those carefree days before the introduction of twenty-four hour rolling news television programmes, it was the sort of stuff that a radio reporter who thought that 'Scruples' were some kind of wall-fixings and 'Ethics' a county to the east of London, could just about get away with.

If that was shabby, the professional pits in my broadcasting career probably came while I was masquerading as a sports journalist and covering a tour of Papua New Guinea, Australia and New Zealand by the Great Britain rugby league team. Since I was on honeymoon at the time and my blushing bride had never been to Australia before, I wanted to show her as much of a good time as was humanly possible, while still paying lip service to my journalistic and broadcasting commitments. So while the Great Britain team

110

and all their other attendant sports reporters headed south to wintry Melbourne for the next Test match, we travelled in the opposite direction, flying up to North Queensland, taking in a few luxurious days on Hayman Island in the Whitsundays, a few more at Palm Cove, north of Cairns, and ending up at a rainforest resort at Cape Tribulation in the far north of Queensland.

My only problem was that I had contracted to do a thirty second update every ten minutes of the Test match for a chain of radio stations back in the UK. As befitted a rainforest that was a World Heritage site, Cape Tribulation was an extremely sparsely populated area, but eventually I found a backpackers' bar a few miles away from where we were staying with a TV and a patriotic, sports loving, fair dinkum Aussie landlord who, for a small consideration, was willing to let me watch the game and use the phone in the lobby to send reports back to the UK. My producer and the radio audience back in the UK will never suspect a thing, I sniggered to myself, as I filed my preview piece and then settled down to watch the game. All went well at first. I watched the match on the TV in the bar, surrounded by twenty or so beer-swilling 'Ockers', filed my reports every ten minutes and the background noise from the drunks in the bar gave the reports just the right sort of crowd atmosphere.

Then disaster struck: Great Britain started winning. Decades of unbroken Australian domination had led the Aussie fans to take victory as a given and the crowd at the ground and, even more so, the customers and landlord of the pub

– patriotic true blue Ockers to a man – did not take kindly to this unexpected turn of events, nor to the overexcited 'Pommie bastard' in the foyer making jubilant broadcasts to the UK about it. As the gap between the teams widened, the atmosphere turned increasingly sour just as, back in Britain, the unexpected scoreline was fuelling demands for ever more score flashes, live updates and reports.

I had just given the final scoreline down the phone and been told that the programme was staying with me, live on air, to capture some of the carnival atmosphere as Britain's players and fans celebrated their unexpected victory, when the furious Australian bar-owner – a true son of the land where second is just the first of the losers – stormed across the bar with a face like thunder and yanked the plug of the TV out of the wall. My Marcel Marceau-style mimed pleas to him to turn it back on, delivered while still prattling down the line to my radio audience back home, fell on deaf ears – if you see what I mean – and once more I found myself in need of psychic powers, uttering a stream of gibberish about British players draped in scarves and hats borrowed from jubilant fans, dancing and singing in front of the main stand, while disconsolate Aussies streamed away from the ground, choking on the ashes of defeat. Such Pommie triumphalism, bellowed down the phone from the Cape Tribulation bar, was continuing to go down like a cup of cold sick with the customers and in an atmosphere of undisguised menace I finished my final report, banged the phone down and sprinted for our hire car, before the tar and feathers – or something worse – could be produced and applied.

# CHAPTER 6

## A Dish Best Served Cold

Back in the Beautiful Dale it was now the autumn of 1983, four and a half years since we'd left the inn, and I was just completing my first production run of the *Good Beer Guide* when one of our former locals rang us to say that the inn, having haemorrhaged customers all year, was once more closed and boarded up, and the gossip in the Dale was that the crooked owners, Stan and Neville, had at last put it on the market.

We first had to confirm that the rumours were true. A couple of paragraphs in one of the local papers, headed '£60,000 for a Quiet Drink' both confirmed the story and revealed the asking price. We did not dwell on the rest of the article, which described the inn as 'The perfect pub ... to a landlord who likes drinking alone,' and noted that 'The inn, the highest in Britain, has driven some of its previous landlords to the brink of a nervous breakdown because of its isolation'.

We made contact with Stan and Neville at once and, as a first step, made an appointment to look over their latest set of cooked books. They were supplied with much nudging and winking about what the true figures would have been if they hadn't been subjected to Stan's creative accounting. When we'd worked for them, their desperation to ensure that we weren't cheating them – we weren't, but their whole system of values seemed to be based on the assumption that everyone was as much 'on the rob' as they were – was matched only by their determination to ensure that they, and on their behalf, their employees, were extracting the absolute maximum amount of cash from everybody else as efficiently as possible. And if they were happy to fleece their customers, they were positively ecstatic if they could find a way to reduce the amount that they were having to pay the Inland Revenue and HM Customs out of their ill-gotten gains.

I never saw the tax or VAT returns they submitted, so I have no idea to what extent they contained the truth, the whole truth and nothing but the truth, but from what I knew of Stan and Neville, I suspected that they would have been happy to submit VAT and tax returns that were such works of fantasy and imagination that they could have been filed under 'Fiction' in Waterstones.

Something in Stan's accounting must have caused suspicions to arise, however, because I still remember the summer morning when he phoned the pub in a state of total panic. 'Take the menus off the tables and hide the blackboard,' he said. 'We don't do food.'

'What do you mean we don't do food?' I said. 'We sold about 150 lunches yesterday.'

'The VAT men are coming to inspect the pub

today. If they ask, we don't do food.'

'For God's sake, Stan,' I said. 'We've got a kitchen full of catering equipment and Sue as a full-time chef.'

'Good point,' he said. 'Give her the day off. And if the VAT men ask...'

'I know,' I said. 'I get it. We don't do food.'

Being put on the spot like that and forced to lie through our teeth to the VAT men, whose cynical, suspicious expressions showed they didn't believe a word we said – and with good cause, since none of it was true – was just another reason for us to hate Stan and Neville's guts. We never heard from them whether the VAT inspection led to any further action, but the next morning the menus and blackboard were back in place and normal food service was resumed. Their wheezes and scams were clearly lucrative; that autumn Neville offered us a free holiday in Tenerife if we'd take £10,000 in cash out of the country with us, hidden in our luggage. Exchange Controls were in place at the time precisely to prevent large sums of money being taken out of the country and, had we done it and been caught, it would have been the most expensive free holiday we'd ever had.

Now they had finally had enough of owning the inn, or else were wanting more time to enjoy their accumulated profits. As a result, we finally had the chance to make good on our pledge to buy the inn. We thought it over, put our house on the market, counted our cash, made an appointment to discuss a loan with our bank manager, and then phoned up Stan and Neville and made what we thought was a fair offer, even though it was substantially less than the £60,000 asking price.

'Not enough,' Neville said, putting down the phone. There was no question of upping our offer – it was all the money we had and could borrow in the world, so we sighed, put it behind us and got on with our lives.

Christmas came and went and 1984 had dawned and was well under way when Neville rang me one night. 'We've had a lot of interest,' he said, 'but we wanted to give you two one last chance to buy it.'

'Sorry, Neville,' I said. 'We'd love to buy it but, like we said at the time, the offer was a final one. We don't have any more money, so we couldn't go any higher, even supposing we wanted to.'

There was a pregnant pause during which I heard Neville place his hand over the receiver and begin a *sotto voce* conversation with someone else, presumably Stan. 'Er, well,' Neville finally said, 'in that case, as a favour to you, we might be willing to consider your offer after all.'

I let a couple of beats of silence pass. 'So there wasn't that much interest, then? Anyway, I'm not sure that offer's still on the table, Neville,' I said, reflecting on the truth of the old adage about revenge being a dish best served cold. 'We'll discuss it and get back to you.'

We talked it over that night and, folie a deux once more as much to the fore as when we'd applied to manage the inn six years before, decided to go ahead, albeit having lowered our offer to reflect both the loss of goodwill after another few months of non-trading and the evident desperation of the vendors. After some huffing and puffing on both sides we agreed a price and arranged to meet them to shake hands on the deal; we made a mental note to count our fingers afterwards.

Why did we want to go back so much? Like parents who obliterate the memory of the traumas of childbirth, colic, teething and all the attendant sleepless nights with their first baby, until the next one arrives to remind them, perhaps we had erased the memory of the drudgery, the hardships and the relentless pressure from our minds, or maybe we really did believe that it would all be different this time. If we were working for ourselves, perhaps it would all seem, if not easier, at least more worthwhile.

It's also hard to discount the impact of the constant pleas from our friends and locals to come back and rescue the inn from the dire straits to which it had sunk under its dismal absentee owners. We liked and respected our locals, by now they were practically family. If we went back, they'd support us and look after us; it would be just like going home. We also had pledges from a few of our old friends from other places where we'd lived in the past that if we bought the inn, they'd either help with the workload or even better, come in as partners with us.

We'd decided that it would only work if we had considerable help with running the inn and if we offered a menu that was sufficiently straightforward to allow us to cope with the avalanches of customers that the summer tourist season would bring. A pub near Manchester – the Royal Oak at Didsbury – offered one model for how that could be achieved. We had often gone there for lunch when we were living near Manchester a few years before. It offered a remarkably simple menu: beautiful bread and an astonishing array of cheeses and pates served up in very generous 'farmers' portions'. Sticking to that simple format, with everything prepared in advance, one or two people could feed an army quite comfortably. We told ourselves we could also have a large pan of soup bubbling on the stove for those who insisted on hot food, or we could cook a big roast every day and serve hot beef or hot pork sandwiches easily enough too. If only we'd stuck to those ideas...

Whatever the reasons, we'd now mentally committed ourselves to returning to the Inn at the Top and we also now had a definite buyer for our house. A few days later, I met Neville in one of Newcastle's dodgier pubs to discuss the terms and timing of the hand-over. All the time we were talking, he kept anxiously looking over his shoulder towards the door.

'It's all right, Neville,' I said. As far as I know, it's not illegal to buy and sell pubs.'

'It's not that,' he said. 'I'm waiting for an envelope.'

Five minutes later, the door opened just wide enough to admit a ferret-faced man with lank, unwashed hair and a promising collection of facial blackheads, who appeared to slide rather than walk over to our table. After an appraising look at me, he pulled a bulky brown envelope from inside his jacket, handed it to Neville with a muttered 'Here y'are Nev, it's all there', and was gone. The envelope disappeared into an inside pocket of Neville's capacious camel-hair overcoat and I at last had his undivided attention.

When we had agreed on the purchase price for the pub, Neville had offered a further discount if part of it, £10,000, was paid in 'poond notes'. We were happy enough with the discount – we were so short of money that even the most dubious of gift horses was not going to have its teeth and gums examined – but we were more than a little wary of Neville's shady friends and opaque business practices.

'If you want cash, you're going to have to come to my bank to get it,' I told him. 'I'm not walking down the street to be mugged by a couple of blokes and then have you coming round the corner, looking innocent and demanding your money.'

Neville gave me a smile as broad as the river Tyne – and as murky. 'I don't know how you could even suggest such a thing, Neil, but if it makes you happy, I'll meet you right outside your bank. I'm not coming in with you, though; I don't want some bank teller recognising me and pointing me out if questions get asked later on.'

Completion day dawned and, never having held more than £200 in my hands at any one time before, I took along two holdalls to carry the cash. To my disappointment and embarrassment, both proved to be entirely superfluous, for it turned out that even the prodigious sum of £10,000 in cash fitted comfortably into a manila envelope. I went outside to meet Neville, who was once again looking anxiously around while awaiting an envelope. I sat in his beaten-up Volvo, while he licked his thumb and counted the money. Neither candidate requested a recount and, beaming like a returning officer at a by-election when the television lights go on, Neville showed magnanimity in victory.

'You'll be needing some new kitchen equipment,' he said. 'The old stuff's seen better days. Anything you want, I can get you, brand-new, half-price.'

'Why, is it stolen?'

His smile broadened. 'No, not yet it isn't.'

We decided to do without the new catering equipment, but I confess that was probably less because of our principled moral refusal to contemplate buying stolen property than because, even at half price, it was still too expensive for us.

The purchase of the Inn at the Top had given us another immediate problem, in that I had to decide whether to give up my continuing attempts to push the boundaries of ethical radio journalism into previously uncharted territories. We already knew from previous experience that running the pub was a very full-time job indeed and I quickly decided that the sports and news journalism, and indeed writing books, would have to be put on hold for as long as we remained at the inn. However, the editorship of the *Good Beer Guide* was high-profile, pretty lucrative and pleasingly part-time, and after much thought and head-scratching, I decided that by utilising the time taken travelling up and down on the train and every spare moment I could find at the pub as well, I could still edit the Guide by working a three day week in St Albans, five or six months a year. The money I earned would be a more than useful addition to the profits from the pub; since we'd borrowed so heavily to buy it, they would all be soaked up in meeting debt repayments for at least the first three years. The downside, of course, was that since the production run of the *Good Beer Guide* began in May and extended into October, I would be away from the inn for those three days a week during the busiest part of the year, but, with our trademark naivety and hopeless optimism, we decided that with some extra help, we'd be able to manage.

The news that we had purchased the Inn at the Top had been greeted with delight by our former regulars, but provoked mixed reactions elsewhere. One article in the trade press noted that 'The couple have been called 'crazy' to buy the pub of their dreams but other people's nightmares, which has defeated many previous occupants'. And others in the pub and brewing industry were already licking their lips in hope or anticipation that we would fail to make a go of it, for my day-job as editor of the *Good Beer Guide* now made me a tempting target for those, not least the giant brewing companies, who resented CAMRA's criticism of keg beer and mega-breweries. After years of claiming that the Campaign didn't know what it was talking about and had no idea about the problems of the licensed trade, some members of the trade press scented a golden opportunity to prove their point; once more the words 'in a brewery', 'a booze-up' and 'couldn't run' probably sprang to their minds...

We had a much warmer response to our news from the doyen of fell-walkers, Alfred Wainwright, the man who had done more than anyone else to popularise walks in Northern Britain's great upland 'wilderness' areas: the Lake District mountains and the Pennine Dales. Mr Wainwright often appeared to regret the popularity – both of himself and the areas he wrote about – that his beautifully illustrated, idiosyncratic walking guides had caused, and he could be shy and sometimes slightly curmudgeonly in person. When he appeared on Desert Island Discs he told Sue Lawley that he 'had once been shy but had grown-up to be antisocial' and he remarked on another occasion that when passing lines of walkers out on the fells, he would only say 'Good Morning' to the first of them 'and that would have to do for the rest of them as well'! Nonetheless he was also one of the most kind, open and warm-hearted individuals you could hope to meet.

One of the first things I'd done after we agreed to buy the inn, was to write to Mr Wainwright asking if it would be possible to buy the original drawings for the pages from his Pennine Way Companion that illustrated the Inn at the Top and its surrounding landscape and landmarks, so that we could hang them on the walls of the inn.

He replied by return of post, a lovely, warm and friendly letter that began 'Thank you for your letter with its exciting news that you are to be mine host at the inn. This must be the biggest venture of your life and I hope it proves successful. I think it will if you can make the summer trade pay for unprofitable winters. I was up there during the summer, when the place was crowded with a dozen or more cars parked on the verges.

The inn has become a popular resort since motorists discovered it: I remember staying there one night in 1938 and I was the only person the occupants had seen for several days. Things have changed a lot since then!'

He added his regrets that the *Westmorland Gazette,* which published his books and owned the copyright, would not release the original pages 'under any circumstances', but said that they would have no objection to copies being made for display. However, he added that, 'you may be more interested in a book on the Pennine Way I have just completed for the publishers, Michael Joseph Ltd, in which I have devoted a few pages to the inn and its surroundings. I think these pages would suit your purpose better, but the book will not be published until spring of 1985. I also have in mind a book of drawings of Yorkshire scenes in which I intend to include a full page drawing of the inn, but there is nothing definite about this yet. I think I would wait if I were you, and if you really wanted something ready for moving into occupation, I think I could find time to do the drawing of the Inn in advance. Life will be quite exciting for you until March 1st (and after!). I hope all goes well for you. Best wishes for the future prosperity of the inn.

Yours sincerely,

A. Wainwright.'

I replied at once, thanking him and taking him up on his very generous offer, and the following month, when he had completed the promised drawing, he wrote to me again saying that, having compared the photograph he had taken of the inn, when passing by the previous year, with the one he had taken way back in 1967, he was 'surprised to note the structural alterations that have taken place in the meantime.' Unaware of the fire in 1973 that had gutted the building, leaving only the walls standing, Mr Wainwright noted that 'the roof now has a steeper pitch and the big chimneys have gone: the inn seems to have been completely re-roofed. The annexe too is greatly changed, formerly having a sloping slated roof. It seemed to me that a more interesting drawing would result by showing 'before and after' illustrations, and accordingly I have done this. If the drawing meets your requirements a small donation to Animal Rescue, Cumbria, sent to the above address, would be most welcome. Yours sincerely, A. Wainwright.'

It really was a heart-warming gesture by a kind, generous and very unassuming man. Mr. Wainwright's *Pennine Way Companion* and his *Guide to the Coast to Coast Walk* which he invented and which he said 'puts the Pennine Way to shame' for the beauty and variety of the landscapes through which it passed, must have been read and cherished by millions of walkers and armchair travellers over the years. However a few of those who had toiled through miles of peat bogs with one of the great man's guides in their hands were sometimes less than enamoured of the author by the time they reached the sanctuary of the inn. One bedraggled walker who was in the middle of the Pennine Way or the Coast to Coast Walk which also passes near to the Inn at the Top, was definitely not a Wainwright fan by the time he had slogged his way up to the inn through the glutinous morasses of peat slurry produced by that year's prodigious rainfall. He vented his spleen by writing in the visitor's book: 'What would I like to do most at the moment? It is not to drink a pint of foaming, cool beer; to eat a huge plateful of steak and chips; to fall into the arms of a beautiful girl. No. It is to take hold of Wainwright and to kick him as hard as possible in the balls!'

Having bought the inn, even at the heavily discounted price we'd paid for it, we had so little money left over that we couldn't even afford a removal van, but luckily some of our neighbours and our old locals were so pleased to see us back that many of them lent us a hand. On 1 March 1984, a typically raw early spring day up on the fells, a strange convoy took the winding moor road leading to the inn: three farm Landrovers, a tractor pulling a horse-box and four battered saloons. Bringing up the rear was a considerably more expensive and up to date Volvo estate, containing a television crew from BBC Newcastle who were there to film a documentary about our first few months as owners of what was arguably the wildest and weirdest pub in Britain. I knew the producer from my earlier incarnation as an exhibition organiser and his ears had pricked up as soon as I mentioned we were buying the inn. Whether he sensed a poignant and moving human interest story, a classic 'fish out of water' tale, or a human train wreck in the making, was not revealed, but we just had to hope it was not the latter.

Although the road itself had been cleared of drifts by snow-blowers and snow-ploughs, there were still several feet of snow on the ground either side of the road as we drove up towards the inn. We paused at regular intervals to allow the BBC crew in their Volvo to drive on ahead of us, set up the camera overlooking the road and then film the convoy as it rumbled past. Just around the next bend or over the brow of the next hill we would pull in and wait while the BBC crew jumped back in their car, overtook us again and then set up the camera once more.

As we reached the top of the hill, parked the car and opened the doors, the familiar icy blast of the wind made itself felt. The splendidly named writer, Edmund Bogg, while roaming 'The Wild Borderland of Richmondshire' in the early years of the twentieth century, had chanced upon the inn and reported that 'Many a weary and benighted traveller has hailed this eyrie haven with as profound delight and thankfulness as any harried being a sanctuary church; the glimmer, though of tallow dips only (or later of kerosene lamp) from the window panes of this public refuge, has been as a beacon light to many a traveller; for in days gone by, before the mines were shut up, when chapmen or Scots drovers crossed the wastes by these rough roads on foot or saddleback, the traffic and the necessity for a half-way shelter and food for man and beast was much greater than in these days of railway journeying and tourists.'

There were no beacon lights or even glimmers of tallow dips visible on this cold, grey day, just the unloved-looking building, shut these last six months, with its ruinous rendering peeling away from the walls, locked doors and shuttered windows. We unlocked the door of the inn and I used a monkey-wrench and a crowbar to undo the bolts on the shutters and prise off a few of the boards nailed over some of the other windows, letting in a little daylight. With the help of our volunteer removal men, we then unloaded our furniture from the vehicles and carried it into the damp, frigid interior of the inn. It was as cold as charity and lighting a fire did little to improve matters, for the blaze smouldered fitfully and the smoke struggled to make its way up the sodden chimney, with much of it escaping into the room instead.

While Sue doled out cups of tea to the helpers, made with a thermos flask of hot water that we'd brought with us, because there was no water to be had at the inn, I began reacquainting myself with some of the things that made the place unique. Having drained the old oil out of the generator and refilled it with the correct grade of light oil – once bitten, twice shy, for we'd spent our first winter at the inn without any power, after the lovely Neville and Stan left us only a drum of reclaimed, second-hand heavy engine oil for the generator – I spent the next few minutes straining, grunting and cursing over the crank-handle, before the generator finally roared into life and the pub lights came on for the first time in six months.

The now brightly-lit interior was not a pleasant sight. The west wall, the one that took the brunt of the wind and weather, was black with damp from floor to ceiling but for now that would have to wait. The only parts of the inn not swimming in damp were the water tanks in the loft, which were absolutely bone dry and, while Sue and her helpers made a start on unpacking the boxes, I set off at once to try and correct that lack of one of life's essentials. I walked across the moor, a spade over my shoulder and with the dog alongside me, gambolling through the snow while the camera crew huffed and puffed and slipped and slided in my wake, as they struggled to keep up.

I found the stream where the ram-pump was sited easily enough. There was only one problem: it was completely buried under the hard-packed snow that filled the gill from side to side. Even worse, the metal 'snow-pole' marking the exact site of the ram-pump had disappeared at some point in the last five years and, try as I might, I could not remember how far down the gill it was. However, when I lay down with my head out of the wind and my ear on the surface of the snow, I could hear the sound of the stream still running underneath. Had the pump still been working, it would have been easy to find by probing through the snow with a long pole, and then listening at the hole for the distinctive bass 'heartbeat' of the ram. Even though the pump had long since stopped, all I had to do was dig a hole through the snow, drop down it and peer up and down the stream beneath the drifts until I found the ram-pump. Then it would be an easy matter to prime it and set it going again. It all seemed so simple...

I dug a hole through the four-foot, rock-hard crust of snow and ice, levered myself into position and then let go. I'm six foot four inches tall and I disappeared from sight completely, leaving a camera crew and one very puzzled dog peering down into the hole from on top of the snowdrift above me. A few feet below them, I could see that the stream had carved a very low 'ice-cave' out of the drifts of snow and ice that had filled the gill. Lit by the dim blue-white light filtering through the remaining snow cover, it was a beautiful sight, but this was no time for aesthetics, there was work to be done. I crouched down and peered up and down the stream, but there was no sign of the ram-pump and without lying full length in the ice cold water of the stream – and, call me soft if you like, but that didn't seem a particularly good idea – I could see no more than a couple of feet in either direction before fallen snow or the low roof of the ice cave blocked my vision. Either I'd have to lie full-length and belly-crawl along the sub-zero stream until I found the pump, or I'd have to dig another hole. It didn't take too much thought before I settled on the latter option.

An hour and a half later, with night falling, I had dug a dozen holes, disappeared down each of them through drifts of snow that were several feet taller than me and still not found a trace of the pump. In the end, I had to give up and head back to the doubtful sanctuary of the inn. Our convoy of helpers had already disappeared back down the road by then, and the BBC camera crew soon followed them, leaving us alone, back in our bleak, freezing and for the moment at least, thoroughly miserable moorland kingdom.

On that first night back at the inn, it was so damp and cold that, after we went to bed, our dog, Gnasher, woke us up because she was shivering so hard. We let her sleep under the quilt at the foot of the bed and the next morning Sue fitted her out with a sawn-off version of one of her old pullovers, which both kept her warm from then on by day and night, and also, with the addition of a scarf and a woollen 'beanie' hat, made a nice picture story for the *Northern Echo* which was then picked up by the *Daily Mirror*. Not only did journalists know that the highest pub in Britain was always good for a story about bad weather, but the *Mirror* was always in the market for animal stories to make its readers say 'Awwwwwww!'.

It was the first trickle of media coverage that would turn into a tsunami of publicity, including the BBC documentary about our first few months as owners of the inn, 'A Foot Or Two Above The Rest' and a certain commercial by a well known double glazing company, that was to make the Inn at the Top nationally and even internationally famous within the year.

When the weather turned warmer, we removed the dog's pullover and, kitted out with a knotted handkerchief on her head and a pair of dark glasses, while posing next to a mug of iced water, complete with straw, she gained us some more valuable publicity under the predictable tabloid headline: 'Just Fur Summer'.

For the first couple of weeks back at the inn we had to get by on bottled water and boiled snow until I finally found the elusive ram-pump under its covering of thick snow. It was an experience shared by a previous landlord, who lost track of it for twelve weeks during the awful winter of 1962–63. Even when the ram-pump was working, the intense cold of winter could freeze the ground to a depth of two feet or more, reducing the flow of water from the spring to a trickle or stopping it altogether. However, it was now early spring and, albeit slowly, the temperature was beginning to rise, so having finally found the ram-pump, all I then had to do was start it. I stood in the stream, with the water lapping just below the tops of my wellies, ducked under the concrete slab that formed the roof of the pump housing and loosened the valve on top of the pump, allowing the water filling the pump chamber to drain out. Phase one successfully completed; all I had to do now was prime and restart the pump.

A ram-pump is a remarkably straightforward thing. It has only two moving parts: a delivery or 'check' valve and a waste or 'clack' valve. Sited in a spring or stream, the force of the water flowing through it provides the necessary power to open and close the valves and force a small part of that water up a pipe to a height of several metres above the level of the pump. Our ram pump was powerful enough not only to push the water all the way up the hill to the inn but also to raise it to the water tanks in the roof space.

To start it, I just had to slowly close the valve and loosen the diaphragm of the pump until the force of water through it triggered a pulse like a heartbeat. It was a fiddly, trial and error process, but at last I managed to get it right and the pump thumped a few times, and then began to settle into a steady rhythm. I had to wait for a few minutes, slowing the beat down a little and as I listened to the steady bass rhythm of the pump, I smiled as I noticed that my heartbeat had slowed its rate in sympathy so that – just like two lovers' hearts – both the pump and my heart were now beating as one.

The pump needed re-priming from time to time, but otherwise never stopped and was utterly reliable, but it supplied only a fraction of the water we actually needed and at such a slow rate that it could not keep pace with the speed at which our tanks were emptied on busy days or when careless visitors left the taps running in the Gents or Ladies. When that happened, I had to drop what I was doing, sprint down the fellside to the stream and set a petrol pump going that we kept for such emergencies, with a flow rate twenty times quicker than the ram. I could leave it running and head back to the customers queueing at the bar, secure in the knowledge that it would stop itself when it ran out of fuel.

However in that frigid Spring, having set the ram-pump going, I had to go back up to the inn, where all the pipes remained frozen and I then spent a couple of hours carefully thawing them out with a blow-torch before I could hear the welcome sound of the first flow of water in months beginning to trickle into the empty tanks. They all then had to be thoroughly cleaned and sterilised before we could actually begin storing drinking water in them again.

# CHAPTER 7

## A Few Yows Short Of A Flock

To say that the inn was not in the best of conditions when we took it over would be something of an understatement. The inn had escaped destruction by fire in 1971 by sheer good fortune. There was no telephone at the time but luckily a BBC TV crew happened to be there, filming for the regional Look North programme, when the fire broke out. The TV crew had a radio and were able to summon the fire brigade with that, and they arrived and extinguished the blaze before it got out of control. However, two years later, in 1973, the then landlord was less fortunate and the inn was completely destroyed by another fire. According to a newspaper report, the blaze had begun with 'a flashback from the still room geyser', and as the inn was then still without any sort of working phone, the landlord and his wife had to drive three miles to the nearest telephone-box to call the fire brigade. By the time the fire engine eventually arrived, the fire had completely gutted the building, leaving only the walls standing.

New owners then bought the ruined inn, but in 1974, while the building was still being repaired from the last blaze, yet another one broke out, gutting the newly restored kitchen, and gale force winds then tore away a large section of the partly re-built roof. The owners went bankrupt three months later and the inn was put back on the market once more.

The purchasers this time were the lovely Neville and Stan, who had bought the wreck and presided over the rebuilding of the place and unfortunately, as we knew only too well from our own bitter experience with them, they were not the sort of men to spend a pound where a penny would do. Every material they had used was the most 'gash', cheap and nasty that they could lay their hands on. The roof had been re-tiled with cheap concrete slates, rather than the traditional sandstone ones because concrete ones were much cheaper, but the wind was constantly driving rain under the slates and threatening to tear the whole roof off again, slate by slate.

The upstairs floors had been laid with the cheapest and flimsiest grade of chipboard. Rather than plaster, most of the walls had been rendered with Artex – hideous stuff that, in the damp air of the inn, never set and clung like clay if you tried to scrape it off. Steel RSJs had been left exposed or clad in dark-stained bits of plywood in a pathetic simulation of 'olde oak beams', and some sort of bizarre hardboard 'panelling' had been used not only on the bedroom walls but also instead of plasterboard on the ceilings.

The exterior of the building had been clumsily rendered and then painted mustard yellow – presumably there was a cheap deal available on that colour as well because only the blind would have picked it out otherwise – it may even have been war-surplus, desert camouflage paint from World War Two – and the rendering was also cracked and stained. By allowing in moisture that then became trapped between the render and the walls of the building, the cracks created the perfect conditions to ensure the dampness of the walls in perpetuity.

An ugly flat-roofed, single-storied, breeze-block extension had been added at one side of the building. How they got planning permission for that in this most prominent of sites within the Yorkshire Dales National Park was beyond belief, though the steel reinforcing rods poking through the roof suggested it had once been intended to build it two storeys high. One of our locals told me that 'It was supposed to have a second floor, right enough, but Stan and Neville hadn't put in deep enough foundations to support it, so it had to be left as a flat-roofed, one-storey monstrosity!'

As well as the black, mildewed interior walls and the roof leaks in a multitude of places, the door- and window-frames of the inn were also filled with a ramshackle assortment of cheap and/or second-hand doors and windows; we counted no less than nine different styles of windows around the building ... and all of them were cracked and leaking like sieves through the rotten frames. They also let in draughts that set the curtains fluttering in even the most gentle breeze and froze the customers to the marrow when the wind was really blowing hard. Since Stan and Neville had drilled holes right through the window frames to hold the shutters in place when they boarded the inn up for winter, each frame also had four half-inch diameter holes in it, all of which admitted a whistling draught until we managed to block them up, and even then, that only reduced, not eliminated the draughts.

The generator was on its last legs and the radio telephone continued to break down at the first signs of bad weather, the very times when we needed it most, but the water supply was the worst problem. Even with the ram-pump working, we knew that the water it gave was insufficient to cope with the demands that our customers would soon be putting upon it; but we had already taken out a huge overdraft to help finance the purchase of the pub and could not raise any more money from the bank. What we desperately needed was a borehole, but the price I was quoted to sink one was a minimum of £5,000 – a hell of a lot of money back then and precisely £5,000 more than we could lay our hands on. A replacement generator would have been at least another £3,000 and that was equally impossible to find, so we just had to soldier on as best we could, though we did at least scrape together the cash to have the generator serviced – for the first time in many years, according to the engineer who did the job.

Neville and Stan had also done the rewiring of the inn themselves, with the result that stray electric cables trailed here and there across the upstairs walls and ceilings and, interestingly, two of the power sockets in the bar were live when they appeared to be switched off. However, their piece de resistance was the new toilet block, opening off the dining room. Once all the concrete they had poured had set, they discovered that they'd managed to lay the drainage channels so that any liquids they contained would overflow back into the room rather than emptying into the drains. Since either they couldn't face doing the job again, or just couldn't be bothered, they'd continued using the old loos and converted the new toilet block into a bottle store, leaving the unusable toilet fittings in situ, presumably in case they ever got around to finishing the original job, with the result that we had to negotiate our way around the useless urinals and toilet-bowls when getting the crates in and out.

Even worse, the last couple that Neville and Stan had employed as managers before selling the inn had been even more slovenly than them. Knowing that they were going to be sacked at the end of the summer season anyway, the managers had systematically worked their way through every plate and bowl in the place, eating from them and then dumping them, unwashed, on the furniture or the floor of the upstairs rooms. Neither they nor Neville and Stan had bothered to clean up, and the plates covered in rotting food had been lying there all winter. That was not only insanitary in itself, but if the rats infesting the gully below the pub car-park had needed any extra incentive to break into the inn, the mangers had duly provided it. When we made our first tour of inspection of the pub after taking it over six months later, I glanced in one of the freezer cabinets and found two dead rats floating there in six inches of melt-water.

If only all the rats had been equally dead...When we went upstairs, we found the bedroom carpets covered in rat-droppings and when I climbed through the trapdoor into the loft, I encountered hordes of rats surfing through the fibreglass insulation, emerging and disappearing as they cleared each joist like dolphins frolicking in the sea. It took steady nerves for us to get to sleep at all on those first few nights and industrial quantities of Warfarin to poison the rats. I also toured the outside of the building, filling every chink and crack in the masonry with cement in which was embedded razor blades, bits of barbed wire, broken glass and anything else unpleasant on which I could lay my hands. I had no scruples about it; this was total war and if it was scarcely within the terms of the Geneva Convention, I was pretty sure that rats had never been signatories to it.

After two weeks of non-stop work, we were more or less ready to open for business. We had planned to remain closed until the end of March while we carried out repairs and renovations, but expectant customers kept arriving on our doorstep and it seemed cruel to turn them away, so we shrugged our shoulders and decided to open a couple of weeks early. What we really needed before throwing open our doors was a period of calm, thoughtful planning, putting the structures in place that would enable us to run the inn in a way that would be as stress-free and labour-saving as possible. That should have covered planning the menus and the work rotas so that in the busy summer season, when well over 100 lunches would be served every day, the kitchen and the kitchen staff could cope with the workload and keep the backlog of orders within reasonable bounds.

We would also have benefited greatly from improving the water and power supply to the inn; neither the elderly and under-powered generator nor the ram-pump in the spring was adequate to meet the demands put upon them. Improving the layout of the area behind the bar to create extra space was also very desirable, bordering on essential. All that was before we even started on the much-needed repairs to the fabric of the building. In the longer term, an extension to provide additional letting bedrooms, a drying room for the clothes of soaking wet hikers, and some additional cellar and kitchen storage space, were also much needed.

However none of the planning was done – there simply weren't enough hours in the day for everything we had to do – and our desperate shortage of capital meant that any thoughts of replacing the generator with a more powerful model, sinking a borehole to guarantee a decent water supply, or remodelling the pub interior, let alone building an extension, had to be put on hold. What little spare money and energy we did have was to be devoted to a perpetual, if metaphorical fire fight, dealing with the worst of the immediate problems like the leaking roof and windows and the chimney from the open fire in the bar that seemed to spew out smoke in every direction except the one that it was supposed to be doing: out of the top of the chimney. Whether it was a damp, still day or blowing a gale seemed to make no difference, smoke regularly filled the bar whenever the fire was lit and since we couldn't do without the fire – only at the height of a summer heatwave was it ever left unlit – we would have to do something about the chimney pronto.

By the time we opened, the inn had at least been cleaned and sterilised from top to bottom, the roof leaks had been fixed, the black damp had been scraped from the walls and the plaster bleached and repainted. The chimney no longer smoked at the bottom and not at the top; when we stripped the hardboard sheets away from the wall of the bedroom above the bar, trying to find out why the room was always so smoky, we discovered that someone, at some time – I was guessing Stan or Neville – had smashed a one-foot square hole straight through the wall and into the chimney behind it and then not bothered to repair the damage. With the repairs done, the smoke from the fire actually went all the way to the top of the chimney instead of filling the bar and the bedroom. Best of all, the resident rats had now been poisoned and eliminated, although – sensitive readers look away now – they tended to breathe their last in obscure corners of the loft or other barely accessible places, and I could only find and remove the last few corpses when the overpowering aroma as they decayed revealed their last hiding places.

Having removed the last pungent traces of our unwelcome rodent guests and cleaned and disinfected all areas, we were ready to throw open our doors to customers. When we did so, to our delight and astonishment, we were deluged with people almost from Day One. They included not just our loyal band of locals and former regulars but farmers, hikers, bikers, cyclists, cavers, climbers, tourists, and the weekenders and holiday home owners, who were moving into the Dale in ever growing numbers. As one friend remarked, when I was trying to get the last few customers to drink up with the traditional pub landlord's query: 'Have you got no homes to go to?' I should really have been calling out 'Have you got no second homes to go to?'

On the first morning that we were once more open for business at the inn, our very first customer, who was also our most regular and favourite customer from our previous spell there, arrived with the postman. Faith was a diminutive, white-haired, frail old lady with skin as wrinkled as a prune that had been left too long in the sun, but she also had a razor sharp wit, an uproarious sense of humour and a remarkably profane vocabulary for a lady of her gentle birth and upbringing.

Still keeping pace with the century, Faith was now eighty-four years old, but the passing years did not appear to have diminished her appetite for strong drink and untipped cigarettes one iota. Nor had they stopped her from using her traditional form of transport: lying flat on a pile of mail sacks in the back of the postman's van. Back then, Post Office vans were not fitted with passenger seats – presumably to discourage the postmen from offering lifts to anyone going their way – so Faith still had to make the bone-jarring journey up to the inn every morning, lying on the mail sacks.

I was fifty years her junior at the time and I would certainly not have fancied the jarring, bumping and bruising that being thrown around in the back of the van entailed as the postman drove up and down the rutted and rock-strewn

141

farm-tracks between the village where Faith lived and the inn. It must have made her old bones rattle like maracas but she seemed willing to endure almost any discomfort, as long as there was a pub at the end of it. The trips to the inn were the highlight of her day, indeed almost her only social contact, and it would have taken a lot more than a few bumps and bruises to keep her away.

With a tear in her eye, she gave us both a bone-crushing hug to welcome us back and then, while the postman had a cup of tea, she settled herself at the bar and ordered a glass of her favourite tipple: 'Large whisky and soda, for the love of God. Just a splash of soda though, don't drown it!'

She downed three of them in fairly rapid succession while we caught up on her news. As before, we ran a 'slate' for her, which she cleared when her pension arrived every week, and if there was sometimes a small shortfall, although Mr Micawber would not have approved, we were happy to write it off, for it seemed a modest price to pay for the pleasure we took in her company. She rarely talked about her origins but, although she could swear like a trooper and had an inexhaustible store of scurrilous tales about her own and others' bad behaviour in her youth, it was clear that she came from an old, monied, genteel and probably titled family.

She did once mention to me that it was the head game-keeper on her family's estates in the North-East who had, as she put it, 'started me on the road to ruin', when she was only eleven or twelve years old – Faith couldn't remember exactly when, but it was certainly not even within sight of the legal drinking age. She claimed the early introduction to whisky had never done her any harm but that's probably not an opinion that her doctor would have shared. 'I used to like tagging along with the head keeper as he made his rounds,' she said, 'and every day, when we got to the half-way point, he would sit me on a stile and give me a raw egg mixed with a tot of whisky from his hip flask.'

'Didn't you choke on it the first time he gave you that to drink?' I said.

'Lord, no,' she said with a laugh. 'I think I asked him for another one!'

Some unspecified disgrace, possibly an extra-marital affair with a man of an 'unsuitable' background or even – heaven forbid! – a servant, had led to Faith's mother being exiled from her home. Like some nineteenth century 'remittance man', she continued to receive a regular allowance for the rest of her life, but the payments were apparently conditional on her never darkening the doors of the ancestral home again. As a result, she lived out her days with her daughter in a small cottage in the remoteness of the upper Dale. It can only have been fifty miles or so away from her family home, but it might as well have been on the other side of the world, for from the day that her mother's exile began, Faith told us that there had never been the slightest trace of contact from any of Faith's grandparents, uncles, aunts and cousins.

She went to the school in the tiny village in the Upper Dale and she must have seemed a rare, exotic creature indeed to the sheep farmers' sons and daughters who were her companions there and who, in that far off, pre-First World War era, had probably never previously met anyone who hadn't been born and bred in the Dale.

When Faith grew up, she stayed at the cottage to look after her mother, and even after her mother's death, she remained in the Dale; she was fated never to leave it. She had married, to an 'off-comer' like herself, but according to our locals, her husband, about whom she never spoke to us, had suffered from mental health issues that had ultimately seen him committed to an asylum. Their only child, Paul, was now well into his sixties, and had also lived all his life with his mother in their tiny cottage. He was a very eccentric character, variously described by our politically incorrect locals as 'not the full shilling', 'a bit touched', or 'a few yows [sheep] short of a flock', but whether the cause of that was a genetic inheritance from his father or something else was unknown.

Paul had once been a postman himself, completing a marathon, twenty-mile round right around the head of the Dale, including the long four-mile trek across the moors to the inn from its nearest neighbour. He delivered the mail every day, in all weathers, continuing to trudge his round through the winter snows, and he even claimed – probably inaccurately as nostalgia or wishful thinking applied a rose-coloured tint to his memories – that he had never once failed to deliver the mail, even during the terrible winters of 1947 and 1963. However, when the Post Office introduced post-vans on all of its mail rounds, Paul, who had never learned to drive, was made

144

redundant. He had never worked in all the years since then, living on unemployment benefit and then his Post Office pension, and spent his time mainly walking the paths and tracks over the moors, daily revisiting his old mail delivery round.

He was a big powerful man, with hands like ham hocks and a bony beak of a nose, but he had an odd, girlish way of speaking, muttering in a breathy monotone and fluttering his long eyelashes with his gaze downcast. He also had a strange haircut – a 'bowl cut' that even Jessie the Cropper might have regarded as too extreme – with his white hair cut in a perfect circle around his head two or three inches above his ears, like a monk without a tonsure. Had he been in the right place, at the right time, his haircut and unusual looks alone would probably have been enough to win him a role as one of the fourteenth century monks in the Sean Connery film, *The Name of the Rose*.

The cottage in the village at the bottom of the hill from the inn that Faith and Paul shared was barely big enough for the two of them. On the ground floor there was a small living room and a tiny kitchen which, since there was no bathroom, was also used when they wanted a wash. There was an outside loo which must have been a real trial by ordeal to use in winter, and upstairs there were just two small bedrooms. Yet despite their lack of space, they also shared their home with nine cats. To say that Paul and his mother did not get on particularly well was the understatement of the century and the fact that they lived in each other's pockets only made matters worse. Paul

145

was a powerful man and could be violent, and on occasions Faith would appear at the inn nursing bruises on her arms or a black eye. Whatever provocation she might have offered did not justify that violence by Paul against his mother, but Faith neither complained, nor would allow any action to be taken against him. 'Whatever happens,' she said to us once, 'he is still my son,' and there the matter had to rest.

The rest of our cast of locals assembled over the following days and weeks. Among them were some very familiar faces like Jed – once seen, his pouched, lined and craggy face was unmistakable. He was probably the last man alive to have earned his living at the ancient trade of droving. As a young man he and his partner had earned their money buying wether [castrated male] lambs from the farms around the upper Dale until they had assembled a drove of several hundred. They then took them to market up to fifty miles away, shepherding them along the droving routes across the moor tops and watersheds that had been used for centuries before enclosures of the land and competition from railways and road transport had rendered them almost extinct.

Some thought Jed had gypsy blood in him, citing as evidence his preference for relieving himself not in the Gents, but in the great outdoors, where he could sometimes be seen using the outside wall of the inn in the same way that a French lorry driver would use the rear wheel of his truck. However, particularly on busy weekends at the inn, when a deluge of human traffic passed through the Gents, he wouldn't have been the only person to have found the great outdoors a more preferable option, and his alleged gypsy origins may have only been the result of feeding the look of his dark hair and swarthy skin through the Dale's ever-active rumour mill.

Sadly Alwyn, who was the Dale's resident ladies man – at least in his own opinion, though his advancing years and his lack of teeth other than the two lonely stumps at either side of his gap-toothed grin made that a questionable claim – was no longer a regular at the inn. He had not abandoned us for another pub; according to Dick, who had often been his foil and drinking partner, Alwyn simply didn't go out at all any more. Dick made repeated efforts to entice him back but Alwyn's days of trying to show the local lads where they were going wrong in their pursuit of the local lasses were over – they would just have to forge their relationships without him – and we now saw him only on the great occasions like the annual sheep show.

However, Alwyn's other close friend, Jimmy, whose pink, scrubbed and shining face belied his years, was still a regular at the inn. His nickname of 'Jimmy Bullshit' reflected his penchant for wildly implausible tales, in which he invariably played the leading role, but he was good and very entertaining company, so nobody really minded that most, if not all, of his stories were probably works of fiction created by his fertile imagination. There were other familiar faces too, but there were also quite a few others who had been mere boys and girls when we'd been running the inn five years earlier. If at all, they had only come in with their parents on special occasions, but they were now grown-up and customers in their own right. We had quite a large following among the late teenage and early twenties age groups. They didn't want to drink in the same pubs as their fathers or even their older brothers and sisters, and we also had the added attractions for them of a pool table and a jukebox ... not to mention a remarkably relaxed attitude to closing time!

Among them was a young man, Norman, who became one of our most regular customers. Norman was a long-haired and bearded twenty year old from the next village to Faith's in the upper Dale and who, usually in company with his two best mates and drinking buddies, Jimmy and Alex, put away pints of beer at a rate I had never seen before or since. Norman's look did not change in decades: long hair, straggling pepper and salt beard and a flat cap permanently perched on his head – the cap's grey now, though like his hair, that might not have been its original colour. He was still wearing it when I caught sight of him while passing through the Dale recently, prompting the thought that he might even sleep and take a bath while wearing it, so that it might never have left his head since the 1970s. He lived only a few doors down from the pub in his local village and though in our era he was also a very regular customer at the Inn at the Top, these days the short journey between the twin pillars of his existence – his house and his local – appears to be just about the full extent of his travels.

Like the fossilised punks who tout for cash in return for posing for photos with tourists around

Trafalgar Square, Norman is still reputedly sharp enough to be happy to pose for photographs with any tourists willing to buy him a pint in return for a souvenir snap of themselves with a 'local Dales character'. It's a business of sorts... And through the money he has put across the bar there, he has probably single-handedly kept that pub in business. As one of its former landlords once remarked to me, 'I remember that when we sold the pub, there was a reference in the accounting books to NP. I wasn't sure if it stood for Net Profit or Norman Parker, though come to think of it, he put so much money over the bar in the course of a year that it added up to pretty much the same thing either way.'

Some new regulars were even younger than Norman. Among them was a boy called Hamish who came up to the inn with his dad. Prompted by his father one evening, I took Hamish behind the bar and, under my supervision, beaming proudly he pulled his first ever pint of beer. He's pulled a few since then; he's been working at the inn for years and is still often to be found behind the bar now.

Although we had Norman Parker and his mates to keep the beer flowing through the pipes at a steady rate, and quite a few of our former regulars maintained the tradition of always coming up to the inn on Sunday nights to talk sheep with farmers from miles around, who might include men from half a dozen different dales, we discovered that winning back some of our old locals wasn't going to be quite as easy as we had thought. After the initial excitement provoked by our return, we began to notice that quite a few of our former regulars were not such frequent visitors as they had been in the past. Such was our naiveté – or possibly our vanity – that it had not occurred to either of us that part of the reason for our popularity on our first stint at the inn was that the nearest rival inn down the Dale was, to put it politely, run by a man whose heart was no longer in the pub trade, if it had ever been. When he was behind the bar, there was a notably cool welcome for all-comers, locals and visitors alike, and as a result many of both sorts had voted with their feet and come up to the Inn at the Top instead.

However, he had moved on during the time we had been away from the area and the rival pub was now run by a much younger and much more enthusiastic couple. Since that inn was also much easier to get to than ours, especially in bad weather, many of our former locals had transferred their affections to it and, rather than being up at the Inn at the Top three or four nights a week as they had in the past, some of them were now only calling in once a week, if that.

We made up our minds to work twice as hard to woo those errant customers back again and meanwhile we still maintained a very good local trade – 'local' not necessarily being the most apt description since even our closest neighbour among them had to travel four miles to reach us. Some of our most loyal older regulars, like our mentor, Dick, and the secretary of the sheep show, Clifford, had been coming to the inn since they were boys. Dick, who was a good bit older than Clifford, used to travel up to the inn, sitting on the farm cart alongside his father when he rode up the hill to collect a load of coal from one of the two mines that then operated nearby.

One of our oldest regulars, Michael, could recall his grandfather telling him about starting work in the pit when he was nine years old. He worked a six-day week, for which he was paid a shilling (5p) a week, and in winter it was dark when he went down the pit in the morning and dark when he came out again, so the only time he saw daylight was on a Sunday. 'And even then,' Michael said with a smile, 'he had to go to chapel, so he didn't see much daylight then, neither!'

Coal had been mined there since the twelfth century and mining boomed in the eighteenth and nineteenth centuries when the lead mines and smelting mills down in the Dale fuelled a voracious demand for coal. The road past the inn was turnpiked in 1770 to make it easier to transport coal (the tollhouse is still there, a ruined stone building at the side of the road a mile or so west of the inn), which was previously carried on packhorses, a mode of transport that was so expensive that it could double or triple the price in the space of a few miles. Road improvements led to a much greater use of carts and wagons and the virtual disappearance of pack horses from the lowlands. However, even after the turnpike past the inn had been opened, the network of rough moorland tracks leading off it, linking the maze of shafts and levels of the coal pits with each other and with the lead smelting mills in the Dale below, together with the severe gradients of the roads in the area, ensured the continued use of pack horses to cross the fells until well into the nineteenth century.

One well-known character from that era, known as 'Awd Helkanah', kept as many as fifty pack horses for carrying the coal he bought from the pit next to the inn and then sold at the farms and villages in the surrounding dales. He earned a place in local legend by his habit of blowing mighty blasts on a large horn to announce his arrival to potential customers.

Like the packhorse trade, the lead industry in the Dale had declined and virtually stopped altogether by the end of the nineteenth century, but two coal mines were still working in the 1930s. One of those mines, just behind the inn itself, was worked by Michael Peacock, the husband of the inn's legendary landlady, Susan Peacock. He not only obtained free coal for the inn but also made a fortune – albeit a short-lived one – during the national coal strike in 1926 when his was one of the very few mines working. However, the 'crow' coal, mixed with bands of shale, was of only moderate quality and under increasing competition from the high quality fuel from the Durham coalfields, the two pits' trade dwindled to the point where both finally ceased operations, one just before and the other just after the Second World War.

There is still plenty of coal down there around and under the inn, but mercifully an application to carry out open-cast mining in the 1970s was turned down, for it would have devastated the area and destroyed the inn as well. Although the mines have gone, traces of 'The Old Man', as previous generations of miners were always known, are found everywhere around the inn, with hundreds of disused shafts, drifts and spoil heaps, and the traces of one old 'horse gin' – a winding engine driven by horsepower, used to raise coal and colliery waste from deep below the moor – are still clearly visible today no more than 400 yards from the inn.

Both the inn itself and the neighbouring buildings – demolished in the 1950s, though there are still traces of the foundations to the west of the present building – had once been mine 'shops' housing the colliery offices and some rudimentary accommodation where the miners might board. However, they also served food and drink to passers-by, for money was not so plentiful in those old, hard times, that any source of potential income could be ignored. The coal miners rubbed shoulders with packhorse traders, who travelled round the isolated settlements of the upper Dales and provided the only 'shopping opportunity' some of the inhabitants might have, and drovers bringing herds of cattle and sheep over the wild uplands to sell at the great livestock fairs like Brough Hill in Westmorland, Malham Moor near Skipton, and Ribblehead near the famous viaduct on the Settle–Carlisle Line. Held for centuries, those fairs have all long since disappeared without trace.

Having bought his coal from Michael Peacock, Dick's father always called in at the inn as well, buying a pint for himself and a ginger beer for his boy, before heading home again. Clifford was a fair few years younger than Dick and by the time his father brought him up to the inn for the first

153

time, the coal mines had closed. Clifford had also maintained his father's tradition of never passing the inn without calling in for a drink, but he had broken with the Dale's traditions in one way. Unlike Dick and most of the other farmers of the Dale, who tended to leave their wives at home when they went to the pub, Clifford very often brought his wife, Jenny, to the inn with him. He recalled that on his very first trip, he and his dad had used a different form of transport from Dick and his father. 'The first time I came I was only a little kid,' Clifford said. 'And I came on the back of my dad's push-bike. Any time we passed by after that, we would always call in and have a drink. Many a time when we called back then, we didn't have the money on us but we could always get a drink and then pay the next time we came in.' Not that it took much money in those days, when beer was only 'three ha'pence' (½p) a pint.

Another farmer always took a pint of milk up to the pub with him and gave it to the landlord in exchange for a pint of beer. The landlord kept a goat, but in winter it was 'dry' and gave no milk, so the pint of cows' milk was as welcome to the landlord as the pint of beer was to his customer. The barrels of beer then were kept in a 'cellar head', a few stone steps down from the bar and right against the outside wall of the inn. 'It kept the beer nice and cold in summer,' Clifford said, 'but in winter it was too cold, so they never had any draught beer, because the pipes would freeze up. So there was just bottled beer in winter.'

Winter at the inn has always been hard – even in the mild years of the 1990s and early 2000's, when the rest of the country had almost forgotten what snow looked like, the Inn at the Top was always cut off for at least a few days by winter storms – but that winter of 1984–85 was nothing compared to our first winter there in 1978–79. In the depths of that winter we had been cut off for an unbroken stretch of eleven weeks and some of our locals in the more remote farms around the head of the Dale suffered almost as much disruption.

One of them, our friend and local, Clifford, saved the lives of two young Dutchmen after they had become trapped by snowdrifts as they attempted to drive over the wild moorland road across the watershed at the head of the Dale. In such savage weather with a blinding snowstorm driven by a gale force wind creating a white-out, it was suicidal even to attempt that road over the high hills, but in their defence, I suppose the Dutch don't have much experience of either white-outs or, indeed, high hills. The two men eventually abandoned their car and tried to make their way back down the Dale on foot but they were floundering in the drifts, freezing cold and unable to see where they were going, and one was already going into hypothermia when they took shelter in a stone hut at the side of the road. Luckily for them, Clifford stored hay in that hut, and there he found them, when he took advantage of a brief lull in the storm to battle his way up the Dale to feed his sheep. Having foddered his sheep, he helped the two men back through the snow to his farm.

'Clifford had an awful struggle to get them down here,' his wife, Jenny, said. 'They told us later that they'd gone into the hut to die. It was three miles back to the farm and Clifford had to get quite sharp with the one who was really bad, just to keep him moving.' He also gave them some sips of whisky from a hip flask which, whether by coincidence or some kind of premonition, he had taken up the Dale with him that morning for the first and only time in his life. The two Dutchmen survived and made a full recovery and returned to the farm, albeit this time in summer, to thank Clifford and Jenny again for saving their lives.

Snow was not the only hazard that they and we had to deal with. Wind and rain could both be almost equally devastating and some storms were so bad that it was a struggle to find the front door of the inn from the inside, let alone the outside. 'Reynard?' one bedraggled follower of a local foot-pack of foxhounds, in the days when such things as fox-hunts were legal, remarked as he stared out through the window at the downpour lashing the inn. 'It never bloody stops up here!'

If you ever visit the inn, you'll see that the edge of the roof is pinned every foot or so with long, right-angled steel bands, that are screwed into the gable ends. The steel bands are not there for show, for without them, the inn's roof slates could easily be stripped off en masse by the force of a storm. When the wind was really blowing hard, it was – and still is – sometimes necessary to get down on your hands and knees and crawl from your car to the front door of the inn, to avoid being blown off your feet. The alternative was to do a sort of controlled falling, allowing the shriek-ing gale, nearly always blowing from the west, to blast you along the front of the inn until you could duck out of the wind around the side of the building and then sneak into the inn by the back door. Unwary motorists foolish enough to let go of their car door as they got out of their vehicles sometimes saw the door snatched from their grasp by the wind, torn from its hinges and sent cartwheeling away down the road.

Our successors as landlords even witnessed a day when not only their post but their postman as well was delivered to their door by the wind. 'He weighed about fifteen stone,' the landlady recalled, 'but when he stepped out of his van, the wind just picked him up and dropped him at the door!' 'Sideways rain' – rain driven horizontally by the force of a gale – was so frequent as not to be worth mentioning, and anyone optimistic enough to hoist an umbrella to protect them from the weather was likely to be chasing it down the moor or doing airborne Mary Poppins impressions.

The upland fells around the inn soaked up the rainwater like giant sponges, feeding the fast-rushing river that, trapped in the narrow steep-sided Dale, often led to flooding. Floods were rarely an issue at the inn, perched as it was, almost at the very top of the hill, but they were not entirely unknown. The remnants of Hurricane Charlie in the 1980s dumped so much rain in such a short space of time that even the Inn at the Top was flooded, with water gushing through the back door of the inn and filling the pub to a depth of six inches. However its worst effects were felt farther down the Dale. The floods swept a bridge away, cutting off one small community and forcing them into a tedious and time consuming detour for months afterwards, and the local pub in that village was flooded three feet deep. Other residents described a wall of water tearing down the Dale, carrying with it huts, greenhouses and garden sheds.

In the villages still further down the Dale the flooding was even worse. One man had to take refuge on the roof of the phone box in one village as water swirled around his feet. Fortunately he had already telephoned for help from the call-box before the rising waters reached the phone and put it out of order, and so was rescued without further mishap. Another man, a visitor, was asleep in his caravan when he felt it moving and looked out to see it being carried along on the flood. Fortunately he too was rescued safely.

Although the Dale was no stranger to floods, that particular one was said to have been the worst since 'the great tempest of 1899' when one village was almost completely destroyed. Sheep, dogs, huts and hen houses were swept away, and the houses badly damaged by the floods, which also washed away their gardens. It was said that the flowers that had been planted in the gardens flowered the following year in the next village, a couple of miles further down the Dale.

In that and similar floods, farmers lost not just their crops and some of their livestock but also the soil from their fields as well. After another terrible nineteenth century flood, one farmer had 'twenty acres of meadow land rendered useless' and another had only five acres of 'good meadow' left out of forty. 'Many thousands of trout and other fish' were picked up from the devastated land when the waters receded.

# CHAPTER 8

## A 240 Volt Ball Of Energy With Shocking Pink Hair

In order to scrape together enough money to buy the inn, we had been forced to take an overdraft from the bank at an eye-watering interest rate and we were desperate to replace it with a brewery loan. In return for the exclusive right to supply beer, breweries then routinely offered interest-free loans to pub owners, based on the barrelage of beer they sold and, given the Inn at the Top's healthy turnover, we had anticipated no problems in securing a loan ourselves. The rep from our chosen brewery, a man in his early twenties with a not very successful moustache and a polyester suit, was equally confident. 'No problem at all,' he said. 'We should have it through for you in a couple of weeks.'

A couple of weeks went by and then a couple more, with no sign of the promised loan, but whenever I telephoned the rep, he assured me that the last 'i's were being dotted and 't's crossed on the loan agreement and the money would be in our bank account any day now. This dragged on for two months while our bank made increasingly strident demands for the repayment of the short-term temporary overdraft facility I had arranged, expecting it to be needed for no more than a couple of weeks. In the end, in sheer desperation, having been given the same worthless assurances yet again, I went over the rep's head and phoned the managing director of the brewery direct. It took a succession of calls before I got through, but when I did, I discovered that the rep – let's call him Walter Mitty, shall we? – had never even passed on our request for a loan and as a result, not only had the paperwork not been completed, it had not even been started.

The fact that the rep was then sacked on the spot was of no help to us and though the managing director offered to fast-track a loan for us, our confidence in his brewery was sufficiently shaken for us to go elsewhere. We approached the Theakston's rep, a glamorous, black-haired woman who, despite her slim build, still seemed to be able to drink even Norman Parker under the table, and never once fell off the four-inch stiletto heels she always wore. She promised us a £10,000, interest-free loan within a week and it was in our bank account even quicker than that. It was the beginning of a long and very successful association between Theakston's brewery and Britain's highest inn, which still continues today.

Among the Theakstons beers that we sold was a powerful brew named Old Peculier (not Old Peculiar, the unusual spelling is because the name is a reference to some obscure ancient official of the town of Masham, where the beer is brewed, rather than its unusual taste). It was a potent dark beer but to my taste buds at least, off-puttingly sweet. However it had its devotees, many of them the same sort of young men who would order the hottest Vindaloo on the menu of their local curry house, just to prove their macho credentials.

However it seemed to me that if you kept Old Peculier long enough before broaching the barrel, since it was a live, cask-conditioned ale, the fermentation process would continue and – as the Holsten Pils adverts used to say – a lot of the sugars would be converted to alcohol. It would make the already fearsomely strong brew even more so, but it would also make it more appealing to those, like me, who preferred a pint of bitter to a bottle of sweet stout or, heaven forbid, a bottle of Newcastle Brown.

I confess that my chance to test this theory came about largely as a result of my own in-experience as a landlord. With the annual sheep show on the horizon, I was carried away on a tide of optimism about the weather prospects and the number of tourists likely to attend the event and I ordered huge quantities of beer. Unfortunately the weather turned the wrong side of 'mizzling' – misty and drizzling – and very few tourists and visitors made the journey up the hill through the mist and rain to sample the delights of either the sheep show or the beer. The locals turned out in force, of course, but on show day they tended to drink whisky rather than beer and though we sold prodigious quantities of whisky during the day, when the show was over I was left with several unbroached barrels of Old Peculier.

Resolving American salesman-style, to make

every problem an opportunity, I decided that this was a heaven sent opportunity to test my theory about Old Peculier. Several weeks elapsed while the number of barrels slowly decreased and the alcoholic strength of the remainder steadily increased. I helped myself to a glass from time to time, purely for research purposes, of course, and found it less and less sweet and as a result, ever more to my taste. The crucial moment came when one of my colleagues from CAMRA, it's justly famous Company Secretary, came up to stay at the inn for a couple of days. He had a pint of bitter as a warm-up and I then suggested that he should try the Old Peculier. He gave me a dubious look but took the pint I pulled for him. He drank it and he liked it. St Paul on the road to Damascus could not have had a more blinding revelation.

'Old Peculier's a bitter beer! Old Peculier's a bitter beer!' he said, shaking his head in disbelief. He had another pint just to make sure he wasn't imagining things, and then, abandoning any pretence at research, he had another just for pleasure, and one more because, as he pointed out, after a drink like that, going back to the ordinary bitter would be like drinking water. In alcoholic strength he had now probably consumed the equivalent of at least a gallon of the beer he normally drank and then, still inspired by his revelation, he borrowed the phone and, slightly slurring his words, began ringing all his friends in CAMRA to bring this wondrous news to their attention.

With the Theakston's loan nestling in our bank account, we were now able to clear the overdraft with its crippling rate of interest and, as our financial worries eased a little, helped not just by the loan but by an improving cash flow as the tourist season got underway, we now had a modest amount of spare money available to pay for some much-needed improvements to the inn.

One of our locals, Jim, was not only a regular at the inn, but a jobbing builder as well, and we enlisted him to carry out some building work for us. As he did so, we kept one eye out for the ghost of the former landlady, Susan Peacock, who ran the inn for over thirty years in the first part of the twentieth century. Her ghost was said to appear whenever alterations were being made to the inn, when she would act as overseer of the work, ensuring it was carried out properly. However, that legend had taken a bit of a dent when she failed to put in an appearance to stop Stan and Neville from generally mutilating the place after they'd bought it, and we certainly never saw her. The only eerie sounds we heard were made by the wind whistling through the rotten windows and the only rattling chains around the inn were those on the snow tyres in winter.

The first essential job was to do something about the black damp in the dining room at the western end of the building, which bore the brunt of the wild weather on our exposed hilltop. The fireplace in the dining room had been bricked up some years before and the chimney stack taken down to roof level, but we felt that with the chimney rebuilt, the fireplace opened up and a log-stove installed, the heat and the flow of air through the room would at least ease the problem, even if it didn't entirely cure it.

So with me as his unskilled labourer, Jim set to work, opening up the fireplace, building a new surround for it and installing the log-stove I had found. We also opened up the dining room area, by removing the ugly timber partitions between the tables – once more Stan and Neville appeared to have used a job-lot of second-hand wood – that had been used to separate the dining areas into a strange approximation of the stalls in a cow byre.

Jim then turned his attention to the roof, removing some of the slates and building a new chimney stack, complete with chimney pot. It was while doing this that Jim began wincing in pain when reaching down each time I passed up the next stone for the stack, or when he twisted or turned awkwardly. He was suffering from the builder's occupational hazard – a bad back – and, though he managed to finish the chimney-stack, by the time he had done so, his back had became so painful that he had to take to his bed and lie flat until the pain eased.

Jim's wife, Rita, displaying all the sympathy that wives normally display for male illness, could be heard muttering to herself about 'man-flu', but Jim wasn't play-acting, he was seriously crocked. He went to see his doctor and then a specialist in back injuries and the only, very depressing, advice that they could offer him was 'You need to look for an alternative career. You'll never be able to go back to building.'

The residents of the Dale were not normally known for their interest in alternative therapies but when a friend suggested to Jim that he might try acupuncture, he was sufficiently desperate to give anything a go. He went to the acupuncturist expecting nothing other than perhaps a little pain relief, but to Jim's surprise, the treatment began to show results almost straight away. It was a sixty mile round trip every time Jim went to see the acupuncturist, and it cost him a significant amount of money at a time when he had no income coming in and had to dig deep into his savings to pay for it. But, such was his growing confidence in the treatment, that he kept going there for several months and at the end of it, contrary to what the specialist in conventional medical treatments had said, Jim was able to resume full time work as a builder with no apparent ill effects.

His next job for us was to do something about the floor in the bar. When we bought the inn, courtesy of Stan and Neville, there was a particularly disgusting worn and stained carpet in the bar, which we ripped up and burned on a bonfire in the car park. The floor beneath it was concrete and we needed something that would cover that, but also add to the character of the place. In a place that daily felt the tread of hundreds of muddy, peat-encrusted hiking boots, carpet was not really a sensible option, and a flagstone floor would have been ideal except that it would have lopped several more inches off the already limited headroom in the bar.

However, thanks to Jim, we found an excellent alternative. He'd heard of a load of old sandstone roofing slates that were for sale, cheap. Once laid on the floor they were indistinguishable in look from a genuine flagstone floor, but took only an inch off the headroom, meaning that almost everyone – apart from the six foot four inch landlord – could negotiate the doorways without banging their heads. The new 'flagstone floor' made the bar look much more attractive and it has certainly stood the test of time – it's still there today. Unfortunately, replacing the steel RSJ beams clad in plywood with genuine oak beams would have been too difficult and expensive to contemplate and, like the rather naff pine panelling in the games room, they had to be left in situ.

We also made one rather less practical improvement by installing a sauna in an unused corner of the upstairs landing. Although it put such a massive drain on the power that it could only be fired up when the pub was closed and everything else switched off, we thought it might be a winter attraction for customers and – not necessarily in that order, also had fond mental pictures of ourselves retreating to this cosy womb when the winter storms were raging around the inn. Meanwhile it was pressed into service in a rather less glamourous role, providing a warm and dry place to store boxes of potato crisps.

When we had bought the pub, it had always been our intention to take on another couple as co-workers and possibly eventual partners. Our reasoning was that all four of us could work the summer season when the deluge of tourists and visitors made it almost impossible for a couple to cope alone, and then in the six quiet months of the year, we could take it in turns to take three months off to rest and recuperate. It was, we felt, the only way that we could sustain the business in the medium- to long-term, and several couples we knew had expressed enormous enthusiasm for the idea of going into partnership with us when buying the pub was no more than a pipe-dream. However, as soon as it became a reality, every one of them, without exception, disappeared over the metaphorical horizon, never to be seen again.

So we advertised in a couple of papers for a suitably deranged couple to come and join us at the most preposterous pub in the country, and received a flood of applications. Having sifted through them and discarded the more obvious alcoholics, fantasists, mentally unstable persons and anyone who filled in their application form in green ink, we settled on a short-list of potential couples and invited the most promising-sounding of all of them to come up for a trial weekend with us, so that we could get the measure of each other and see if the work suited them and, just as important, that we were compatible.

One major obstacle presented itself as soon as they walked through the door. The couple were friendly and enthusiastic, the only problem was that the woman was around a size twenty-six, and since the space between the bar and the shelves behind it was so narrow that two standard-sized people could only pass each other by holding their breath, she formed an impenetrable barrier wherever she stood behind the bar. In order to get past her at all, she had to emerge and then someone else could go in. It must have been humiliating for her and after a couple of hours of this, it was clear that either she would have to go or I'd have to embark on a major reconstruction of the bar, and

I wasn't quite sure I was ready for that.

The coup de grace was administered during the night. I was awoken from a deep sleep by a crash, and when I went to investigate I discovered that the unfortunate couple's double-bed had collapsed underneath them, with its legs splayed out like an overloaded seaside donkey. They didn't say anything then, but they left at first light the next morning, without even waiting to say goodbye. We tried a few more couples, all unsuitable for a variety of reasons, and then pretty much gave up on the idea, resigning ourselves to using whatever casual hired help we could find instead.

We had expected that finding staff to work at such an impossibly remote location would be our biggest problem but in fact it proved to be one that largely solved itself. Jim's wife Rita, a one person cleaning cyclone and waitressing whirlwind who had worked for us when we managed the pub five years before, would have been a very welcome addition to our workforce but was sadly not available. After years of working the summer season at the inn and then being unemployed through the winter, she had opted for the year-round security of a full-time job with the local council, working at an old people's home. Although Rita conceded that working at the inn was a lot more fun than her council job, she could not be persuaded to come back and work for us again, but our other local helper, Mary, another real hard grafter, rejoined us, helping with the cleaning in the morning and then staying on to serve customers during the lunchtime rush.

The rest of the motley crew of employees that we

eventually assembled pretty much picked themselves, often literally. Soon after we took over, we hired a joiner to do some running repairs to the woodwork for us, including repairing the worst of the window frames, and he moved in for a few days while he was doing the job, bringing his mercurial eighteen-year-old punk girlfriend, Ruby, with him. By the time the joiner had completed his work and was ready to move on, Ruby had evidently decided that she liked the idea of life at the pub much more than that of life with him and volunteered to stay on with us as a barmaid. The joiner travelled down the Dale alone, while Ruby installed herself behind the bar. A feisty, motor-mouthed 240 volt ball of energy with spiked, shocking pink hair, Ruby at once became one of the prime visitor attractions in the district and within a week, a row of awe-struck, tongue-tied and thoroughly besotted farm-boys were lining the bar every night to gaze in wonder at her.

Their romantic hopes were dented a couple of weeks later when three hikers stopped at the inn. They were halfway through their long-distance walk along the Pennine Way – two weeks down and two weeks to go – but although three had entered the pub from the south that evening, only two of them carried on to the north the next morning. Ruby had taken a fancy to the third, Liam, a powerfully-built character with a suitably punk haircut: three spikes of gelled hair, like a triple-pointed Mohican, with his dark hair bleached blond at the tips. Liam explained to me that as he was broke, he was reduced to achieving his bleached blond look by lowering the tips of his hair into a bucket of Domestos and had then used soap instead of hair gel to make the spikes of hair stand on end.

Whether it was the hair or his party trick of doing press-ups while balancing on a single knuckle of one hand, or something else entirely that had first caught Ruby's attention was not revealed, but she soon persuaded Liam of the wisdom of staying behind while his friends set off to complete the rest of their long-distance walk without him. In the still hours of that and every subsequent night, the pub echoed to the sound of the newly bonded couple's frenzied lovemaking, and in daylight we had the benefit not just of a barmaid but of a willing, if understandably pale and tired sous chef for the kitchen.

Our other two full-time employees also arrived by accident. Two Australian backpackers, confusingly both named Alan, and promptly rechristened 'Big Alan' and 'Little Alan' to make identification easier, strode up to the door one day, taking in Yorkshire as part of their gap year – although it was already much longer than that – tour of Europe. They had been planning to move on after a quick drink, but once more, just like their co-workers, they never actually got any further. 'I've been travelling for two years,' one of them said, 'and this spot is just how I imagined England to be. There are not many places left like it, so we just thought we would stay.'

We welcomed them with open arms and they became full-time resident handymen/builders by day and barmen by night. Little Alan was of medium height and dark-haired and Big Alan was blond and tall, and both were good-looking in a rough-hewn sort of way and built like the proverbial 'Outback dunnee'. Word about the two Australian hunks went round the Dale like wildfire and the queues of lovelorn farm-boys gazing wistfully at the gorgeous but now unattainable Ruby were soon joined by an equally long line of farm-girls gazing at the much less unavailable Alans. If the younger men and women of the Dale worshipped Ruby or one or both of the Alans respectively, their fathers adored Sue and, despite the total lack of supporting evidence, I tried to convince myself that I had my share of secret admirers too; they were probably just being ultra discreet.

Our resident work force was now occupying all but one of our guest bedrooms, but we thought that the lost bed and breakfast income was a small price to pay for the sharing of the workload, and the pleasure we derived from having them around. In theory at least, our augmented workforce might also allow us to take an occasional night off and – unless we were really busy – an hour off during the afternoon. In fact we almost never did so but in any case, the early months back there at the inn were more pleasure than toil. It was like a party every day for us and our motley crew of staff, full of laughter and private jokes at which our customers were often bemused onlookers. It wasn't necessarily good for business – whatever that was – but it was very enjoyable, and we took a particularly perverse pleasure in clocking the facial expressions of some of our more tweedy customers of a certain age, as they arrived in the heart of the Yorkshire Dales, no doubt expecting the blazing open fire, flagstone floors and oak beams of an archetypal Dales pub.

All those ingredients were indeed present and correct – even though admittedly the beams were fake – but what they also got was often either the pub owners and staff cackling with laughter as they fought it out with soda syphons at five paces, or an earful of Siouxie and the Banshees screeching out 'Helter Skelter' or Frankie Goes to Hollywood's 'Relax'– banned by the BBC, but still on the jukebox playlist at the Inn at the Top – and an eyeful of the luridly, if scantily attired Ruby, pogo-ing away behind the bar. A few of our potential customers got no further than the doorway before beating a hasty retreat, but since we were busier than we could humanly cope with anyway, it seemed a small price to pay for our wholesome family entertainment.

Some of our other would-be customers of a certain age were doubtless also put off by another regular phenomenon associated with the inn: bikers' rallies. The inn had always been popular with bikers, who loved burning up the twisting, undulating and little-used roads around us and, while they had been banned from many other pubs in the Dales, sometimes for a variety of misdemeanours, but often simply because the landlords didn't like bikers, they had always been welcome at the Inn at the Top. Several different clubs held their rallies and annual reunions up there and, despite their sometimes intimidating reputation, we never had the slightest trouble from any of them.

Knowing that their welcome at the dwindling number of pubs that would still accept them depended on there being no trouble, the biker clubs policed their own events, setting up an admissions desk outside the door to vet the arrivals for known trouble-makers, running their own security with the help of a couple of the burlier members of the clubs, and they even brought their own portaloos and set them up on the car park as well. They camped on the land next to the inn, left the bar without argument as soon as we called 'Time', and cleared up all their litter before they left; if only some of our supposedly more civilised customers had been even half as polite, neat and tidy, running the inn would have been a dream!

While we were happy to accommodate the bikers, we needed a crash course in maintaining sufficient stocks of their favourite drinks. Whenever a group of bikers from Tyneside, Wearside or Teesside was there, we soon learned that the bitter, lager and stout that most of our usual customers drank would remain largely untouched. What the male bikers wanted was either 'bottles of broon' (Newcastle Brown) or pints of Snakebite – a fifty-fifty mix of lager and cider, sometimes with a dash of blackcurrant thrown in as well – and what most of their women drank was 'Pernod and black'(currant). All of them tasted equally disgusting to me, but the bikers clearly liked them and, after all, the customer is always right.

Before the first bikers' weekend we hosted, I fielded repeated requests from the organisers to 'make sure you've got plenty of Newcastle Brown in'. I looked at the towering stacks of crates in the cellar and convinced myself and the bikers that we already had plenty. The bikers duly arrived on Friday evening and by the Saturday lunchtime I was making a frantic circuit of the off-licences, supermarkets and the other pubs in the neighbouring towns and villages, buying or borrowing every bottle or can of 'broon' I could lay my hands on. Even then we ran out of both Newcastle Brown and Pernod again before the bikers headed for home on Sunday lunchtime.

We also played host to motor enthusiasts of a rather earlier vintage – both the motorists and their vehicles – since both the Scott Trial, a seventy-mile off-road event for vintage motorbikes, and the Beamish Reliability Run, a 150 mile tour of Northern roads for vintage cars, motorbikes and commercial vehicles registered before 1956, passed by the inn and used it as a pit-stop, having laboured up the savagely steep hill from the Dale. The radiator of many a vintage motor was boiling like a tea kettle by the time they reached the top!

Sadly one society we were eager to see more of – The British Naturists Society – who had inadvertently provided us and our regulars with much free entertainment and amusement when they chose the Inn at the Top for a camping weekend during our previous spell at the inn, failed to put in an appearance this time. We suspected that the cold-related shrinkage of their appendages was too recent and bitter a memory for them to risk further frostbite by trying to pitch their tents again on our cold and wind-blasted hilltop, and that instead, they had found

174

some more sheltered lowland location in which to air their differences ... if you see what I mean.

In addition to our punk bar staff and Aussie handymen cum bar staff, we had also acquired one other member of permanent staff: a bantam cockerel named Eric who had been donated to us by someone who had sold up and was leaving the area. Eric seemed happy enough in his new kingdom at first, but the lack of any female company soon got to him. He went off his food, entered a profound depression and was only crowing at one tenth of his normal volume. In desperation – and, it must be admitted, with one eye on its publicity value – I placed an advertisement in the lonely hearts column of the local newspaper, seeking a mate for him. As I told a reporter who, as we had hoped, followed up the advert with a feature article, 'We would love to find Eric a partner before winter sets in. There are only grouse up here and they fly too fast for him!'

To Eric's vocal delight, our search was rewarded not just with one mate for him but with two, and he was soon making up for lost time with all the enthusiasm you might expect, but sadly, the story does not have a happy ending. One ill-starred night a marauding fox sneaked into the backyard of the inn and killed the entire menage a trois: Eric and his two blushing brides, though we were able to console ourselves with the thought that he had at least died happy.

# CHAPTER 9

## Your Boss Will Never Suspect A Thing

We were now happy with the staff we had somehow managed to assemble, but the hope that the rats that had been in residence when we moved in and the former owners Neville and Stan, and their assorted managers, would be the last of the unpleasant characters that we'd have to deal with proved to be foolishly optimistic, and a few more shady types kept appearing at the Inn at the Top from time to time. There is an old motto in the licensed trade: never employ anybody who has ever worked in a pub before. We began to see the reason for that over our first few months as owners of the inn. Virtually everybody we came across seemed to be on the take and our naiveté and relative inexperience in the trade – at least as pub owners – made us prime targets: fresh meat.

I had been warned to watch out for the brewery draymen and so I scrutinised our deliveries like a hawk. A few expensive weeks went by before I discovered that you had to pay equal or even greater attention to the crates of empties going back. The draymen had a nice little earner, conning inattentive landlords by underestimating the number of crates of empties, all of which – bottles and crates alike – had a deposit on them. They would then add the extra crates on to the tally of one of the landlords with whom they had a cash-in-hand arrangement.

There was no shortage of other scams. One hiker who called at the inn had claimed to be walking from Lands End to John O'Groats, raising money for charity along the way, and many trusting souls donated some money to him. He was later arrested by police after they discovered that, for him at least, charity began at home, and all the money he had collected, allegedly some £25,000, had gone straight into his own pocket.

Early one morning, not long after we'd taken over, I met another charming chap. A middle-aged man, an ex-military type with sandy hair and a moustache, and wearing a tweed jacket and cavalry twill trousers, came into the inn as I was stocking up the shelves behind the bar. He glanced round the deserted bar and then fixed his gaze on me. I was, I admit, unusually young for a Dales publican and I probably cut a rather less than dashing figure, dressed in my customary pre-opening hours garb of blue boiler suit, wellies and black, woollen 'beanie' hat.

'Good morning,' he said. 'Anyone else around?'

'No, just me.'

He leant across the bar in a confidential way. 'You work in the bar, do you?'

I nodded.

'Well,' he said. 'I'm a freelance stocktaker. I work with quite a few pubs around here, doing their stock-checking for them.'

He leant even further forward and dropped his voice a little more. 'You and I could have a nice little arrangement between us here. You recommend me to your boss, I come in once a month and do the stock-taking. The figures all add up perfectly, but you and I get a nice little taste out of it and, best of all, your boss will never suspect a thing.'

I straightened up and studied him for a moment. 'He probably will,' I said. 'I am the boss.'

He recoiled as if he'd been stung, hesitated a moment, perhaps trying to calculate if irreparable damage had been done, then turned on his heel and hurried out without another word.

I decided to do my own stock-taking – after a fashion. I was often too busy and tired to make a proper job of it, but I always made a point of wandering around at least once a week, holding a clipboard and a pen and pursing my lips and tutting as I counted the bottles on the shelves and consulted a long list of random figures I had scribbled down on a sheet. I think our bar-staff got the message; if they were fiddling, it was too subtle and too small scale for me to worry about ... or at least I think it was...

The small scale dishonesty of a few of our customers was no more than a minor irritation compared to the losses we could have suffered if we had succumbed to some of the traditional licensed trade scams or if any of our staff had been seriously 'on the rob', but it was tedious nonetheless. Coach parties vied with hikers as souvenir hunters or, to put it less politely, thieves. Our bill for replacement ashtrays and glasses was astronomical, but most irritating of all, though less expensive, was the visitors' habit of nicking the toilet rolls. Every morning we'd clean the loos and place two or three new toilet rolls in each one. A passing hiker or tourist would then use the loo and place all the surplus loo-rolls in their bag or rucksack for their own private later use, with the result that the next customer would find the equivalent of a pub with no beer: a loo with no loo-paper.

Whenever they approached the bar and explained the problem, we would supply a fresh loo-roll but, whether through shyness or sheer fury, or because they did not discover the lack of paper until they had already passed the point of no return, some did not do so and made alternative arrangements. Some wrote abusive messages on the walls or doors but one enterprising customer pulled strips of wallpaper off the walls and used that instead of loo paper. Unblocking the loo, which was now clogged with wallpaper, and then redecorating the walls after that, was just one more job to be fitted in. Fortunately most of our customers, both locals and tourists, were a pleasure to serve and in the favourite mantra of the Yorkshire Dales National Park were content to 'leave only footprints and take away only memories'.

One customer who had already given us more than our fair share of good memories, Faith, continued to be a near-daily visitor to the inn, but her long life and the long years of hard drinking and heavy smoking were beginning to take their toll on her. She was as thin as a moorland grass stem and, partly as a result of that, no doubt, her capacity for drink was not what it was, and she became drunk quite quickly. That did not matter as much up at the inn, where she had us and the postman to look after her and make sure she got home safely, but it made her much more vulnerable when at home, not only to Paul's sporadic bursts of violent temper, but also to people preying on her.

Although she was not by any means a wealthy woman, Faith's cottage was full of valuable small antiques and curios that she had inherited from her mother. A few dealers in antiques and 'bygones' travelled up and down the dale from time to time looking for bargains and when a pair of them knocked at the door of Faith's cottage one day, they must have licked their lips at what it contained. Faith wasn't interested in selling her possessions and the dealers went away empty-handed on that occasion, but they had learned enough about her to plan a return visit.

When they came back a couple of days later, they brought a bottle of whisky with them and having plied Faith with several glasses, either she agreed to them taking their pick from her antiques, or else she was so drunk that she was unaware that they were doing so. They disappeared down the Dale, taking a rich haul of her antiques with them. When they heard what had happened, a few of our locals were very much looking forward to making the acquaintance of those dealers when they next returned to the Dale and were planning to exact some retribution for the way they had ripped off Faith but, having already stripped her of some of her most valuable possessions, they did not show their faces again. Even people who might have been expected to be a little more sympathetic to her were sometimes also the beneficiaries of her alcohol-fuelled generosity; someone from the Dale who really should have known better was spotted emerging from her cottage one day with one of her heirlooms under his arm.

If Faith was particularly vulnerable when strangers were about, however, it was her nearest and dearest who was sometimes the greatest danger of all to her. Living cheek by jowl in their cramped cottage, there was constant friction between Faith and Paul. They argued bitterly and he had hit her on several occasions, but her refusal to make any formal complaint against him meant that, even when the police were called, there was nothing they could do but give him a verbal warning.

The nine cats that shared their home showed much more affection for Faith than they did for Paul, but he nonetheless insisted that one of them was his cat, not his mother's, and tried to prove it by keeping it locked in his bedroom. That added another layer to the already eye-watering smell of cats in the cottage and, unsurprisingly, the cat was also so desperate to escape its cramped and less than fragrant quarters that it made a bolt for the door whenever Paul opened it to come in or out. One day that summer, as Paul entered the room, the cat made its customary escape bid. He made a grab for it and as he struggled to hold on to it, the cat lacerated his face with its claws. Paul shouted in pain and fury and then vented his temper by hurling the cat against the wall with such force that he broke its neck.

When Faith discovered what had happened, she went for Paul herself, and the ensuing fight was the most violent that even that volatile couple had ever had. Paul was almost uncontrollable and it was more by luck than anything else that Faith, though badly bruised, was not seriously injured or even killed. She managed to escape him and fled to the house of her neighbours, an old couple who settled her by their fire, locked their door and then phoned our friends Gavin and Ruth, who lived in a neighbouring village, and asked them to help.

Fearless and furious in equal measure, Ruth, a trained nurse, went straight round there. Having called the doctor to check Faith's injuries and reassured herself that she was in no immediate danger, Ruth went up to the cottage. It was brave of her to do so, for Paul was still boiling with rage and in no mood to listen to reason at first but, knowing that he was very wary of dogs, she'd taken her pet sheepdog with her, and the presence of the dog and Ruth's measured but no-nonsense approach slowly calmed Paul down.

Having examined Faith, the doctor called in social services. It was now obvious that Paul posed too great a danger to his mother for them to continue living in the cottage together – if he attacked her again, or even if he just pushed her over, the stone-flagged floors would have broken her brittle old bones – and she was taken to a temporary safe environment while a more permanent solution was found.

Without his mother to feed him, Paul was incapable of looking after himself and he was taken to secure accommodation in the neighbouring Dale. With the help of the right medication and freed from the stresses caused by living with his mother and their menagerie of cats, he then resumed normality – for Paul at least – and I saw him occasionally, still with his unusual hair styling, pedalling his bike around the grounds of his new home.

Faith had hoped to live on alone in her little cottage but, now increasingly frail, she had reached the point where she could no longer look after herself either. She had to give up her home and went to live in sheltered accommodation in the nearby market town, while her cats were collected by the local animal rescue charity, which found them new homes.

We missed Faith's visits to the inn – another link with the old days at the Inn at the Top had been broken – but when the time allowed, which wasn't as often as I'd have liked, I'd pop over and visit her at the care home where she was living. One thing hadn't changed; the first thing she always asked me when she saw me was 'Are we going for a drink?'

I'd take her to the pub just down the road, run by the parents of her favourite carer from the home, and I'd buy her a whisky and soda: 'Just a splash of soda. Don't drown it!' Then we'd sit by the fire while I listened to a few of her tales. I'd probably heard them all by then but, no matter how many times I heard them, I still enjoyed her retelling of her favourite anecdotes, her eyes alight with mischief.

She also had one or two ghost stories in her repertoire, one of which 'The Hand of Glory', had allegedly occurred in a building that had once been a coaching inn, just across the moor from the

Inn at the Top. She told it to me, one dark winter afternoon, with rain rattling against the windows and a fire crackling in the grate and – call me suggestible if you like – she was sufficiently convincing as she lowered her voice and glanced around as if expecting the characters from her tale to come bursting in through the door at any moment, to raise the hairs on the back of my neck.

According to her tale, in the last years of the eighteenth century the old coaching inn had been run by a man called George Alderson with his wife and son, and a maidservant called Bella. The inn was a long, narrow stone building set at right angles to the high road which crossed the wild and lonely moor on the ancient route from York to Carlisle. The lower storey of the house was used as stables for the stage-coaches which changed horses at the inn and the other storeys were reached by a flight of ten or twelve stone steps leading up from the road to a stout oak door. The windows on either side of it were deeply recessed into the thick stone walls and protected by iron bars.

One cold October night, the curtains were drawn across the windows and a log fire was spluttering and crackling on the hearth. George Alderson and his son were sitting by the fire talking of the money they had made at the fair on Brough Hill that day, all of which was stowed away in a bedroom cupboard. Alderson's wife and Bella sat at their spinning wheels across the room from them. The last stagecoach of the day had been and gone and the door was barred and bolted for the night. A storm was blowing outside, with rain lashing the windows and fierce gusts of wind rattling the casements and stirring the curtains, when suddenly there was a knock at the door.

'Open the door, lass,' Alderson said to Bella, 'I wouldn't leave a dog out on such a night as this.'

'Best just slacken the chain first,' his more cautious wife said.

When Bella went to the door, she saw an old woman on the step and at once opened the door wide and invited her in. She was bent and stooped and dressed in a long cloak and hood that was drawn close over her face. As she walked feebly to the armchair by the fire, rain streamed from her clothes and collected in pools on the oak floorboards. She was shivering violently, but refused to take off her cloak to have it dried. She also refused the offer of food or a bed for the night, saying she was on her way to the South and must set off as soon as there was enough daylight. All she wanted, she said, was to rest beside the fire; she could get all the sleep she needed in the armchair.

Alderson and his wife and son went to bed soon afterwards, leaving Bella alone with the shivering woman. When Bella tried to engage her in conversation, she got only short surly answers in reply and although the old woman's voice was so low that Bella had to strain her ears to hear, it did not sound like a woman's voice to her. When the old woman stretched out her feet to warm them at the fire, Bella caught a glimpse of a horseman's gaiters showing under the hem of her skirt. Deeply uneasy, instead of going to bed, Bella resolved to keep watch. She lay down on a wooden bench at the far side of the room, out of the glow of the firelight and pretended to fall asleep.

After a few minutes the person in the chair stirred and stood up. No longer bent and stooped, it was the figure of a tall and powerful man. He stood listening intently for some time, then took from the folds of his cloak a brown and withered human hand. Next he produced a candle from his pocket, lit it from the fire and placed it in the dead fingers of the hand. By now, Bella's heart was beating so fast that she could hardly maintain the regular deep breathing of pretended sleep. She froze as she saw the man moving towards her, holding his gruesome candlestick in front of him and she clamped her eyelids tightly shut. She sensed that the man was bending over her and that the light was being passed to and fro in front of her eyes, while the man muttered in the strange, masculine voice that had first roused her suspicions:

*'Let those who rest more deeply sleep,*
*Let those awake their vigils keep.'*

The light then moved away and through her eyelashes Bella saw that the man's back was now turned to her and that he was placing the hand in the middle of the long oak table, while muttering

*'O hand of glory, shed thy light,*
*Direct us to our spoil tonight.'*

He moved a few steps across the room, opened the curtains and said

*'Flash out thy light, o skeleton hand,*
*And guide the feet of our trusty band.'*

At once the light flared up, casting a brilliant light into the room, and the man then walked to the door, drew back the bolts and unfastened the chain. Bella felt the cold blast of night air rushing in as the door was flung wide open. She kept her eyes half-closed as the man looked back at her and then, drawing something from under his cloak, he blew a long shrill whistle. Hearing no answer, he went down a few steps and whistled again. The next moment, rushing through the door, Bella pushed him in the back, sending him tumbling down the steps on to the road below. She ran back inside, locked and bolted the door, and then raced upstairs to wake the Aldersons. However, although she shouted and shook them, they slept on, their snores echoing through the building. Her attempts to wake their son were no more successful, for he too slept as if in a trance.

She heard the sound of angry voices outside the inn and there was a thunderous battering on the door. Bella ran back downstairs to the kitchen, where the Hand of Glory was still burning with a vivid light. She picked up a cup of milk that had been standing on the table and doused the flames with it. Almost at once she heard footsteps on the stairs and George Alderson and his son rushed into the room carrying firearms in their hands. The robbers continued to batter at the door, threatening the landlord with death if he did not unlock the door and give them his valuables, but Alderson's son opened the window and fired his blunderbuss at them. There was a groan and the sound of someone falling and after a muttered conversation among the robbers a voice called out 'Give up the Hand of Glory and we will not harm you. By way of reply, the boy fired another shot and the robbers eventually retreated. When daybreak arrived, there was no trace of them to be seen. According to the story, the Aldersons kept possession of the withered hand 'for sixteen years after'.

A 'Hand of Glory' – the mummified left hand of a hanged murderer, severed below the wrist at midnight by the light of a full moon – often featured in occult lore. Once lit, just as in Faith's story, it was supposed to render everyone unconscious. Nothing would wake them until the flame was extinguished, which could only be done with milk because water had no effect. Even more alarmingly, if the victims were not roused by the second cock-crow of morning, they would die, and their souls burn in hell. As that suggests, Faith's story was an ancient one; she said one of the old farmers in the Dale used to terrify her with it when she was young.

However, it must also address some deep-seated human fear, because I've heard many variants of it since, all involving a man dressed as a woman, including one in which a motorist picks up an apparently female hitchhiker in a long cloak. The driver spots a pair of man's boots poking out from under the hem of the cloak, and in one version, glimpses a concealed meat cleaver. Once more, however, just as in The Hand of Glory, the driver succeeds in tricking the dangerous stranger and pushing him out of the door, and escapes alive.

When Faith had told me her tales and drunk her whisky and soda, I'd drop her off back at the home an hour or two later, and her last words, not unlike her first ones, though slightly more slurred, were always the same: 'You'll come again soon, won't you? And we'll go for a drink, shall we?'

Faith is now long gone to the great public bar in the sky – I was one of the pall-bearers at her funeral – but I still think of her often and never pour a glass of whisky without offering a silent toast to her. Like so many of the local characters from those Inn at the Top days, they broke the mould with Faith; we'll never see another one like her.

We almost lost another of our favourite locals soon afterwards. Dick, our mentor in the ways of the Dale, almost from the day we'd first arrived there, was one of the warmest, gentlest and kindest people I ever met. In his late sixties but still a solid and robust figure, with a barrel-chest and a ground-eating stride up the fell-sides that invariably left me gasping in his wake, he was universally admired, respected and well-liked, and seemed almost as timeless, unaltering and indestructible as the fells themselves. So it came as a huge shock when he became so ill that it was feared he would die.

The first blow to him was not a disease but an horrific accident. Dick had been using a chain-saw to cut up a fallen tree for firewood, when the chain of the saw hit a strand of barbed wire that had been buried deep in the bark of the tree he was cutting. The wire must once have been fixed to the tree as part of a fence line, but over the years, the tree bark had grown over it, hiding it from view. The rest of the fence must have either rusted away or been removed years before but that strand of wire had lain there, invisible, until Dick's saw-chain had snagged on it. The chain broke and the loose end lashed Dick across the throat, almost beheading him.

Fortunately, although Dick's son wasn't around, Dick's wife, Peggy, was nearby and phoned 999 at once. Helped by their next-door neighbour, Peggy then did what she could to staunch the bleeding and the air ambulance was with them within minutes, but Dick had lost so much blood that he was close to death by the time he reached hospital. There they managed to stop the bleeding and saved his life.

He returned home apparently little the worse for his ordeal, but not long afterwards, he fell seriously ill with what was thought to be pancreatic cancer. He was back in hospital for some considerable time, and when he at last returned home, he was a frail shadow of his former self. For a long time it seemed as if he would never recover. I hadn't seen him in months and by the time one of his friends brought him up to the inn, Dick was so pale and stick-thin, and his face so wasted compared to the robust figure he had been, that I almost walked straight past him without recognising him.

I was privately convinced that it might be the last time I ever saw him, and I was far from alone in thinking that, but to the great delight of everyone who knew him, Dick then began to rally – perhaps all it took was a couple of pints and a good argument about sheep! He started to gain weight, re-ained his normal healthy skin colour and a few months later was back to the solid, powerful figure we remembered, with only the livid white scar across his throat as a reminder of what he had been through.

One of our other regulars was also facing troubles that year. Doug, one of the butchers in a market town at the foot of the fells below the Inn at the Top, had been supplying us with our meat since we moved in. Doug did not come out often in the evenings, since his working day began at four o'clock in the morning, but when he did, he made the most of it. Accompanied by his partner, Sylvia, whose face showed the lines of a life hard lived, but whose severe expression was belied by the warmth of her personality, Doug would dress to the nines for his night out in a sharp suit, white shirt with gold cufflinks and a silk tie. He was old school: if he put £50 into his wallet for his night out – and that was a lot of money back then – he wouldn't go home until he had spent all of it. He would march into the inn, stand a round of drinks for the house and then hold court at the bar, telling tales, cracking jokes and making everybody's night.

He was also a very good butcher, selling the best meat in the town where they lived, but when he was diagnosed with cancer, his business nose-dived. His more superstitious customers abandoned him in droves, largely because there was an old wives' tale circulating in the Dale that, like cold germs or food poisoning bacteria, the taint of cancer could somehow be passed on and absorbed by contagion, and those who believed that did not want Doug handling the meat they were going to eat. We kept buying our meat from him and we're both still alive and well, so the superstition wasn't true, but that was little consolation to Doug, who saw his business collapse at the very point where he had more than enough stress in his life already. After some harrowing chemotherapy and radiation treatment, he made a slow recovery and was in remission for some years but he never regained quite the drive and energy he had had before, and nor did he regain his lost customers. The business eventually folded and he ended his working days as a butcher in a local supermarket, before the cancer he had battled for so long finally claimed him.

One morning, while I was on a 'supply run' down to the market town on the other side of the hill from the Dale, I met another of the extraordinary local characters who seemed to spring up like mushrooms from the soil of those cold Northern fells and dales. A flash of bright colour was normally as rare as a rainbow in the uplands. Except for a few spring weeks, the fells remained clothed in a muted range of greens and browns and the sky was more often grey and blue. The farmers dressed in wool clothing, dyed in dull, natural-looking shades of green and brown that matched the colour palette of the fells, and even the upland sheep were more grey-brown than white, except for the new-born lambs and the dazzlingly white fleeces of the just-clipped sheep in early summer. This muted colour range made the Day-glo cagoules usually worn by the hikers stand out like electric shocks on the fells, but even those paled beside the astonishing sights often to be seen around the small market town at the foot of the hills leading to the Inn at the Top.

I was leaning against a wall on a typically grey Pennine morning, day-dreaming as I chewed absent-mindedly on a sandwich – I'd set off from the inn to pick up supplies without having had breakfast first and was now starving. Just then, a scarlet slash of colour flashed over the roof-tops. My first thought was that it was a parrot, but since wild parrots were even more rare in northern England than the proverbial rocking-horse droppings, I filed it away as one of life's unsolved mysteries and was preparing to return to the ruminative destruction of my sandwich when the red flash reappeared.

This time I was quicker to react, and was rewarded with the unmistakable sight of a parrot disappearing from view among the chimney pots. Clearly an escaped pet, I thought to myself, resolving to avoid any involvement in lengthy missing parrots reports to the local police by ignoring it. Just then, however, a pair of them flew over, squawking loudly, before also disappearing among the rooftops. I looked down, to meet the eyes of a couple of local farmers regarding me with sly amusement. Their faces were as old and wrinkled as their caps, but the eyes watching me were as keen as a winter wind. I knew that there was nothing the local farmers enjoyed more than the chance to 'work' an off-comer by spinning him an initially credible, but increasingly implausible yarn, so I tried to resist the temptation to ask for an explanation and went back to munching on the sandwich.

The farmers waited impassively as my common sense fought an unsuccessful battle with my curiosity. 'What were those birds?' I finally enquired.

'Oh, they're jays,' one replied, with a ghost of a

wink to his friend.

I gave him a sceptical look – as my mother used to say, I was green but not entirely cabbage-looking. 'Unusual colour for jays, red and gold,' I said. Almost the colour of parrots.'

'Ah, they're Eden Jays, though,' the second farmer said, eager to claim a share of the credit when the story came to be retold to their peers in their local later on.

'Those will be the ones that eat the wild grapes you see growing around here, I suppose,' I said sarcastically, determined to go down fighting.

'That's the trouble with townies,' the first one remarked with a triumphant smirk to his friend. 'They can't tell the difference between grapes and gooseberries.'

'Nor jays and parrots,' his companion said, laughing loud enough to drown the noise of the parrots overhead.

I gave what I hoped was an enigmatic smile and returned to my sandwich, resolving to leave the solution of the avian mystery until I could obtain incontrovertible evidence with my own eyes. A couple of weeks later, my patience was rewarded when I saw a flock of parrots and macaws circling around the trees in the garden of a large, impressive-looking house, a short way outside the town. I resolved to enquire within at the first available opportunity.

The parrots were obviously a matter of some local entertainment and not a little local pride to the inhabitants. After my first encounter with them, I saw them often and I too, soon grew to enjoy the spectacle of strangers to the town, gazing up in jaw-gaping surprise as a group of vividly coloured, screeching parrots flew overhead, then looking furtively around to see if anyone else had noticed this extraordinary phenomenon.

The next time I came down to the town to pick up supplies, I allowed myself an extra hour to attempt to solve the mystery of the parrots. I left the car in the centre of town and walked out alongside the river, raising a chorus from the semi-wild, semi-tame ducks lurking near the bank in the hope of a few crusts of bread. The path followed the 'backs' of the town, passing a flat-roofed concrete cricket pavilion that looked as incongruous as a multi-storey car park in this far corner of the fells.

As I walked along, soon enough, punctuating the steady drone of traffic from the main road, the cawing of the rooks and the babble of bird-song from the hedgerows, I could hear the songs of birds that would have given an unsuspecting ornithologist nightmares for weeks, for the calls of an endless variety of macaws, cockatiels and parrots came echoing from the trees lining the gardens of the large house across the fields.

The house was an impressive Victorian gentle-man's residence, surrounded by fine mature beech trees, each of which contained an unusually large nesting box. As I walked up the drive, I could see that the gardens also housed several aviaries that were full of both exotic species and the local wild birds, availing themselves of the rich pickings to be had. Through the windows of the conservatory I could also spot an indoor aviary, that I soon discovered was used for birds that either felt the cold or were sick, or in need of hand-rearing.

I rang the door-bell and introduced myself to the owner of the house and the birds. Michael Parker could only have been an Englishman. He had been born and raised with all the material advantages that any man could wish, and seemed to live the life of a gentleman farmer, with no apparent financial worries to trouble him, passing his time in a fine house in a beautiful and peaceful corner of the country. Despite these advantages, however, I sensed a certain sadness in him. He seemed a man isolated by his wealth and position, imprisoned by his shyness, unable to express himself except to his birds, and perhaps closer to them than any other living thing. His sandy hair was thinning and his eyes were soft and sad; they seemed the eyes of a man too much alone. He had travelled abroad as a young man, but now seemed settled into the long autumn of his life in these grey fellsides, caring for his birds.

He made me a cup of coffee and told me his history. As a boy, his main interest had been in butterflies, before a chance encounter set him on the way to his consuming passion for birds. His mother's labrador picked up a badly injured racing pigeon, and for the first time,' he said, 'I saw beauty in a bird. I nursed it back to health, but my father told me I had to return it; it had a ring on its leg, so we knew how to contact the owner. I was heartbroken to give it back, but in gratitude the owner gave me some squabs, which I reared.'

After receiving a budgerigar as a gift, he then kept and bred them for several years, but he was so upset when a weasel got into his aviary and killed thirty-five of them, that he had transferred his affections to larger, more easily defensible birds from then on. We walked out through the garden, with Michael identifying every bird and relating its history. His birds had all the home comforts that they could possibly want. Food supplies were plentiful, ample nest boxes and shelter had been provided, and there were even heated shelters to keep out the Northern cold, though he said that these were little used, except by the few birds that could not fly.

The dazzling aerial displays over the nearby market town were the result of his determination that his birds should live as natural and free-flying a life as possible. 'Birds should be encouraged to fly,' he said. 'If they don't, their flight feathers atrophy. I was given one that had been a pet all its life; it's twenty years old and can't fly, and since they can live to be a hundred, that seems a bad thing.'

Despite their freedom to fly where they wanted, he said that he had lost remarkably few of his birds. 'How do you start them off free-flying?' I asked. 'Are you not scared that they will just fly off and you will lose them?'

'Once a bird is in good "yarrock" – that's a falconry term for being in good health and the right weight to fly,' he said, 'I get them going. To start with, they fly well without being too much in control; they don't know where they are going to land. I lose a few before they get to the stage of being able to land where they want, but no sensible parrot flies off deliberately, he won't want to leave a place where he's comfortable and well fed. The nervous birds are doubly difficult to get flying free. I let the hen go first and the cock keeps her around by calling to her. When she's got used to flying around and coming back for food – and when a bird has had food once, she will never forget where she got it – then I let the cock bird out as well.

'I lose more cockatiels than anything else. On their first flights, they go spiralling up into the sky, literally out of sight. I have to keep stirring up the others, trying to make them call, which is what draws the other ones down again, but I lose more of them than anything. I also learn about their inter-relationship from watching them free-fly. Three blue and gold macaws got too matey; like humans, two is normally company and three over-crowding. The three of them flew right over to Newton Aycliffe in County Durham. It was a lovely spell of June weather, clear and sunny, with no wind. Two days later, two of them returned absolutely exhausted, and it took another two days for them to recover. Two months after that, I saw one advertised in the paper, which had been captured after it had crashed in a field of corn. I picked it up over in Newton Aycliffe, thinking that if it was mine, it would recognise its home surroundings immediately. As soon as I released it, it flew directly to the very small exit from what is a very large aviary, so it was clearly the same bird. Someone else told me they had seen it at Scotch Corner.

'One green-wing macaw – they are notorious wanderers – took itself and five others to Bowes.

The weather broke and we had a nearly complete white-out, but two days later, there it was, absolutely bedraggled, clinging to a tree in the garden. A friend had seen it on Stainmore. It's pretty unique for them to come back from so far away; usually if they fly more than two miles, they're gone.'

'So like the sheep,' I said, 'your parrots are "heafed" to the fells?'

He nodded. 'I suppose they are.'

'And could they survive without you and become a permanent wild colony?'

'No, because the birds can't feed themselves the whole year round. I was worried by the provisions of the Wildlife and Countryside Bill, and I wrote to the Minister, but he wrote back to say: "Since your birds cannot survive for 365 days a year without being fed by you, it is perfectly legitimate for you to have them flying free".'

To my surprise, Michael said that his birds foraged more successfully in winter than summer, for there were more fruits and berries then for them to eat. Only in a really hard winter would the native birds, such as fieldfares, completely strip the hedgerows of berries. He had two Indonesian King Parrots, which could go missing for up to three months at a time in autumn and winter, living on fruit, crab apples, hawthorn berries and the peanuts and fat put out for wild birds.

As well as caring for his own birds, Michael was also an inadvertent, but very willing feeder of large parts of the wild bird population as well. 'When the weather is bad, there are literally thousands of wild birds flying into the aviaries to feed,' he said. He also put out food for the wild birds and had a conservation field full of rare grasses, herbs and wildflowers, and a lake, where ducks and geese could feed and rest on their migration flights. Owls and jackdaws often also took over the parrot nesting boxes in his garden. 'Lots of people try to encourage owls to nest,' he said, 'often without success, but I have two pairs of tawny owls that breed every year in my parrot boxes.'

He also unintentionally provided food for sparrow hawks, though to his relief, given the choice, they usually seemed to prefer good, plain British food to a more exotic diet. The cockatiels had a one-way entrance hole to their aviary, for they had to be inside at night or the owls would eat them, but one night, he said, a sparrow hawk had got in as well. 'I heard terrible noises from them, but it hadn't taken a single one. They go into the big aviaries to catch the wild birds, though. I saw one take three wild birds once and then fly sluggishly away. I didn't like to watch without intervening,' he said, shuddering at the memory, 'but I had to know, and hawks do only kill to eat.'

His aviaries had almost reached saturation point, but he still harboured an ambition to breed African Grey Parrots, although hand-rearing was a major commitment and imposed a considerable strain on him. 'Hand-rearing is always the result of the same problem: breeding too late. They have to be fed twice a day from September to March. I had to go to hospital a few years ago, and my gardener, Arthur, saved Moses' [one of his parrots] life by feeding him while I was away.'

I thanked him for his time, took a last look at the extraordinary technicolour spectacle in his garden and then went on my way, heading back up to the Inn at the Top in time for the lunchtime rush. The last time I saw them, both Moses and Arthur, and indeed, Michael Parker himself, were all still thriving.

# CHAPTER 10

## A Sheep Identity Parade

Like farmers everywhere, most of our locals tended to be right wing in their politics – conservative with both a small and a capital 'c' – even though the way they lived their lives and supported each other through hard times seemed to have more in common with the anarchist's creed of mutual aid or Karl Marx's dictum 'From each according to his ability, to each according to his needs'.

Without hesitation, without even needing to think about it, our locals would go to the aid of any one of their friends and neighbours who had fallen ill, had an accident, lost his job, or suffered a bereavement or some other misfortune. It was done without ostentation, and not in the expectation of thanks, reward, or the return of the favour at some future time, but simply because the centuries that they and their ancestors had lived among these wild fells had taught them that mutual aid and mutual support were the only ways to ensure their survival under the harsh conditions that they daily endured.

When help was offered, it was always diplomatically phrased and carefully gradated, so as not to embarrass the recipient or hurt his or her pride. If a gift of food was being made, for example, it would often be left with a throwaway comment like 'I made too much, we've more than we can eat already and it seemed a pity to waste it.' And if cash was needed, for example by someone who had lost his job, it would usually be offered in return for 'a bit of a hand with some gap-walling' or some other job that supposedly needed doing, even though the farmer offering the work was perfectly capable of doing the job by himself.

In addition to individual acts of kindness, there were certain times of year when everyone lent a hand, above all, at hay-time, the most crucial time in the farming year and which, in nine years out of ten entailed a frantic race against time and the elements to get the crop in. There is probably nowhere in Britain with hay meadows as beautiful and as species-rich as those of the Dale. Walk through the hay meadows – keeping to the paths, of course – in late May or June before the hay-crop is gathered and you will be knee deep in wild flowers like meadow buttercup, self-heal, pignut, red clover, wood cranesbill, hawkbit, cuckoo flower, meadow vetch, bugle, bird's-foot trefoil and spotted orchid. There are less common flowers too like eyebright, yellow-rattle, betony, bistort, and some, like the globeflower and lady'smantle, that are unique to these upland hay meadows. Growing among the wild flowers there are also scores of different grasses like common bent, sweet vernal grass and crested dog's-tail. Where the soil is damper, near the streams running down from the fellsides to feed the river, you will find meadowsweet, marsh-marigold and the beautiful and beautifully-named melancholy thistle. These meadows – virtually untouched for a thousand years – are now almost unique in Britain and are carefully managed by the farmers, in partnership with the Yorkshire Dales National Park, to preserve them. No artificial fertilisers are used and the hay crop is never cut until the flowers and grasses have set seed, ensuring the richness and diversity of species will continue into the future.

Further down the Dale and throughout the lowlands, most grass for winter feed is grown from single species seed and cut and stored either as silage in airtight big bales, 'clamps' or silos, or as 'haylage' – which, as the name suggests, is a halfway stage between hay and silage. The resulting fermented grass stinks to high heaven and produces silage run-off which if not contained, can cause serious pollution and poison watercourses. Where hay is made in the lowlands it's usually made up into round 'big bales', weighing about 450 kilos. In the uplands, the traditional small rectangular bales of hay are still made – the largest size that a farmer can conveniently carry on his back up a fellside, or sling from the saddle of his Dales Galloway pony, or – more likely these days – carry on the back of his quad bike, when foddering his sheep.

Even under ideal conditions, once cut, it takes between three and five days for grass to turn to hay. The crop is cut when it is fully grown but not so mature that it results in hay full of tough grass-stalks. Relying as much on his own local knowledge and intuition as on the forecast from the Met Office, each farmer will make his own decision about when to cut the grass and, once made, the decision is irrevocable. When the weather looks set fair for a few days, the grass will be cut first thing in the morning, often with the dew still on it. The task was once carried out by hand, with a line of men advancing across the meadow swinging scythes in slow, steady, rhythmic arcs, but it is now universally done by a mower pulled behind a tractor.

Those farmers who can afford modern equipment may use a mower-conditioner that crimps the cut grass between rubber rollers, perforating the stalks every ten centimetres to allow faster evaporation of the moisture they contain. A Macerator which crimps each grass stem every couple of millimetres and speeds up the drying process even more, can also be used, particularly if the weather looks threatening, but all such equipment is expensive to buy or hire, and the lower profit margins on upland sheep farms means that most farmers there have only the most basic equipment.

Once cut, the grass is dropped by the mower in windrows, and a tedder may then be used to toss and spread the grass across the field, allowing it to dry faster. The hay will also be turned regularly with a mechanical rake to speed the drying process. When the hay is completely dry and again arranged in windrows, a mechanical baler picks it up and compresses it into the familiar bales, bound with the baler-twine that is used for a multitude of purposes around the farm – everything from an emergency repair to a gate with a broken hinge, to keeping up a farmer's trousers in place of a belt.

Once the hay is baled, it is more secure from the weather, because it can be stacked and covered with a tarpaulin to keep the worst of the rain off, and even if left uncovered for a little while, the moisture will not penetrate more than an inch or so into the bale. However the farmer will not completely relax until all the bales have been loaded onto his trailer and hauled and stacked under the cover of his barn roof. It needs to be carefully stacked too, leaving adequate gaps for ventilation, because the hay generates heat as it completes the 'curing' process, and new hay that has been too tightly packed has been known to spontaneously combust.

At one time every meadow contained a stone barn where the hay from that field would be stored to feed livestock overwintering in the stalls below the hayloft. Those stone barns still punctuate the hay meadows of the Dale, though most of the hay crop is now usually stored in 'big sheds' close to the main farm building.

In the Upper Dale, the weather can change in the blink of an eye and it can be pouring down around the head of the Dale even while tourists are sunbathing in the principal town twenty-odd miles away. So our local farmers always kept one eye on the weather blowing in over the watershed to the west and the least glimpse of a lowering black cloud was enough to drive them into even more frenzied efforts as they raced to get the crop in before the rain began to fall.

Most years they succeeded in finding enough sunshine between the showers to gather the hay but every now and again, there was – and still is – a summer so wet that much of the precious crop would blacken and become mildewed as it lay in the fields, too wet to gather in, while the farmers' prayers for 'just a couple of days of sun' went unanswered. With their own crop ruined, the only option left to them then was to buy in hay from more fortunate areas of the country, further eroding the upland farmer's already slim profit margins.

Everyone in the dale helped at hay-time and even the sons and daughters who had left the family farm to earn a living further down the Dale or elsewhere in the country, would usually return, timing part of their summer holiday to help gather in the precious crop. Those unable to help in the fields, would take part in other ways, cooking meals for the hungry workers or minding young children for their parents in the meadows. Hay-timing, as it was called, could last from first light or even earlier, until well after dark, and took several days to complete, but once the very last bale was safely stowed in the barns, most farmers would head for the inn to wash away the dust, seeds and pollen with a few well earned pints.

It could easily be eleven at night before they even arrived at the inn on the last night of hay-timing but, whatever the licensing laws at the time might have said, and no matter how tired we were ourselves, knowing how vital the hay crop was to them, we were always happy to keep serving them, sometimes until dawn was already streaking the eastern horizon. Our locals had earned the right to a celebration of a successful hay-time, though I suspect the dominant feeling was usually more one of relief than of elation.

Throughout the rest of the year, our locals also offered help to those in need of it, in all sorts of different ways. Farming has always been a hazardous occupation and one of our locals, Clifford, was seriously injured when his tractor suddenly set off on its own and ran over his legs while he was fixing his shearing machine. It left his wife, Jenny, with a seriously injured husband and 500 sheep to gather off the fells and shear.

The isolation that was an accepted part of their working lives could then seem even more severe but their friends rallied round at once. 'You don't meet people in your everyday life,' Jenny said. 'We go up to the sheep on the moor and if you see someone on the road as you're heading up there, you might stop for a chat for five minutes and that's about it, but when something goes wrong, you know there's always someone there, which is great. Let something happen and they are here like a shot.' The morning after Clifford's accident, one of their friends from the far side of the hill that closed off the end of the Dale appeared at the farm with his son. They went up and gathered all Clifford and Jenny's sheep and brought them down off the moor for them. 'He'd have had 1000 of his own sheep to clip,' Jenny said, 'but he just dropped his own work and came to help. The next day they came back again with some other neighbours and did the shearing for us as well.'

Others with less life-threatening problems also benefited from the help that was offered by their friends and neighbours. Some of the older residents of the Dale were grateful for the kindness of Bernard, one of the gamekeepers on the grouse moors owned by 'Lordy' – the derisive nickname given by our locals to the owner of the shooting rights in and around the Dale, to satyrise his manner and pretensions as much as his birthright. Bernard was a great bear of a man, with beetling brows and a florid complexion. When he was wearing his thick, winter overcoat, with its pockets crusted with blood, fur and feathers, it made him look even more huge, like a mythic creature from some Norse fairytale, but despite his considerable size, he was a far from intimidating figure, and in fact was one of the most gentle and generous men in the Dale.

Bernard often made a point of dropping off some of the rabbits he had trapped on those whose budgets did not extend to such luxuries, and when Christmas was approaching, despite his day-job, one or two of the older or poorer residents of the Dale might wake up on Christmas Eve to find that a hulking, shadowy figure – an anonymous Father Christmas – had already done his rounds and left a pheasant for them, dangling from the handle of their back door.

Bernard's duties as a keeper included having an

eye out for poachers but, while he was relentless in pursuing those trying to poach on a commercial scale, if he caught a couple of local lads out trying to poach a grouse or a pheasant for the pot, or a couple of trout from the river, he was less likely to involve the police than to let them off with a warning or send them off home with a clip round the ear. Bernard had worked as an under-keeper on the estate for many years and when the head keeper retired, he and most other people in the Dale assumed that he would be in line for promotion to the top job.

However a man with such close ties to the people who lived in the Dale, and moreover one with such a generous heart, did not appear to be at all Lordy's idea of the ideal head keeper. Instead he recruited a man who had been working on a shooting estate a considerable distance away and who had no connections with the Dale whatsoever. The new broom's approach to poachers, whether local lads or organised gangs from one of the big cities, was allegedly the same. Either the police would be called and the miscreants charged, or he and his cronies would administer a dose of rough justice. If the latter, there were unlikely to be any subsequent complaints; disputes in the Dale were often settled without recourse to outsiders, and the fact that most of the population lived in rented farmhouses or tied cottages owned by Lordy's estate was a further inhibiting factor.

Whether, having been passed over for promotion, Bernard grew resentful or careless, or whether Lordy's agent had been seeking a pretext to get rid of him anyway – a number of other local

209

keepers were also 'let go' around the same time – a little while later Bernard was summarily dismissed. With a wife and three children and, without a reference, no prospect of work as a keeper in the Dale or on a shooting estate anywhere else, he was forced to leave the Dale altogether and take a menial job in a town to survive.

Even those who did not depend directly on Lordy's shooting estates for their income could find that their living and their future was in his hands. It was a serious hurdle to clear when the time came for an old farmer to retire, for almost none of them owned the land that they farmed. Nearly all were Lordy's tenants and though it was the custom for the tenancy to be passed on, father to son, a 'modernising' landowner like Lordy, who owned virtually the whole of the Upper Dale and its surrounding moors, could intervene. A number of farms had already been forcibly amalgamated, with the surplus buildings sold off as country cottages for weekenders, the good grazing land on the lower slopes consolidated into a handful of large farms and the upland sheep grazing rights retained by Lordy but not used.

There was constant friction between his game-keepers and the local farmers but if Lordy and the keepers held the whip hand in some ways, the farmers were not completely powerless. As one of them said to a keeper during one ferocious argument, 'Well, when it's nesting time, I can take a long stride or a short stride.' He meant that he could either step over the grouse eggs and chicks in the nests that he passed while up on the moor or he could tread them underfoot. It's doubtful if he would ever really have done that, but it was a reminder that life in the Dale worked better when keepers and farmers were in harmony, not opposition.

Even if Lordy himself did not intervene, when a farm changed hands, the moment when it passed from the father to the eldest son could sometimes be an abrupt and even brutal transition. An old farmer who had spent his life raising his sheep and working his land, might almost find himself persona non grata on that same land, his lifetime of accumulated knowledge ignored, his advice spurned by his son. We watched one or two old farmers practically dwindle before our eyes. Their raison d'être removed, they often cut forlorn and lonely figures, whiling away the remainder of their days, under their wives' feet if they stayed at home, but with little better to do than sit on a bench and exchange a few words of conversation with passers-by if they ventured outside. Very few farmers were book-lovers, and daytime TV was almost non-existent back then and in any case, in those pre-digital days, television reception was very patchy in the Dale, so there was little else for the old farmers to do. If we felt sorry for them, we could see the other side too, for their sons might have been chafing under their fathers' often harsh regime for twenty or thirty years, given all the menial tasks to perform, but with their opinions and advice similarly ignored or dismissed. The transition didn't have to be like that, of course, and most farmers and their sons worked quite happily in partnership, but there were enough of the other sort to remind us that farming could sometimes be a cruel occupation in all sorts of different ways.

Lordy's grand plans for the Dale were an even crueller business, in my admittedly biased opinion. His master plan of greatly reducing the number of sheep 'stints' – grazing rights – on the open fell was carried out in the belief that reducing sheep numbers would increase the numbers of grouse. He believed that there was more money to be made in selling additional grouse shooting days to plutocratic 'guns' than there was in collecting the modest rents from hill-farmers. If the price of that was the depopulation of the upper Dale and the destruction of communities that had survived, little altered, for centuries before he and his ancestors had acquired his title, then Lordy had already demonstrated that it was a price he seemed to be perfectly happy to pay.

However, the belief that grouse numbers would rise if the sheep were removed remained untested and controversial. Farmers argued that the sheep actually helped to preserve the grouse in snowy winters because, by scraping at the snow with their hooves, they exposed the heather for themselves and the grouse to feed on. Grouse were also always subject to periodic epidemics of disease that killed huge numbers of them, and overpopulation was believed to be one of the principal causes, so eliminating their predators and removing competitors for the heather that was their principal and, at certain times of the year, their only diet, was only likely to lead to overpopulation and ever more frequent epidemics. In any case, depriving local men of their livelihoods, so that bankers and businessmen could role-play as country sportsmen in brand new tweeds and toting shiny new Purdey shotguns, did not sit well with me or most of the other inhabitants of the Dale, though strangely, the National Park authorities seemed to take it all in their stride.

Lordy's defenders advanced the rather specious argument that the annual influx of 'guns' during the grouse shooting season, the employment opportunities for keepers and the temporary casual work available to beaters driving the grouse on to the guns, more than compensated for the lost income from sheep farming. A dubious claim in itself, it also took no account of the impact on the upper Dale communities of the loss of a substantial part of the long-term, full-time population.

When our friend Jenny was a girl, growing up in one of the most remote parts of the Dale, her family's farm was one of a community of eight farms around the dale-head, including one very near neighbour. 'I had three brothers and a sister,' Jenny said, 'and on the other farm there were four children. We used to play in the beck for hours and hours during the summer, building dams across the beck to see how deep we could get the water. We'd walk a mile and a half across the fells to the village school then, which had twenty-five pupils in those days. If we were caught out by bad weather – fog or snow – on the way back, there was a wall we could follow and it would lead us home. Being the eldest, I was the child in charge and I was always being told 'Jenny, see they don't get left behind.' I hated that! There were more boys than girls and a few lads together could be a bit of a problem!'

By the early 1980s when we were running the Inn at the Top, the number of farms around the head of the Dale had been halved from eight to four. The village school a mile and a half away had closed for lack of pupils and Clifford and Jenny's two children had grown up on their farm without any other children of their own age to play with. The pattern had been repeated further down the Dale as well and, quite apart from the lost farms, houses, pubs, post offices and bus services, and the missing customers for the remaining shops and pubs that those lost farms represented, the fact that, with several small village schools closed, the nearest primary school was now ten miles from the settlement at the head of the Dale and the nearest secondary school twenty-seven miles away, spoke for itself.

Lordy, whose father had reportedly inherited the title only on the grounds that he was the second cousin once removed of the childless relative who had formerly held the title, eventually grew bored with moving the human pieces around his own private rural Monopoly board, sold the estate and moved on, but by then the damage had already been done. However, the current owner of the estate, a much more private individual, is generally well liked in the Dale. He supports the local events like the village shows, but does so in a discreet way, not looking for publicity or thanks for it, and according to one of the farmers I spoke to, there is a much better relationship between his keepers and the farmers these days. 'He appreciates that sheep and grouse have always gone together,' the farmer said, 'whereas Lordy always seemed to think that sheep were the enemy.'

While, unlike some of Lordy's employees, most inhabitants of the Dale would help each other out in the blink of an eye – and that powerful sense of community had been one of the strongest attractions for us when we returned to the inn – living in remote rural areas with few fresh faces ever moving in could also have its downsides. Gossip was a fact of life in the Dale as in all small communities, but it seemed a natural, if sometimes intrusive and occasionally hurtful part of rural life. However living cheek by jowl in small, isolated communities could also foster emnities that sometimes escalated into bitter, lifelong feuds.

Two brothers lived in a tiny, isolated hamlet of no more than a handful of houses a few miles from the inn. They were almost next-door neighbours, and yet, according to our regulars, the two men had not exchanged a word with each other in decades. Our locals had either never known or could not now recall how the feud had started – it may well have been a dispute over land or sheep, the principal cause of most arguments in the Dale – and it was possible that even the brothers themselves could not now have remembered the causes of their feud, but that did not lessen its intensity. Although it had not tainted relations between their children, the two men remained apparently implacable in their hostility to each other.

Neither of them were big pub-goers, but they would be out and about on the big days of the farming year, including the night of the autumn tup (ram) sales and, of course, the annual sheep show at the Inn at the Top, but if one entered the bar and saw the other one there, he would either disappear into the other bar or turn on his heel and walk out again. We found it inexplicable, because both men individually were as warm, friendly and likeable as you could wish, but they could not stand a second in each other's company, and as far as I know, they carried the feud, whatever its cause, with them to the grave.

With the possible exception of those two feuding brothers, there was a remarkable degree of trust among the farmers of the Dale. Their doors were routinely left unlocked, whether or not they were at home, and if someone else's sheep strayed on to their land, they would round them up and return them to their rightful owner as soon as possible, wanting if anything at all – nothing more than the price of the winter feed they had consumed. Up on the fell-tops there were few fences or walls separating one flock from each other and though they were 'heafed' to their own patch of ground, wind, snow, wild weather or just sheepish curiosity perhaps, could see them stray and finish up as intermingled as a well shuffled pack of cards.

Every farm had its own markings, a combination of patches of dye, and lug – ear – marks, or horn marks, all listed in the sheep-farmers' bible, the Shepherd's Guide, so that any farmer could readily identify the owner of stray sheep, though most of our locals claimed to be able to identify every single one of their own sheep by face and by name. However, a system built on trust requires everyone to be trustworthy, and though the vast majority of farmers would as soon have shot their own sheep as have stolen someone else's, there were, it was said, a handful of exceptions. Sheep rustling, it turned out, was not just something from the history of the Border reivers or from tales of the old Wild West, it still went on then, and indeed still does today.

Farmers were resigned to losing a few sheep every year to natural causes: lambs which were still-born, or had their eyes pecked out by crows when just born, or which were too weak to survive a late Spring snowfall. Others were run over by tourist cars, or taken by foxes, but not all the predators up on the moors had four legs. Every now and again, we would hear the farmers talking about sheep that had disappeared and though sometimes unscrupulous townies were to blame, driving up to the moors to rustle sheep that would then be slaughtered for meat in some illegal abattoir, there were also times when the farmers were convinced that the culprits were some of their own.

From time to time, prompted by a chorus of complaints from angry farmers, the local police would launch a crackdown on rustling. The farms of suspected sheep rustlers would be raided, any sheep for which they could not account would be confiscated and a 'sheep identity parade' would then be held in one of the local auction marts, at which farmers who had lost stock would try to find them among the sheep lined up for their inspection, watched by a couple of hundred other farmers who had turned up more out of curiosity than to find missing sheep of their own.

In one series of police raids, 150 yows – worth

between £100 and £150 each – were recovered from hill farms in the North Pennines. Forty of them turned out to have been stolen from farms in the Dale and six people were arrested in connection with the thefts. One of the farmers at the identity parade described the rustling as: 'A disgrace to the farmers concerned but, to me, it's also a disgrace on the farming community. The whole thing is based on trust. You turn sheep on to a common and you expect to get them returned because you trust everyone.'

Some of the rustled sheep were positively identified and restored to their rightful owners, but a number of others could only be classed as being of 'doubtful origin', meaning that the farmers examining them could not be certain about the ownership of the sheep. If the earmarks and other identifying features had been tampered with or removed, it was even possible that the sheep's owners might never be identified, for so widespread had the breed become over the years that they might have been stolen from any hill farm within a radius of 100 miles.

Some of the arrested men, although not from the Dale itself, came from farms within a few miles of the Inn at the Top, and although the police had led the investigation so far and had promised prosecutions, few farmers seemed to have much confidence that the courts would administer the swingeing punishments they felt appropriate. There were mutterings among some of our locals that a more old-fashioned brand of justice might be administered instead and there would certainly have been no shortage of volunteers to carry it out, for though our regulars disagreed about almost everything else, the one thing that they were unanimous about was their hatred of sheep rustling and sheep rustlers.

# CHAPTER 11

## Young, Innocent and Ignorant

As spring began to give way to early summer, the number of customers arriving at the inn increased day by day. If that was helping to ease some of our financial problems, the long hours and the relentless workload were also building up a sleep debt in us that was unlikely to be repaid before the winter. But whenever our workload began to seem too heavy, there would be a reminder of why we had wanted to own the inn in the first place: a raucous, laugh-a-minute night with the locals; an eye-opening chat with a customer from some far-flung part of the world who had somehow made his way to the inn; a spectacular display of the stars and the Milky Way overhead on one of the treasured handfuls of clear, moonless nights; or a stroll over the moor on a sun-drenched early summer morning with the air full of the songs of larks, the liquid bubbling call of the curlews, the monotone pipings of the golden plovers nesting among the tussocks of moor grass and the gabbling cries of the grouse as they burst from the heather almost at our feet and sped away downwind, skimming the contours in the way that earned them their local nickname 'low flyers'.

We also had our entertainment delivered to our door every day, as a fresh cast of characters arrived and entertained, amused, or very occasionally, irritated us, before moving on. That variety, never knowing who or what was going to come through the door next, was one of the great attractions of the Inn at the Top, to us and to the people who visited it or made it their local. It was a strong contrast to most of the other pubs in the Dale, where pretty much the same cast of characters tended to assemble, day after day, and week after week. That constancy and predictability was either the joy or the bane of living in such small, isolated rural communities; very little changed in such places from month to month or even from year to year. Depending on your mood at the time, that could seem reassuringly timeless or irritatingly predictable. If that was to an extent true at any time of the year, it was even more so in winter, when there were few tourists or visitors to enliven the local scene. In most rural and village pubs then, the cast of characters and the conversation among them could often seem to consist of very minor variations on an extremely limited theme.

That was never the case at the Inn at the Top. Whenever the roads were open, in addition to our locals and regulars – and one of the latter was a man in his sixties who told us that he'd been cycling to the inn for decades, having made his first visit when he was 'young, innocent and ignorant', and still made the 150 mile round trip from Preston on his bike at least once a month just to have a pint at the inn – there would be a constant stream of visitors and tourists arriving from all parts of Great Britain and from the wider world beyond.

Without even straining my memory, I can recall chatting to people from almost every European country and region, including such exotic locations as Macedonia and Transylvania, and from Argentina, Patagonia, Brazil, Costa Rica, Canada, the US, Iceland, South Africa, Australia, New Zealand, Fiji, Korea, Thailand, Japan, India and even Mongolia, in the wider world beyond. Life at the Inn at the Top may have been hectic and exhausting but it was never dull. Many of those foreign visitors had never even heard of the Inn at the Top until they came to the Dales. Some were recommended to visit the inn by the owners of the B&Bs where they were staying and others had read about it in books or magazines, usually written in rather less purple prose than the Chairman of the Cyclists Touring Club Council who was quoted in a newspaper in the 1950s as describing the inn as standing 'enthroned upon the moors. Round it, the moors prostrate themselves, the winds of Heaven gyrate, the lark sings, the grouse cackle, the heather blooms. It is a height of Olympus provided with a pub. If Omar had lived in England, most likely he would have squatted with his book of verse, his wine and "thou" at the inn.' Most likely he would, indeed.

Apart from the beauty of its surroundings, the principal attraction for summer visitors to the inn was simply that it was the highest inn in Great Britain ... and therefore, since no other country possesses bona fide inns, the world. Fortunately modern visitors were rarely as curmudgeonly as a London Daily News journalist, W Fitzwater Wray, who, under the pseudonym Kuklos, wrote a book, 'A Vagabond's Note-Book', about his travels around Britain by bike in the opening years of the 20th Century. Chancing on the inn in October 1906, he wrote that 'the wild moor presses up to the house on all sides and the grouse pick up the crumbs at the back door.' Standing on the sanded floor of the inn with his back to the fire 'under the pendant pork' (the flitches of bacon hanging from ceiling hooks) he remarked, with his tongue firmly pressed in his cheek, that 'it is not easy to explain why the inn that has most dirt underneath it should be more sought and sung than, say, the inn with the widest back door in Kent, or that with the longest black list in Wales.'

Despite Kuklos's scepticism, the chance to have a drink at the highest inn continued to draw thousands of visitors every year and once they'd seen the beauty of its surroundings and the character of the inn – and of its locals – many of them returned again and again. The allure of the place to so many of its visitors was illustrated in a letter that one man, Keith Davis, sent to me while he was reading *The Inn at the Top:* 'In 1970 I went to work in the laboratories of a large chemical company based in Oldbury, West Midlands,' he wrote. 'It was there that I struck up an enduring friendship with another fresh-faced twenty year old, despite the fact that he was a Black Country lad and I was a "Brummie"! We were both enthusiastic walkers, and so it was that one summer we found ourselves camped near the river in the upper dale, enjoying the delights of a bacon and midge sandwich. Having completed our repast, we decided to wash down our invertebrates with a pint or two at the fabled inn.

'We set off up the narrow lane in my Mini van and as we climbed higher, the weather turned decidedly "mizzling" as we approached the inn! Despite the beer it was a memorable night. The army was ensconced in the pub, or at least a sergeant was, who was sitting with a pint in front of him talking into a microphone connected by a coiled lead that snaked out through a partially open window to his Land Rover parked outside. Occasionally, he would bark utterances into the 'mike' such as, 'Where the **** do you think you are?' from which we deduced that a bunch of squaddies were out on the moors on a route-finding (getting lost!) exercise. As the night wore on, the pub started to fill up; to the point that eventually anyone passing out would have remained standing!

'Eventually, with enough anaesthetic inside us to dull the pain of sleeping on cold hard ground, we drove off down the road. I recall that we had not gone too far and were driving along an elevated section or embankment, when we heard a plaintive cry for help. We stopped, and after a few seconds, a figure emerged from the mist and scrambled up the bank. As we drove on down into the dale it transpired that our new acquaintance was a local farmer's son and of a similar age to us.

'As we chatted, we noticed that he was taking an inordinate amount of interest in our travel plans;

the reason for which soon became clear. It appeared that he had spent most of the day at a local village show, and he had borrowed his father's car so he could finish his drinking marathon at the Inn at the Top. Unfortunately, on the way back he had rolled the car and was now working on an escape plan, involving us, so that he did not have to face his father's wrath. At first, we could not understand why he was so terrified of facing his father until he revealed that more or less the same thing had happened the year before, and on that occasion he had received a sound beating from his Dad. Finally, we did convince him to 'man up' and face the consequences, perhaps selfishly, because he was quite a big lad and we only had a two-man tent!

'I have wondered from time to time what happened to our erstwhile friend. I expect – if he survived his father's punishment – that he would be "sixty something" now and probably a respectable pillar of the community. Strangely, despite my wife's family being Dalesfolk and living in Wensleydale, I have never been back to the Inn. Perhaps I will when I have finished reading your book.' And if the by now sixty-something erratic driver is still around, perhaps they will renew acquaintances when he does!

We were now well into the merry month of May and the annual Sheep Show at the Inn at the Top was looming. Although the local breed of sheep with their distinctive black faces and white noses are now found on upland farms throughout the British Isles, when the breed was originally developed back in the 1920s, refining the black-faced sheep that had roamed the uplands since the days of the Vikings, the sheep breeders drew a circle on the map with a pair of compasses. Fifteen miles in radius, that circle defined the boundaries within which the breed would be perfected, encompassing a dozen different dale-heads in three different counties. The spot on the map on which the point of the compasses was placed – the exact centre of the circle – was the Inn at the Top, so there could have been no more appropriate site for the sheep show that decided the annual 'World Championship' of the breed, held every year on the last Thursday in May.

All the once popular local sheep shows had died out in the 1930s, mainly as a consequence of the effects of the Great Depression, and with the Second World War then intervening, it wasn't until 1951 that the tradition was revived with the new show at the Inn at the Top. Given that depressing background, it must have represented something of a gamble to do so, but within a couple of years the new show had established itself as one of the highlights of the Upper Dale's year and by 1954, one cyclist who arrived to see the show noted that 'the landlord told us that when the police had counted 400 cars, they got tired and gave it up.'

The timing of the show was quite deliberate. After the rigours of winter and then lambing-time, late May was the first occasion in the year when the local farmers had enough spare time and energy to turn their thoughts to showing their sheep, while the sheep themselves had had time to regain condition after surviving the hard times of the winter, so that both sheep and shepherds were looking at their best.

The popularity of the local sheep breed was based on their hardiness and the good mothering qualities of the yows (ewes). Crossed with a blue-faced Leicester ram, their offspring – strangely known as 'mules' – had the right conformity and carcass for the meat trade, whereas the pure-bred sheep's value lay principally as breeding stock. The outer layer of the fleece is coarse and wiry, with a denser and warmer layer of wool beneath it. In the old days selling the fleeces after clipping used to provide a welcome additional income for farmers, but by our time at the inn, the locals were already complaining that it was barely worth the labour of clipping the sheep. If that situation has changed at all in the intervening years it has largely been for the worse, not the better. However a cottage hand-knitting industry supplying a shop in one of the villages of the upper Dale has provided a market for at least a little of the wool and many tourists now return home with a pullover, cardigan, scarf or a pair of gloves knitted from the local wool to keep them warm in winter.

The sheep show at the Inn at the Top also ushered in June, the one month of the year when sheep farmers in the upper Dale could afford to relax. 'The best time of year is June,' one said. 'Winter's over, lambing's done with and the hay not ready to be cut.' Many farmers – or at least, those of them who took holidays, for not all of them did – would go away for a week or two in early June, usually to Scarborough or Whitby on the Yorkshire coast or to the Lake District, for few of them strayed far from their own 'heaf', even when on holiday. By July it was back to the hard graft: sheep shearing, hay-time and also peat-cutting in the days when every resident of the Dale had the ancient right of turbary on the moors and cut peats for winter fuel.

The tup sales in the autumn then led on to 'tupping time', when the rams were turned out to serve the flocks, on a date that had never varied from generation to generation. It was always the earliest possible date that would also ensure that the resulting lambs would be born late enough the following spring to avoid the worst of the late winter weather, though, given the uncertainties and excesses of the weather around the Inn at the Top, that was always more a hope than a certainty. Once tupping time was out of the way, the farmers were back once more to feeding the animals through the winter, always with one eye cocked towards the horizon, looking for the brooding, pewter-coloured clouds that heralded a big snow storm.

There were few attractions other than the sheep themselves at the inn's annual show. The Lofthouse and Middlesmoor silver band from Nidderdale always played there – and still do – as they had since the very first show in 1951, when they happened to be passing on their way back from a concert elsewhere, and stopped to see what was going on. In our first year as owners of the inn, the show was being filmed by the BBC crew as the last act in the documentary they were making about our early months there, and they filmed the band in action. If you ever happen to catch the documentary on one of its now infrequent re-showings on BBC TV, you will see the band's leader and conductor approaching the bar with a beaming smile, waving a fistful of notes. That was the fee the band had received from the BBC for the rights to use their music in the documentary and in fact the money never left the inn, because by the end of the evening, the band had passed every penny of it across the bar in exchange for endless rounds of beer and whisky, though they seemed perfectly happy with that arrangement as they clambered unsteadily back onto their coach for the journey home.

Apart from the pens of sheep and the show ring, there were also a handful of stalls at the sheep show, but they were targeted almost exclusively at farmers, not tourists, and sold wet weather gear and veterinary products, rather than tourist trinkets. Otherwise, there was nothing to be seen but the sheep and the men who bred them. If, to the untrained eye at least, the sheep looked virtually indistinguishable from each other, all with peaty-coloured, off-white fleeces, black faces and white noses, the farmers – or at least the clothing they wore – were just as identical, all clad in flat caps, tweed jackets, moleskin trousers, wellingtons and Barbour-type coats.

The sheep show at the inn might have looked homespun and unassuming, compared to the village shows elsewhere in the Yorkshire Dales, let alone the Great Yorkshire Show at Harrogate, or the Royal Show at Stoneleigh in Warwickshire that were also held every year, but as one farmer said to us, 'There are classes for our sheep at the

Royal Show, but the winner there might not even get a ticket [an entry] to this show. This is where you'll see the best tups and yows to be found anywhere.'

The prizes for the show at the Inn at the Top were nothing to get too excited about. None of them were worth more than a few pounds and most were donated by agricultural suppliers, resulting in prizes as prosaic as 'Two Gallons of Battle's Summer Dip', 'One Bag of Minerals', and 'Five Litres Top Clip Worm Drench', but the prestige that went with having bred the supreme champion was priceless to the farmers. If they needed a financial reward beyond that, they usually got it at the autumn tup sales, where the champion tup from the show at the Inn at the Top might sell for as much as £50,000.

For years there had been a close rivalry between our mentor Dick and a farmer from a different dale, Lenny, who had never won the Supreme Championship at the show, though he had been placed second on two or three occasions. Although I didn't know Lenny particularly well, since he was not a regular at the Inn at the Top, he seemed to me to be everything Dick was not – and not in a good way. Always dressed in a three piece suit with a gold watch chain across his paunch, Lenny was boastful where Dick was reserved, noisy where Dick was quiet, and he seemed a bit too quick to disparage others, whereas Dick never had a bad word for anyone, not even Lenny.

Dick had bred the Supreme Champion at the sheep show the previous year, the first time he had taken the title in twenty years, but this year rumour – mainly, it has to be said, emanating from Lenny himself – had it that Lenny had a champion tup, though almost no one had actually seen it since he kept it under lock and key at his farm.

The tension mounted throughout the show day, with ourselves and most of our locals rooting for Dick, while a much smaller group of Lenny's friends and admirers supported him. Dick drew first blood by winning the 'tup hogg' class. Sheep are divided by age into different categories: Lambs are young sheep that have not yet been weaned from their mothers' milk; 'hoggs' are young sheep that have been weaned – a painful separation from their mothers in the summer of their first year, when they always fill the air with their pitiful bleatings; 'shearlings' are sheep that have been sheared once (and since they are not sheared in their first year, this means a two year-old sheep); and finally the older sheep are classified as just plain 'tups' or 'yows' – rams or ewes – though just to make it even more confusing, female sheep are also called 'gimmers' and rams judged by their owners not to be of sufficient quality to be used for breeding are castrated and are then known as 'wethers'. A female sheep becomes a yow when she has given birth to two sets of lambs – she gives birth to her first set as a gimmer shearling, and is therefore three years old when she delivers her second set of lambs.

Despite Dick's initial success, Lenny, keeping up a non-stop stream of propaganda about the wonders of his own shearling tup, beat Dick's tup hogg into second place in the overall champion tup class. As one judge wearily muttered in an aside to his mate that was picked up by the TV crew's microphones: 'It's a job with a man like that, he talks folk into it.'

Whether he had 'talked folks into it', or because his tup really was a champion, Lenny went on to win the overall championship for the first time ever, and, as was the tradition, celebrated by filling the silver cup with a bottle of whisky and passing it around the pub for all his peers to drink to him. I couldn't help noticing that even those who were drinking their full share – and sometimes rather more than that – of his whisky, barely waited for the door to close behind him before launching into a withering critique of Lenny's heavy-handed lobbying for his tup, and a dissection of the judges' errors in reaching their verdict.

The tourist season was now in full swing and the inn was packed every day. We flattered ourselves that part of that was due the skill and charm of the new owners, but in our more self-aware moments we also had to concede that a considerable part of the reason for its popularity down the years might also have been connected with the fact that the inn's landlords and their customers had never paid too much attention to the licensing laws. As a result, it had always been a notorious after hours drinking spot ... and it was not a reputation that we did anything to change.

Our hyper-extended opening hours were certainly good for business. Sue and I were discussing our rapidly increasing wealth – or at least our rapidly diminishing levels of debt – one night, when the metaphorical light bulb suddenly went on. 'No wonder were making money,' I said. 'We're both working 110 hours a week – that's three full time jobs each.' However the prodigious number of hours we were working were much less good for our health. Permanent black shadows had appeared under our eyes, both of us had lost weight and once more my normal charming, good-natured self – in my opinion anyway – was, with increasing frequency, being replaced by a passable impersonation of Basil Fawlty.

In that far off year of 1984, once more the world was continuing on its merry way, while we, in our Yorkshire Shangri La above the clouds, were barely more than dimly aware of what was happening beyond the fells surrounding the Inn at the Top. In the course of that year, Michael Jackson had been badly burned while filming a Pepsi ad, the Boat Race was postponed for twenty-four hours after the Cambridge boat struck a barge and sank, the miner's strike had begun over threatened pit closures, with violent clashes between police and striking miners culminating in the vicious 'Battle of Orgreave', the women protesters had been evicted from outside the US Cruise missile base at Greenham Common, policewoman Yvonne Fletcher had been shot dead outside the Libyan Embassy in London, Ronald Reagan had arrived in China for an historic visit, scientists had discovered the Aids virus, the Soviet Union had pulled out of the Olympics in Los Angeles in retaliation for the American boycott of the Moscow Olympics, Sinn Fein leader Gerry Adams had survived being shot by Loyalist gunmen, Indian troops had raided the Golden Temple in Amritsar,

York Minster had been engulfed in flames after a lightning strike on the roof, the UK and China had agreed a date for the handover of Hong Kong, India Prime Minister Indira Gandhi had been assassinated, and an IRA bomb in a hotel in Brighton had almost wiped out Margaret Thatcher and her Cabinet.

However, all of these more or less earth-shattering events were to pass largely unnoticed at the Inn at the Top, where they were mere background noise to our own vital concerns: Was there any water in the tanks? Would the generator manage to limp through another day? Would the brewery dray arrive before we ran out of beer? Would the interval between customers ordering lunch and being served with it exceed one hour? And, linked to that, would the Basil Fawltyesque owner manage to get through the lunchtime peak period without blowing his top at some hapless customer?

The first few months back at the inn had been pure pleasure, with fine spring and then summer weather, and every day a fresh barrel of laughs. However, as the grind of sheer hard work, endless days and sleepless nights took its inevitable toll, the laughs became a little less frequent. I was now also embroiled in the annual production run of the *Good Beer Guide,* and my three-day absences in St Albans every week, while providing a welcome boost to our working capital for repairs and renovations, added to the stress and the workload for both of us.

The dawn commute over the moorland road every Monday to catch the first London train of the day at 6 a.m. from the station twenty-five miles away also nearly cost me my life. I was running late one beautiful summer morning and squinting in the low light of the rising sun, I was bombing along the single-track road just after five o'clock, confident that at that ungodly hour, I would have, not just the road, but the whole of the North Pennines to myself. As I rounded a bend, flat out, I came face to face with a JCB, speeding towards me, bucket lowered, beyond which I could see the grinning face of one of our locals from the far side of the moor, making a similarly early start on his way over the tops to a job in the Dale. I stomped on the brakes so hard that the twin streaks of rubber on the road surface were still visible weeks later, while the JCB driver did the same, and I screeched to a fish-tailing stop with the front bumper actually touching the steel bucket. Half a second later on the brakes and it would have been me, not the bumper that made contact with it. I survived and drove the rest of the way at a slightly less reckless speed.

Throughout the production run, I travelled down to St Albans first thing every Monday morning, worked on editing the *Good Beer Guide* all the way down on the train, steadily working my way through the mountains of dog-eared, beer-stained, survey forms, supplied by the CAMRA members, sometimes with additional details added on torn-up beer mats. I carried on working through the next three or four days and all the way back up on the train on the Wednesday or Thursday night, and then, to assuage my guilt at having been away from the pub for so long, I threw myself back into the bar work with renewed

234

frenzy, before collapsing into bed and falling asleep in seconds.

By mid-summer, the combined pressures of running one of the busiest pubs in the Dales while simultaneously trying to put together that year's *Good Beer Guide* was exacting a heavy toll, and my relationship with Sue had become almost non-existent. We were so busy that we never had time to talk, other than to bark orders for food and drinks at each other, except for last thing at night, when we were both usually too tired to speak, and if there was any simmering sexual tension in the air – and given our exhaustion, there wouldn't have been much anyway – it was less between each other than between Sue and the taller of the resident Alans, and me and the punk Ruby. Trouble was definitely brewing at t'inn...

However, I take full responsibility for that. Although returning to the inn had been a dream that we both shared, there was no doubt at all that I had played the leading role in making it happen. In my blind enthusiasm for the idea, I had played up all the benefits to myself and to Sue and waved away any thought of the problems that might arise in finding the money to buy the inn in the first place, and I had barely given a thought to the cold, sober realities of what might happen if we proved to be successful in that. At first, swept along on a tide of adrenaline and bonhomie, it had been a great success and a barrel of laughs, but what had started as something of a Whitehall Farce was now in danger of degenerating into a full blown Shakespearian tragedy – though, with luck, without the attendant murders.

Although it had not been a conscious impulse on my part, in any conflict between the needs of our relationship and the requirement to keep serving the customers at the inn, the latter had always won out. The biggest source of friction was the lunchtime food rush.

Even at the busiest points of the year I managed, just about, to keep pace with the drinks orders across the bar, but even with a couple of helpers in the kitchen, as the pub got busier, the delay between ordering food and actually receiving it grew longer and longer.

By the start of the school summer holidays, those arriving at the inn after twelve-thirty were sometimes not receiving the meals they'd ordered for an hour or even more, and each passing day seemed to make matters worse. It wasn't acceptable and on top of my heavy workload at the bar, I was also having to deal with an ever growing stream of understandably irate customers demanding to know what had happened to their lunch. All our discussions before we took over the inn about how to cope with the food rush had been forgotten, we were serving the wrong kind of food, in the wrong place, at the wrong time, and the kitchen staff couldn't cope.

As a result, the stress levels for both of us had gone through the roof and that gave another turn of the wheel to our deteriorating relationship. By now it was probably too late to turn back the clock. We were trapped in the inn and in a by now thoroughly miserable relationship with each other. Although neither of us articulated it at the time, it was clear that before very long something would have to give, but for now we soldiered on in an increasingly tension-filled atmosphere.

Our efforts to restore and revive the inn had proved only too successful; turnover had gone up over fifty per cent, but the strain on ourselves and our staff rapidly began to show. The relentless grind of pub work, rising at seven ready to feed breakfast to the departing hikers and clean up and bottle up before Faith and the postman arrived, but still being in the bar till at least at two a.m. the following morning, when we were trying to speed the last of the farmers on their unsteady way home, proved too much in the end.

Maintaining a ready smile in the face of the great British public after month after month of endless drudgery and exhaustion, would have taxed the patience of a far more tolerant individual than my namesake, Basil Fawlty. The only persons to whom Sue and I could be thoroughly unpleasant were each other, and like many landlord and landladies before us, our relationship deteriorated to the point where, on a busy August morning, the stresses finally got too much for her. She had reached breaking point and left the inn that day, driven off down the hill in a friend's car. The fact that the taller of the two Alans followed her down the road very shortly afterwards was a double blow; my feelings of betrayal and rage were accompanied by a more pragmatic consideration: I had just been deprived of two staff members simultaneously – and at the height of the tourist season as well. The farmers' daughters of the Dale were almost as disconsolate, they now had only one Alan to lust after.

I had rather more pressing concerns than that at the time. As any landlord will tell you – if he can find a spare moment – running a pub is incredibly hard work. The Inn at the Top in particular, open all day and most of the night, and requiring huge amounts of work to restore it to decent condition and hours of extra labour just to provide the basic amenities – heat, light, power and water – that others got just by flicking a switch or turning on a tap, was hard enough work for two, and for one it was probably going to be absolutely bloody impossible. However, I was too busy serving customers to ponder any long-term implications at the time. My dominant emotion was probably mindless fury at being left to cope with the busiest period of the entire year on my own.

I have only the most blurred memories of that awful day or the miserable few weeks that followed. If I had intermittently resembled Basil Fawlty before, I was now his living, breathing, splenetic reincarnation. Sue did return three weeks later in an attempt at a reconciliation, but the relationship had deteriorated too much for any realistic chance of that, particularly when any attempts to mend fences had to be fitted in around the demands of running the busiest pub in the Dales at the busiest time of the year. After a few more largely miserable and reproachful weeks, she left again, this time apparently for good.

Until that moment you would have been hard-pressed to find anyone in the Dale who had a bad word to say about Sue. Unfailingly warm and welcoming to everyone, no matter what ungodly hour thcy arrived at the inn, she had also managed the difficult balancing act of being well-liked by the farmers' wives despite their husbands' open adoration of her. However, back in those distant days, the ripples of the women's liberation movement had barely begun to trouble the placid waters of this remote Dale, and leaving your husband was not an option that the older farmers' wives there had ever felt was open to them, no matter how severe the provocation.

Their sons and daughters might have viewed things a little differently, but to the middle-aged and older generations in the Dale, marriage really was a life sentence. If your husband was a drunk or a lecher or even if he raised his hand to you once in a while, that was just the way it was. 'I made my bed and I must lie on it', was a saying that was often heard in the Dale. So, while there may have been some sympathy for Sue, tied to the treadmill of working at the pub with a husband she no longer loved, there was also disapproval of her among at least some of the farmers' wives that was perhaps tinged with some resentment that she had seized a chance to escape that was not available to them.

Many of their husbands – no keener than their wives to see such new-fangled ideas take hold – were equally disapproving and, after learning of my plight, some of our regulars offered to sort out the problem in the way that a few things were sorted out in the Dale: by tracking down the offending couple, paying them a visit and giving Big Alan 'a reet good hammering'. However, pleasing though the thought was in my darker moments, it seemed unlikely to do any good and, not without some reluctance, I had to turn down their generous offer. It would not have been an easy pledge to fulfil in any case, for Sue and Big Alan had apparently decamped to an island in the Outer Hebrides, proving that, in Sue's case at least, the search for ever more remote and inaccessible dwelling places still went on.

By now I was so sick of the whole pub business that one early autumn afternoon, I took advantage of the fact that the bar was miraculously empty for a few minutes and, for the first time since we'd taken over the inn, I closed the door between the official lunchtime and evening opening hours. Having locked and bolted the door, I then made myself a cup of coffee and settled down to enjoy a leisurely read of the newspaper; I couldn't remember the last time that I'd enjoyed such a luxury, usually it was thrown away unread, except by our customers. Barely had I taken my seat, however, when the first of an endless succession of would-be customers began knocking at the door, tapping on the window and, having spied me lurking in the shadows, shouting self-answering questions through the letterbox, like 'Are you open?' and 'Can I use the toilet?'

My only response was to close the curtains and sit back down again. It seemed to do the trick; most of them gave up after a few minutes and either sought relief among the rocks behind the inn, or headed on down the Dale in search of a warmer welcome, but one particularly persistent customer just would not give up. Getting no response at the front door, he made his way round to the back and tried that one as well, then came back round to the front and began banging on the window. I stood it for five minutes and then, bursting with self-righteous indignation, I leapt to my feet, scattering coffee, biscuit crumbs and bits of newspaper in all directions, ran across the room, threw open the curtains and, through the window, subjected the hapless customer to a barrage of foul-mouthed invective and offensive gestures. I then re-drew the curtains, gathered up my newspaper and sat down again. I'm not proud of myself for it, but the unfortunate and undeserving customer just happened to be the recipient of an entire summer's worth of exhaustion, frustration, misery and bile.

I was just getting ready to reopen about half an hour later when the phone rang. 'My name's Marshall,' a voice said. 'I've booked a double room at the inn tonight.'

'Ah yes, Mr Marshall,' I said, now back in full oleaginous Basil Fawlty mode. 'We're looking forward to seeing you.'

'You won't be,' he said. 'I called at the inn half an hour ago and the rudest man I've ever seen in my life gave me such a mouthful that I decided not to stay there after all. I've booked a room elsewhere.'

'Mr Marshall,' I said, playing for time and thinking fast ... and the first reaction of a scoundrel is always to reach for a lie: 'I'm deeply shocked and I can only apologise. I went to town to buy some supplies this afternoon and left my barman in charge. Rest assured that he won't be working here the next time you pass this way.'

I cringed every time the door opened for the next few days but, perhaps mercifully and, come to think of it, unsurprisingly, Mr Marshall never returned and as my workload eased with the coming of winter and the pain of separation began to fade, Basil Fawlty also put in less regular appearances and I became at least semi-human once more.

With the pub much quieter, I could even leave one of the bar staff in charge for a couple of hours once the lunchtime rush was over, and I spent a lot of my new-found spare time running over the moors around the inn and revelling in their beauty as the purple blooms of the heather faded and the autumn shades of red, orange and russet spread over the moors.


# CHAPTER 12

## Conquering Everest

During that summer, with the considerable assistance of our resident Australian jacks of all trades, we had managed to fix some of the worst of the problems with the building, though plenty still remained. We'd removed the cracked and leaking render from the entire building, exposing the original stone walls, though the Alans had first insisted on lovingly chipping away the old rendering to leave a twelve-foot long, mustard-yellow outline of Australia on the otherwise pristine wall and it was a couple of weeks before I could finally persuade them to administer the coup de grace to this homage to their homeland. They had then re-pointed the walls and re-painted the exterior woodwork and we had meanwhile commissioned a beautiful new pub sign, so the inn looked an absolute picture. The generator had been patched up and serviced and had already managed to limp through most of the height of the tourist season, and the roof leaks had been repaired, though the supply of water in the pipes as opposed to through the roof, remained a constant concern.

We'd also rebuilt the chimney stacks, relined the main chimney, pulled up and burned the disgusting carpet in the bar and in its place laid the traditional flagstone floor, albeit made of stone roofing slates to avoid reducing the ceiling height to an impossibly low level. We'd opened up the blocked-up old fireplace in the dining-room and installed a log-stove there but, despite the new open fire in that room, the west wall still sprouted black damp at regular intervals. That meant it had to be repainted every couple of months, but the only alternative seemed to be to demolish and rebuild the entire wall and that was not a job we felt qualified to do ourselves, and nor could we afford to hire someone else to undertake it.

The other major problem was the state of the windows. We couldn't afford to replace them and although the worst of them had been patched up by our joiner back in the spring and all of them had since been repainted, they were still almost as cracked, leaky and draughty as ever, letting in wind and water in summer and howling gales and snow in winter. On our previous spell as managers at the inn, on wild, winter days I had even found drifts of fine, powder-dry snow seven or eight feet long extending right across the floor of the pub from the chinks in the window frames and the cracks round the doors, and I was anxious to avoid any repetition of that.

One evening back in the carefree days before we'd taken over the inn, when such things as watching TV in the evenings were commonplace, not unimaginable luxuries, I'd been staring vacantly at the flickering image on the TV during the commercial break in whatever programme we were watching. As I watched Ted Moult extolling the virtues of Everest double-glazing, a sudden thought struck me. 'You know the Everest double-glazing ads?' I said. 'How come they're always about sound-proofing – helicopters landing outside on a manicured lawn, while Ted Moult stands inside, saying 'You can't hear a thing!' and all that kind of stuff – or about how tough they are, like the one with a wrecking ball failing to break the toughened glass? Why do they never film one that's to do with keeping out wind and wild weather instead?'

'I don't know,' Sue said. She didn't add, 'Who cares?' but her expression showed that that was definitely what she was thinking. I filed it away under Life's Unsolved Mysteries and didn't give it another thought, but as I was standing behind the bar one autumn evening, pondering what to do about the cracked and rotting windows at the inn, that long ago conversation came back into my mind. Inspiration had struck and, leaving Ruby and her boyfriend Liam to see off the last handful of customers, I disappeared at once into what we laughingly called 'The Office' – the sauna cum crisp store at the head of the stairs. Twenty minutes later I had knocked off a letter to the Marketing Director of Everest Double Glazing, pointing out their terrible sin of omission and suggesting, a) that it was high time that the company got its act together and filmed such a commercial, and b) that there could be no finer place to film it than at the most wild, woolly and godforsaken inn in the United Kingdom. I gave the letter to the postman the next morning, but never really expected even the courtesy of a reply.

Three days later the phone rang. 'Mr Hanson?' a suave voice said. He introduced himself as the account executive of a large advertising agency; responsible for the Everest account. 'Your letter was passed to me,' he said, 'and we'd like to come up and have a look at your inn tomorrow.'

The next morning I heard the thunder of helicopter rotors, audible even above the keening of the wind over the moor and a helicopter appeared, swaying alarmingly in the force of the gale as it went in to a hover before making an unsteady landing on the car park at the side of the inn. A gaggle of power-suited advertising agency execs and a couple of creative types, including the director who would be shooting the new Everest commercial, emerged from it, ducking low as they scurried across the car park beneath the still-turning rotors and then straightening up as they strode into the inn.

They shook hands and introduced themselves, and we exchanged a few words before I left them to have a good look round inside and outside. They came, they saw and they liked it. Even though they were trying to be noncommittal, I could tell they were excited by what they were seeing. Characterful pub interiors might have been ten a penny in Britain, but there was no pub anywhere in the country that had surroundings quite like the wild and windswept moorland around the Inn at the Top. As an Emily Bronte fan had remarked to me one day, 'It makes Top Withens look like Regent's Park.'

They took another good look at the exterior of the inn and at the moorland surrounding it, and then came back inside for a final word before departing. 'We will pass our recommendations on to the company,' the ad agency's account executive said, 'but obviously the final decision rests with them.' He paused. 'However, if we do decide to go ahead, you'll be able to supply some suitably wild weather, won't you?'

'We can supply a suitable location, as you've seen,' I said, 'and we can provide some suitable food and drink as well. The weather isn't really under our control, but it rains 250 days a year here and there are only a handful of days when the wind isn't blowing, so the odds are pretty good.'

'Some snow would be nice,' he said.

'We'll do our best,' I said, 'and if you can delay shooting the commercial until the far side of Christmas I can pretty well guarantee some, but even up here, we don't normally see much in November.'

'There's no question of delaying the shoot, I'm afraid,' he said. 'It has to be in the can by the end of November, so I suppose we'll just have to take pot luck.'

I hid a private smile of triumph; this time he was talking as if the location had already been decided. It turned out that they had been on the brink of filming a new commercial anyway, and had already researched a few locations, including another remote inn, the Jamaica Inn on Dartmoor, but had rejected it, so the director said, because of the 'ugly clutter' of electricity pylons and telephone poles nearby. From the pictures I've seen, it doesn't look too ugly these days, so those must have been tidied up at some time in the last thirty-odd years, or they hadn't been that bad in the first place, but I certainly wasn't about to start arguing the merits of someone else's inn with him.

I suspect that no one from Everest or their advertising agency had even heard of the Inn at the Top before I wrote to them – after all it was in the North, or as one of the creatives charmingly referred to it while talking to me: 'Out here in the sticks'. However, having been made aware of its existence, they now seemed only too eager to embrace the inn and indeed 'the sticks'. They promptly shelved their original idea for the commercial and within a week had scripted a new one, based around the Inn at the Top. We would provide the location and, with luck, some suitably foul weather; in return they would supply us with some new Everest double-glazed windows.

After two young men, armed with tape

measures, clipboards and pens, had visited the inn to measure all our windows – and just to make their lives difficult, no two windows were exactly the same size – Everest made its bid. Authorised by the CEO of the company, a man who had built up the business from scratch and clearly knew the value of a pound when he saw one – perhaps he was from Yorkshire, like me! – their initial offer was to replace only the windows that would actually be in shot during the filming. I thought that this was a less than generous offer, and after a bit of to-ing and fro-ing with the agency account executive, I pointed out the negative publicity that might result if someone, heaven forfend, should happen to let slip during a press interview that the flagship building in Everest's brand-new advertising campaign, while it certainly had gleaming new windows around the front, was shipping water and letting in howling drafts through the rotting windows around the back. A revised offer was then rapidly made: they would replace all the windows after all.

The deal was done and within a fortnight, three enormous wagons were lumbering up the winding moor road, causing traffic jams for miles as they struggled to negotiate the tight bends, steep gradients and stretches of single track road with passing places. When they arrived, it was blowing the customary gale. The fitters parked their wagons as close as possible to the outside of each window as they replaced it, but the wind was blowing so strongly throughout the time they were there, that, in every case, as soon as the old window was removed, a howling gale screamed through the gap. The curtains were standing out parallel to the floor in the wind and it took four strong men to wrestle each window into place and then hold it there while it was wedged, fixed and silicone-sealed. If the company ever gives out gold medals, they should reserve a set for those crews of installers. Meanwhile the inrush of freezing wind that accompanied each removal and replacement of a window was dropping the ambient temperature in the bar by a few more degrees. By the time they'd finished, the inn was as cold as it had been when we'd moved in the previous spring and once more the dog was shivering when we went to bed that night. It took twenty-four hours after they'd finished before the place even began to feel slightly warm again.

Two days later, the film crew arrived on site, bringing with them the star of the show and national treasure, Ted Moult. A Derbyshire daisy farmer, Ted was a self-made businessman and a largely self-educated man who, although he had left school at the age of seventeen with minimal qualifications and even less money, had already bought his first dairy farm by the age of twenty-two. He had first come to prominence in the 1950s on BBC Radio's Brain of Britain quiz show. Even though he was actually eliminated in the first round, Ted's warmth and unpretentious common sense, coupled with his quick wit, photographic memory and a natural flair for comic timing, had already charmed the BBC producers and the listeners alike, and he soon became a regular on radio and television quiz shows, panel games and discussion programmes. He appeared regularly on

Ask Me Another, Any Questions, What's My Line and Call My Bluff, and was the guest on the first ever episode of Countdown – the programme with which Channel 4 was launched.

As his fame grew, he also made a number of cameo appearances in films and television programmes, including one as the aspiring beau of the housekeeper Mrs Hall in the hit series All Creatures Great and Small, much of which, coincidentally, had been filmed just down the road from the inn. He had also guest-starred on TV shows with stars like Kenneth Williams, Kenny Everett and Dame Edna Everage, and appeared in The Archers for a while, with the character 'Bill Tinsley' being specially created for him. The quirky group 'Half Man, Half Biscuit', also recorded a tribute song to him: D'ye Ken Ted Moult. Chosen for an appearance on Desert Island Discs in 1959, Ted picked classical music by Beethoven, Brahms, Handel, Mendelssohn, Sibelius and Vaughan Williams, but also found room for Eartha Kitt and Jimmy Shand and his Band, and then chose The Pickwick Papers as his book and some drawing equipment as his luxury.

Ted was also credited with introducing the idea of Pick-Your-Own strawberries – he began advertising Pick-Your-Own on his farm way back in 1961 – and made a point of personally greeting his customers as they arrived at his farm. Everest were shrewd enough to recognise the appeal of a man who was universally liked and trusted by the public, and he had enjoyed a long and lucrative association with them, acting as the public face of their advertising campaigns for many years.

Our locals were agog at the thought that film cameras and, best of all, a TV star who was also a farmer, would soon be appearing in their midst, and excitement was building to a peak as the date set for the filming of the commercial approached. However when the great day finally dawned, the filming did not get off to the best possible start. It was only November and I had already pointed out that we couldn't necessarily guarantee snow that side of Christmas, but the company's schedules required it to be filmed at once, so that the advertising campaign could begin immediately after New Year, and even without snow, the inn and its surroundings could still cut a pretty grim and miserable figure on a grey, cold and windy winter's day. Sod's Law prevailed, however, and the day they began shooting was one of those handful of days in the entire year when the wind didn't blow and the sun was beating down from a cloudless sky. The film crew hastily rescheduled and shot some of the interior scenes that day, instead of the exterior shots they had been planning to do.

The locals had turned out in force, eager for whatever diversions the filming might provide, and several of the farmers were promptly recruited as extras, propping up the bar while the director called for take after take of each shot. It was as they were about to re-shoot a scene for the fifth time, that the assistant director noticed that one of the farmers, our mentor in the ways of the Dale, Dick, had continued to drink his beer between takes. 'Hold it!' he said. 'Can you fill that up again please?'

He turned to Dick who, though never known to think twice about the offer of a free beer, was looking slightly puzzled about what he'd done to earn it. 'It's for continuity,' the assistant director said. 'You need to have the same amount in your glass each time we re-shoot.'

Dick had probably never even heard the word 'continuity' before, but like all the farmers of the Dale, he was never slow on the uptake. I saw him exchange meaningful glances with his mates, and as soon as the director called 'Cut' at the end of the next take, all of them drained their glasses and presented them for refilling, 'For continuity,' Dick said, with the air of a man who had been working in the film industry for decades. Continuity was preserved on so many occasions during the course of the afternoon that by the end of shooting for the day, Dick had fallen off his stool and one of the other extras was sleeping it off in a corner.

The film crew and 'the talent' weren't staying with us, but at some rather more sumptuous accommodation in a town twenty-five miles away, and they gave me some dark, reproachful looks as they set off that night. 'I thought you said this place was guaranteed to have wild weather,' the director said – rather testily I thought – as he got into his chauffeur-driven limo.

I gave a feeble smile. 'Only death and taxes are guaranteed,' I said. 'But today's has been really unusual weather for up here. I'm sure it will be back to normal tomorrow.'

He shrugged and the convoy of vehicles disappeared down the road, taking all their equipment with them, apart from the location caterers, who left their van on site. That evening, to my relief, clouds were soon streaming in from the west, blotting out the stars, and the wind got up until it was howling over the moors around the inn, so I locked up and went upstairs to bed that night happy that normal weather service had resumed. In the middle of the night, I was woken by a loud crashing sound. Half-asleep, I blundered out of bed and prowled through the building, checking the doors and windows by torchlight. Nothing seemed to be amiss, so I went back to bed and, despite the deafening noise of the wind, I fell back asleep at once.

The film crew arrived at first light the next morning, to discover that we had good news and bad news for them. The good news was that the promised wild weather had duly arrived, with horizontal rain driven by a shrieking gale that was rocking the building. The bad news was that if they wanted breakfast, they'd have to buy it from us, because the location caterers' enormous heavy wagon, injudiciously parked in the open, rather than in the lee of the inn, had been unable to resist the full force of the wind during the night, and was now lying on its side in the car park. It took the combined efforts of two farm tractors to pull it upright again and, from the accompanying sound effects, any catering equipment, crockery and glassware that had not already been smashed on the way down, got its comeuppance on the way up again.

To their eternal credit – a credit which must have come close to reaching its limit as they paid for all their replacement food, crockery, glassware and fittings – the caterers managed to get themselves up and running again later that day. Once 'the talent' had been fed, the film crew and extras were allowed to eat too, whereupon the farmers, over-excited at the discovery that free food as well as free beer was now on the menu, descended on the catering wagon like a biblical plague of locusts and cleared it of just about everything the caterers had managed to scrape together.

Despite these minor hitches, Everest duly got their commercial in the can. On that second morning, having first placed powerful lights in every room at the front of the inn to give it that welcoming glow when seen from the moor, the crew disappeared outside to film the opening sequence of the commercial. It required Ted Moult to stand on the fell above the inn, leaning into the wind as he set the scene, shouting to make himself heard above the screaming of the wind, and then having his flat cap blown off by the gale. Since the wind could not be trusted to oblige with a gust at just the right moment, one of the film crew's 'gofers' gave a tug on a piece of fishing line, discreetly attached to the great man's cap, to send it flying off towards the distant Dale.

Ted was a hardy Derbyshire farmer, but even he was unused to the kind of weather served up at the Inn at the Top. After filming outside for all of five minutes, another of the film crew's gofers came running in to ask if I might have any spare warm underclothes that Ted could borrow. I sorted him out with a set of brand new, bright red thermal underwear, bought in anticipation of the long, cold winter to come. Ted disappeared upstairs to change and was so warm and contented in his borrowed gear that when filming was over the following evening, he set off for home, still wearing my thermals, and I never saw them, or indeed him, again.

One would-be customer, a Mr White from Sunderland, turned up that morning in the middle of the shoot and had to travel on without slaking his thirst. In those days he was a keen walker of the fells around the inn and often called in for a pint. Although it had previously been managed by summer-only landlords, he knew that we had taken it over and were keeping it open throughout the winter, so he'd set off for a walk over the fells that November, in the confident expectation of a pie and a pint when he reached the end of his hike.

He walked up the Pennine Way from the tiny village in the bottom of the Dale and reached the inn at about noon, where he was, he said, 'amazed to see the inn standing in front of me like a beacon. All the front windows were brightly lit up from inside and I took a picture of this unusual vision. On trying to enter, the door was locked and knocking on it, Neil opened it clutching a brick-size mobile phone to his ear and asking what I wanted. I said "a pint".'

It went against the grain to turn any customer away, not least one who'd walked all the way there, but I was now getting earache from the director of the commercial, about holding up the shoot. He was booming down his mobile phone 'He's in the shot! He's in the shot!' He had insisted on the pub being closed for the day, and with an extensive set of new windows and a guarantee of massive TV exposure, I wasn't disposed to argue with him, so I passed the message on, pointing towards the fell behind Mr White.

'I turned round to see a large number of cameras and floodlights in a row on the moor embankment just beyond the road,' Mr White recalled. 'I had found myself in the middle of the Everest advert shoot. So with a dry mouth I travelled on.'

Our dog, Gnasher, should have been enjoying her moment of fame, starring in the commercial alongside Ted Moult. When they had finished the exterior shots and were ready to start the interior ones, I placed her at the end of the sofa, gave the command 'Sit' and went back behind the bar. The director called 'Action' and Ted made his entrance through the front door and walked across the bar. As soon as he did so, the dog set off to greet him, wagging her tail with great enthusiasm that was only slightly diminished by the director shouting. 'Cut! Get that bloody dog out of the shot.'

Repeated commands to 'Sit and stay' had nil effect on Gnasher, and after several aborted takes, the director realised that, just like her owner, the dog wasn't too good at taking direction, and the shoot had to go ahead without her. Banished to the kitchen, she left with what I took to be a reproachful look in my direction.

The commercial climaxed with the 'money shot' – as makers of a rather different genre of film might have called it – with Ted Moult standing by the front window of the bar, dropping the famous feather to demonstrate the efficiency of the window's draught-proofing, and then uttering the immortal line: 'You only fit double-glazing once, so fit the best – fit Everest.'

I'm sure the falling feather shot would have worked perfectly anyway, but with one eye on the gale still howling outside, the film crew sealed the outside of the window frame with gaffer tape just to be doubly sure. One of the gofers climbed a small aluminium ladder and dropped the feather, which was then retrieved by one of the other gofers and passed back to him so that he could drop it again. Meanwhile, at the other end of the bar, there was the surreal sight of a dozen grown men – director, creatives and advertising agency executives – with a combined income that must have been well into seven figures, grouped around a monitor screen and groaning with disappoint-ment or gasping with childish delight as they watched the playbacks of take after take of the feather, drifting down past the window and settling on the sill. Finally they had the shot they wanted with the feather performing a perfect set of parabolas before landing right in the middle of the sill.

The director called 'Cut. That's a wrap,' where-upon the gofers, wranglers and other strangely-named film crew dogsbodies began dismantling their equipment and loading it onto their trucks with a haste that suggested they did not altogether share our enthusiasm for our wild moorland kingdom. They disappeared down the road soon afterwards, leaving us to bask in the still unaccustomed warmth of our new draught-proof windows, and the rosy glow of anticipation for the fifteen seconds of fame that would be ours when the commercial began to air.

The celebrated feather did not travel back with the film crew and occupied a pride of place in a glass case in the bar for many years, while many tourists – who clearly should get out more – used to pose for commemorative photographs in front of the very window where the falling feather shot was filmed.

Ted Moult was a genuinely nice guy. As soon as each shot was finished, he settled down with the farmers, chatting away to them about fat stock prices and sheep breeds, and he was affable, genial even, with all those around him, going out of his way to make everyone feel at ease. At the end of the shoot, before he set off down the Dale with the rest of the crew, Ted took me outside and we sat on the bench under the inn sign with the dog between us, while the advertising agency's stills photographer took a few shots. A couple of weeks later a courier arrived at the inn with a large parcel. Inside was a framed photograph of the three of us: Ted, the dog and me, which he had inscribed 'From one draught expert to another!' I still have it in pride of place in my office, in memory not just of my time at the inn, but of one of the most thoroughly decent men I have ever met.

However, Ted Moult's story ended tragically. With a substantial income from the Everest ads, an apparently successful farm and a life of considerable achievement behind him, you would have thought that Ted would have been as happy a man as you could meet, but it turned out that his genial air concealed a hidden, private and troubled soul, prone to bouts of depression. In September 1986, nearly two years after the commercial shoot at the Inn at the Top, he took his twelve-bore shotgun and killed himself in a barn at his home, Scaddows Farm, near Ticknall in Derbyshire. He was just sixty years old. Some said he had been worried about his health, while others claimed that the incessant wet weather that summer that had prevented him harvesting his grain, had been preying on his mind.

# CHAPTER 13

## Keeping the Gales Off The Ales

The Everest commercial began airing right at the start of January, just a few weeks after the film crew had departed from the inn for the last time, and Everest were absolutely delighted with the look of it and even more so with the results of the advertising campaign. The TV ads and the accompanying print campaign that proudly claimed that Everest windows had 'kept the gales off the pub's ales' and had proved so effective that 'the only draughts you now find in the bar come in pint glasses', proved to be their most popular and successful campaign ever. Everest told us that they had never had so many enquiries nor sold so many windows in such a short space of time. More than twenty years on, viewers of a Channel 4 television programme obviously shared their enthusiasm when they voted it one of their fifty favourite TV commercials of all time, and Everest even revisited the inn and filmed another commercial soon after the twentieth anniversary of the first one, intercutting the new commercial with fragments of the original one. If you look really carefully you can even catch a glimpse of the dark-haired, bearded and frighteningly young-looking landlord behind the bar in the original commercial. How times have changed, in every way, since then!

We had enjoyed a few weeks revelling in the warmth created by our new double-glazed windows, with many of our customers discarding their jackets inside the pub for the first time ever, but it was not the last we were to hear of the new windows. One morning, a letter arrived from the Planning Officer of the local District Council. 'It has come to our notice that the windows at your public house have been replaced,' he wrote. 'It is a Grade II listed building and planning permission is required for any alterations.' He went on to tell us that we would have to apply for retrospective planning permission, justifying the change, and we were warned that if the council were not satisfied with our arguments, the windows would have to be removed and the original ones reinstated. That would have proved rather difficult. The glass had all been smashed and thrown in a skip and the rotting window frames had been burnt on a bonfire in the car park. The Planning Officer added that, in his opinion, the new windows were completely unsuitable for the building and that, if replacement ones had to be fitted, sash windows should have been used instead.

I replied at once, pointing out first that the pub was a listed building because of its history, not because of any architectural merit, of which it possessed precisely none. The inn had been gutted in a fire ten years before. Little of the original building remained intact and all of its original windows had been destroyed. As we had discovered when we first came there, Neville and Stan had refurbished the building using the cheapest available materials. When it came to the windows, they had purchased an assorted joblot. I had the photographs to prove that the windows we had removed came in no less than nine different styles: side-opening, top-opening, bottom-opening, with and without a quarter-light, some with 'Regency' panes, some bottle-glass, some plain. The only kind of windows that emphatically had not been present were the sash windows he was insisting we should now fit.

The Planning Officer had raised no objection to any of these monstrosities at the time Stan and Neville were fitting them, nor to the single-storeyed, breeze-block, flat-roofed extension that they had built – scarcely in the vernacular tradition of the Dale and definitely not improving its looks – why, I asked, was he now picking on us after we had done so much to restore and improve the place?

I supplied chapter, verse and photographs to justify my claims, together with a copy of the documentary film shot by the BBC when we had first moved in to the inn, which clearly showed the appalling state of the mismatched old windows, all of which evidence was promptly acknowledged and just as promptly rejected by the Planning Officer. Having failed to move him, I decided to appeal direct to the voting public and their elected representatives, and contacted the local paper. They ran a front-page story, the national press picked it up as well and the television news then followed suit.

As the story took hold – everyone loves the story of a plucky underdog battling a faceless bureaucracy! – to the great delight of Everest, their advertisement then became the first commercial ever to be shown in its entirety on the BBC Six o'Clock News. Experts, pro- and anti-, were wheeled out for interview, and I had the pleasure – more pure schadenfreude – of hearing an expert architectural historian, regularly consulted by the Yorkshire Dales National Park, and the man who originally recommended the building for Grade II listing to the Department of the Environment, say that in his opinion, the design of the new windows was much more in keeping with the character of the building and also truer to the original style of the multi-paned windows fitted to the inn when it was built in the seventeenth century, than the sash windows that the Planning Officer was demanding.

Despite the testimony of this very expert witness and the wealth of supporting documents, photographs and film, the Planning Officer remained obstinate and obdurate, and the case at last had to go before the Dale's equivalent of the Supreme Court, the local District Council chamber, where the issue was debated at length by the full council. I attended the hearing feeling rather anxious about the outcome, but I found my smile broadening by the minute as the Planning Officer was revealed to be in a minority of one, with councillor after councillor speaking favourably about our improvements to the pub and the welcome boost to other local businesses as a result of the Everest advertising campaign, not to mention the publicity from the subsequent controversy over planning permission. As one of them said during the debate, 'the windows have improved the pub and brought a bigger boost to tourism to the area than the council ever could'.

When the vote was finally taken, to my great delight, and the considerable embarrassment of their Planning Officer, the councillors voted unanimously in favour of leaving the windows in situ. The Planning Officer slunk out of the council chamber, but he never forgot his humiliation. Years later, when our successors as owners applied for planning permission to build an extension to the inn to house some extra bedrooms for hikers and tourists, he made them install sash windows in it. However even that proved to be a pyrrhic victory for him. The Inn at the Top had always been a part of Yorkshire until local government reorganisation in 1974 when some bureaucrat – clearly not a Yorkshireman – decided to move the county boundary just to the south of the inn, leaving it, horror of horrors, in County Durham. It made no sense whatsoever. All the council services

– such as they were – were provided by North Yorkshire, not Durham, and in fact the only connection with that county was that the inn was policed from Barnard Castle in County Durham. It was a round-trip of forty miles, which was a considerable stretch even for the long arm of the law, so the police only made it with the greatest reluctance. If arriving after the scheduled closing time, they also took the precaution of making an anonymous phone call to tip us off that they would be visiting us, so that they wouldn't find us serving a bar full of customers when they got there, which would force them to do something about it and probably require them to make regular repeat visits.

A campaign to end the iniquitous state of affairs about the county boundary had rumbled on for years, but in the end, it was simple economics – the cost to County Durham of having to pay North Yorkshire County Council to supply the services to the inn that County Durham should have been providing themselves since the inn was transferred to that county – that persuaded them to reinstate the inn where it should always have been: within the boundary of Yorkshire. As their Chief Executive told a special meeting of the council's Policy and Resources Committee: 'the fact is, we don't have a powerful case against the boundary change on the technical front and even if we did, we would be taking on a financial liability.'

As a result, though not until some years after we had left the inn, on what some might have seen as the appropriate date of April 1, 1991, the inn was at last restored to its rightful home. Even more pleasing to me was the fact that the District Council, for which our nemesis the Planning Officer had worked, was itself abolished some years later, and his job with it. What was that about revenge being a dish best served cold?

The Everest commercial had one more unexpected consequence for me. It had showed me pulling a pint of keg beer for one of the farmers, rather than a pint of 'real ale' from a hand pump, and as a result of my shocking betrayal of CAMRA's raison d'être, I was then the subject of a proposed Motion of Censure at CAMRA's next AGM. I tried to point out that a) the director of the commercial had insisted that I stand at the end of the bar where there were no hand pumps, and as the recipient of £20,000 worth of free windows, I wasn't in a position to argue with him, and b) that most of the farmers preferred keg beer anyway. As a dedicated consumer organisation, we were supposed to be about ensuring freedom of choice, even if that meant serving keg beer rather than real ale, but to the more hard-core CAMRA members this was no excuse for my treachery and I was roundly booed when I took the podium at the next AGM.

I consoled myself with the thought that every single editor of the *Good Beer Guide* had received exactly the same treatment. My predecessor had been booed at the AGM when I took up the reins, while I received an ovation, but that was simply because I had not yet produced an edition of the Guide for the members to hate. As soon as the members saw that, just like my predecessors, I was the owner of a red pen and was prone to use it on their rambling pub descriptions, which often dwelt extensively on the fact that the landlord was a CAMRA member but told you nothing at all about the pub itself, then I too was booed to the rafters whenever I showed my face at one of their gatherings. My keg beer heresy had only made matters even worse.

However, I could live with that, so I continued to wield my red pen with equanimity. As well as taking an axe to pub descriptions that resembled *War and Peace,* in length, if not in quality, I also excised as much as possible of the arcane codes and language that CAMRA members used to communicate with each other, but which were useless, or worse, to the ordinary members of the public at whom the *Good Beer Guide* was supposedly aimed. 'Basic local', for example, was often used to describe pubs so lacking in facilities that only the most dedicated and hygiene-averse beer lover would risk a pint there. Some of the more hard-core CAMRA members would also try to exclude from the Guide any pub that offered any more exotic foods than pork pies, pickled eggs and potato crisps. Having spent my share of evenings in their company, I can confirm that, while the average CAMRA member back then was able – or claimed to be able – to detect every subtle nuance of flavour in the beer they were drinking, their palate for food was often rather less sophisticated and didn't usually seem to extend far beyond pie and peas or curry. My attempts to convince them that some potential purchasers of the book might be interested in eating as well as drinking were met with harrumphing or pitying looks.

Some CAMRA members may not have been impressed by the Everest commercial, but large numbers of the Great British public undoubtedly were and many of them turned up at the inn to tell us so in person. The Inn at the Top had always been well-known locally but had previously been little-known outside its Northern heartlands, but the publicity generated during the Everest campaign and the subsequent 'War of the Windows' with the council Planning Officer was now to make it famous throughout the land. Already incredibly busy during the summer season, the pub would now become a madhouse the year-round – except when the snow was falling – and be heaving with customers from soon after dawn until well beyond dusk. However, in the weeks before the commercial aired it was possible to take my foot off the gas occasionally and myself, Ruby and Liam could all take turns to indulge in the previously unthought of luxury of regular evenings off.

I had now worked my way through the classic stages of the Kubler-Ross 'Grief Cycle' after separation from a loved one:

1)Shock – 'Initial paralysis at hearing the bad news'.

2)Denial – 'Trying to avoid the inevitable'.

3)Anger – 'Frustrated outpouring of bottled-up emotion' (my favourite, I spent a long time there).

4)Bargaining – 'Seeking in vain for a way out'.

5)Depression – 'Final realisation of the inevitable'.

6) Testing – 'Seeking realistic solutions'.

And now, finally, I'd reached Stage 7) 'Acceptance'.

I was now a bachelor again – *de facto* if not yet *de jure* – for the first time in twelve years and after a decent interval of ... well, two or three months anyway, I was even ready to take the first tentative steps in the search for my next life companion. The grey little town at the foot of the moors to the west of the inn and particularly its idiosyncratic night-spot would prove to be a happy hunting ground for me as I began to build a social life outside the restrictive confines of the inn. However in one of the town's pubs I first had to suffer one of the more severe humiliations in a long line of only intermittently successful attempts to interest the opposite sex in my manly charms.

I had spent an evening indulging in authentically British male behaviour, drinking beer and directing long, meaningful looks, designed to showcase my brooding intensity, at a particularly beautiful woman across the room. The fact that she was sitting with a man friend was no obstacle to my increasingly inebriated attempts to establish eye contact. Reluctantly I decided that it was time to move on, but I paused at the top of the two steps leading to the back bar, to direct one last haunting look in her direction.

Unfortunately, in so doing, I missed the top step, stumbled and hit a farmer at the bottom of the steps squarely between the shoulder-blades. The impact caused him to fall against his companion, emptying his pint over her in the process.

I watched, horrified, as the collisions and spillages spread outwards like ripples on the surface of a pool. Having replaced more drinks than could ever have been spilt in the human dodgems I had created – farmers may be slow talkers, but they are quick thinkers when the situation requires it – I left the pub with burning cheeks, a heavy heart and an empty wallet. I had never realised until then that the saying 'pride comes before a fall' was supposed to be taken literally.

Fortunately, I had more success elsewhere and, making up for lost time, in fairly rapid succession I went out with a doe-eyed au pair who was working for one of the local 'toffs'; a sultry, raven-haired divorcee from a market town at the foot of the fells; a leather-clad motorbike-rider from New Zealand who happened to be passing through the area and stayed around for a while; and a half-Armenian, half-French dancer living in London, whose beauty and exoticism on her visits to stay with me did wonders for my standing in the Dale.

After all these tempestuous liaisons had flared and burnt out, I began another relationship, this time with a woman from the Dale, who was trapped in a loveless, childless marriage. In almost any other part of Britain, she would simply have got a divorce, but tradition was a powerful and sometimes suffocating force in the Dale, and as I knew from when Sue had disappeared over the horizon with an Alan in hot pursuit, divorce was still regarded more as a stain on an individual and a family than a sensible solution to an intractable problem.

It was also the way things were around there that men taking up with married women were asking for trouble. The services of a couple of local 'enforcers' had been offered to me when Sue and Big Alan went off together, but now I was the one who was breaching the Dale's unwritten moral code by embarking on an affair with – let's call her 'Jane'. However, we were both lonely, there was a strong mutual attraction and if there was a risk, it was one we were willing to run.

Usually we met on my afternoon off, at a hotel in a market town a safe distance from the Dale. While downstairs in the tea rooms, ladies of a certain age indulged in afternoon tea and cream cakes, served on bone china with lace doilies and all the trimmings, Jane and I would be upstairs doing our best to make the earth move. Meeting once a week was never going to be enough for a couple in the throes of a passionate affair, however, and we began to seize the chance of clandestine meetings in the Dale as well. I took what I thought were adequate precautions, but how wrong I was, and quite how much of a chance I was taking, was not fully apparent to me until my patron and mentor in the Dale, the old farmer, Dick, beckoned me over to a quiet corner of the bar one evening.

'I was passing Jane's house the other night,' he said. 'And there was a car just like yours parked about a hundred yards up the road.' He held up a hand as I started to splutter a disclaimer. 'Of course I know it wasn't yours,' he said, with what might have been the trace of a wink. 'But if it had have been, that wouldn't have been the wisest place to leave it. You see, you probably don't know this, but a cousin of Jane's farms further up that road and he passes the house most nights on his way back from the pub. Well, he's the sort of person that likes to know everybody's business and, you know what people are like round here, they might just put two and two together and make five … and if they did, there might be trouble.'

As ever with Dick, it had been done with infinite kindness, tact and discretion, but it was just as stark a warning nonetheless as if he'd said 'Listen idiot, if you want to be beaten to a bloody pulp by a bunch of Jane's husband's friends and relatives, keep doing what you're doing'. He glanced at me, just to make sure I'd taken it in. 'So if it were me,' he said, 'and I was ever wanting to be out that way again, I'd probably leave my car in the village and walk up.' He gave me another ghost of a wink and went back to his mates in the corner of the bar.

From then on I followed his advice and walked from the village and, perhaps as a result, with the exception of the two I broke on the steel generator casing during the deep-frozen winter of 1978–79, I still have all my own teeth.

# CHAPTER 14

## One Of The Great Eccentrics

As autumn turned to winter, although my social life was definitely on the up, I had yet to reach a decision about how and if I was to continue at the pub. Sue and both the Alans were now long gone, and though Ruby and her boyfriend Liam remained, I wasn't convinced that, only just turned eighteen, they were ready for a managerial role just yet. My problems were exacerbated when my mother was diagnosed with cancer. She had had a bad fall when out walking a few months before. It had been witnessed by a family friend who told me that 'the curious thing was that she didn't even put out her hands to protect herself, but just dropped face down on the ground'. Apart from being bruised and bloodied, she had appeared okay and although she'd had a series of tests at the hospital, she assured me that they'd shown nothing to be concerned about other than a virus. That may or may not have been true, but I could only take her word for it.

The first intimation that there really was a serious problem came when she again suddenly collapsed, this time halfway down the stairs of her house. Luckily Sue had called in for a visit at the time – although we were separated, she still had a warm relationship with my mother – and she hung on to her, but was struggling to stop my unconscious mother from falling the rest of the way down the stairs. Holding on with one arm, Sue managed to reach the phone and dialled first an ambulance, and then me at the inn, but from sixty miles away, all I could do was phone my mother's neighbour and get him to run round and help take her weight until the ambulance arrived.

After a few days in hospital, my mother was allowed home, but the prognosis was grim; she had cancer of the brain, which had already spread through her body and she did not have long to live. I didn't want to see her end her days in a home or a hospital ward, but my only close relative, my brother, lived in New Zealand and could scarcely be expected to come and look after her, and if I was going to do so, I first had to find someone to run the inn for me.

A possible solution presented itself almost at once. Our silent partner in the inn, who lived in the Lake District, had a drinking buddy, a hotel chef called Gerry, who was looking for a change of scene. The silent partner had got to know him well during their regular after hours drinking sessions in their local pub. That set a few alarm bells ringing with me – giving a problem drinker an inn to run was like giving a lunatic the keys to the asylum – but given that the Inn at the Top was another notorious after hours spot, I re-assured myself that at least the chef would be used to late nights. He came up for an interview soon afterwards and though he did seem a bit too full of himself, with big tales of what he'd done and where he'd been, in my desperation at that time, I would probably have jumped at an even less reassuring character, so long as he was available to start at once. I took him on and told him that if everything worked out well, there was a possibility of him becoming a partner in the inn a little further down the track.

One serious worry was that he did not have a car and had not driven for fifteen years, ever since – so he said – his parents had been killed in a car-crash. It was not quite impossible to run the inn without being able to drive, but it was exceedingly difficult, because it was so far from anywhere that many suppliers would not deliver. The inn was definitely not on a bus route and even down in the Dale, country buses had almost the same rarity value as golden eagles in the British landscape – sometimes you might see one, sometimes you might hear one, but the chances of actually catching one were close to nil.

There was a taxi service in the town ten miles away but country taxis often doubled as the school bus and the local hearse, or at least as a funeral car, which could cause problems and delays if your need for a ride happened to coincide with the school run or with a burial. If the latter, you might have to wait for an hour or more while the driver helped to speed the departed, and you could then find that, from force of habit, he insisted on driving the entire way at ten miles an hour.

Sometimes an enterprising and car-owning local could be persuaded to do the job in return for a few quid in cash and no questions asked, but often a taxi would have to be summoned from elsewhere, at sometimes inordinate expense. One time, carless and desperate to get back to the inn, I had to hire a taxi from a town twenty miles away. As we drove along, its driver regaled me with tales of the extortion visited on his peers on their annual taxi drivers' outing to Blackpool.

'Thirty-two of us made the same journey in eight taxis and no two of them had the same reading on the meter,' he said. 'It's a bloody disgrace.'

'But your meter's not even switched on,' I pointed out, helpfully.

'No, it's a standard charge for this journey.'

'You get a lot of people travelling this route, then, do you?'

'No, I think you're the first one,' he replied, without a trace of irony, before trousering an enormous fare.

In order to avoid such problems, it was essential that Gerry drove but he assured me that he was now over the personal traumas caused by the tragic death of his parents and would be happy to take up driving again. So I hired him on the spot, introduced him to Ruby and the rest of the staff, stayed for 48 hours to show him the ropes, and then set off for my mother's, leaving Gerry in charge of the pub, with my Landrover as his transport.

Sue had volunteered to help me care for my mother which, given the state of our relationship was a) very noble of her and b) fraught with potential personal difficulties, but somehow we made it work well enough and I'm sure that my mother drew much comfort from the thought that her terminal illness might at least have the virtue of bringing us back together. Whether anything could really do that was far from certain but, out of consideration for her, we certainly did nothing to dispel the idea when we were with her.

Over the next few weeks her condition steadily deteriorated. She needed constant care and attention, but during the early stages of my mother's terminal illness, once a week I was able to leave Sue to take sole charge of her for twenty-four hours, while I went back to the inn to allow Gerry some time off. However, as the cancer progressed, it became impossible to leave her, and in any case, the perilous state of the roads in January and February and the possibility of a sudden snowstorm made it too risky to attempt the journey for fear that I might find myself once more trapped at the inn by snowdrifts while Sue was left to look after my mother by herself.

On one of the last journeys I made before winter really closed in, on a bitterly cold, late December day, I had safely negotiated the first of the dales that I had to cross on my way up to the inn and had climbed to the top of the watershed barring the way down to the next dale. As I approached the start of the long descent, I saw a puzzling sight ahead of me. A crowd of people – hikers in full winter gear – were standing at the top of the hill, staring down the far side. I wonder what they're looking at, I thought, as I bombed over the brow of the hill, which ran down, steep and straight for a couple of miles, between the wall of the fell on one side and the steep drop on the other.

It turned out that what they were looking at was a trickle of cars, trying and failing to drive up the other side of the hill, the top end of which was covered in sheet ice from an overflowing stream that had spilled over the roadway and then frozen in the previous night's savage frost. There had been no warning: one minute I was driving along a road that, though flanked by piled-up snow, was perfectly safe to drive on, and the next I was on an ice rink, already moving fast and accelerating more as gravity took hold.

I couldn't brake hard, if at all, because the slightest touch on the brakes set the back end drifting out as the car went into a skid. Luckily I'd already changed down a gear because that would now have been suicidal too, but all I could do was hold on, pray and, as the car sped towards the gaggle of cars stuck on the upslope, keep steering into the skids to keep some vague control over the car. As I looked down the road ahead, I could see one car pulling over to the left, obviously preparing to do a three-point turn. If it did that, there was a very good chance that I'd be hitting it broadside. I flicked my headlights onto full beam, put my hand on the horn and left it there, so that I was blaring out a warning as I sped down the hill towards the gaggle of cars.

I missed the first one by inches, swerved round the next two with slightly more to spare, but then found myself drifting dangerously close to the drop on the left hand side of the road. Trying to correct that – all this while plummeting downhill at approaching sixty miles an hour – I got into another skid, over-corrected that, and skidded again, so that I was carrying on down the hill in a series of fish-tailing slides from side to side.

Ignoring the *son et lumiere* of my horn and headlights, the driver of the car I had spotted had now begun his three-point turn. He managed to turn across the road easily enough, but when he put it into reverse, unsurprisingly the wheels began to spin and slide. For long agonising seconds, the car was parked sideways across the road, completely blocking it. I sped towards it, fighting the wheel and uttering every swearword I had ever heard. I glimpsed the white, frightened face of the driver turning towards me – my own face must have been even more pale and terrified – and then I saw a spray of grit as his wheels slid onto a clear patch of road and gripped for a second and the car shot backwards, embedding its rear bumper in the banked snow. I had already hunched my shoulders, bracing myself for the impact when I saw the gap opening up between the car and the edge of the road. Still sliding from one skid to the next, I aimed for the gap and barrelled through it, so close to the car that his bumper clipped my front wing, causing another heart-stopping skid.

Then I was through, and as I reached the bottom of the steep hill to the summit and the gradient became more gentle, I managed to get the car under some sort of control and, by gently pumping the brakes, I eventually succeeded in slowing the car and finally stopped it altogether. I was still shaking as I got out of the car, scooped up a double handful of snow and buried my face in it. I gave myself five minutes to recover and then, a

278

little older and a lot wiser, I drove the rest of the way at a very stately fifteen to twenty miles an hour. I managed to reach the inn without further incident, and after an anxious twenty-four hours, scanning the massing clouds, I left again before the snow began to fall. This time I made my way back using a lengthy detour right down the length of the Dale and down the A1 before turning back to the west to reach my mother's house without having to cross any serious hills or watersheds at all.

My brief visits to the inn had done nothing to reassure me that my choice of Gerry as relief manager had been the right one. Right from the start there had been some worrying signs that not everything at the inn was running as smoothly and sweetly as I would have liked. There were rumours of drunken late night disagreements between Gerry and a couple of customers, which had nearly come to blows, a mysterious hole had been punched in the roof of the porch which he was unable or unwilling to explain and, though it could just have been because of the winter weather, some of our most regular and loyal customers no longer appeared to be coming up to the inn at all.

It was troubling, but with more serious issues filling my mind, there was little I could do about it now. To make matters worse, Gerry had also managed to wreck his only transport: my Landrover. The very first time he'd taken it out, possibly while he was drunk – the jury was still out on that – he'd gone off the road at the very first bend down the hill from the inn. He had then left it upside down on the fell all night, so that all the oil had drained out. Once the Landrover had been righted by one of our local farmers pulling it back onto its wheels with his tractor, Gerry had then set off in it again without replenishing the oil, with the inevitable result that the engine had overheated and seized. That cost me several hundred pounds to fix, but accidents will happen, so I paid the bill with a sigh and left Gerry to carry on.

A couple of weeks later, I arrived to discover that Ruby and her boyfriend had split up and he had quit soon afterwards. Ruby also told me that Gerry had then appeared in her bedroom the following night, drunk, and tried to get into bed with her. When I asked him for his version of events he claimed it was a misunderstanding. Under normal circumstances that would probably have been the moment to have sacked him, but these were not normal circumstances and having given him a major bollocking and a warning about any repetition, I felt I had no option but to let him carry on for now. Once my mother was dead and buried, I could re-take charge of the inn and try to sort out the problems.

Unfortunately, if understandably, Ruby was no longer willing to wait for that to happen and, faced with the prospect of having to share the inn with Gerry on her own, she chose to follow her ex-boyfriend down the road, leaving Gerry in sole charge. The following week, he wrecked the Landrover again, this time going off the road and colliding with a rock, causing even worse damage. This time, with my patience exhausted, I asked the garage to keep hold of the Landrover when they'd completed the repairs and told Gerry that he would have to manage with taxis from now on, or get everything he needed delivered, either by the local shops or by me on my weekly visit. In the depths of winter, with few customers about, that was not going to pose such a problem as it would have done in the summer season, so I was still confident that he would be able to manage well enough.

My mother was now near the end and she died shortly afterwards, still in her own bed with her younger son at her side as she drew her last breath. After the funeral, I spent a couple more days clearing her house and settling her affairs, and then went back to the inn. Sue had also stayed to the end and, though we were now going our separate ways again, my mother's fatal illness had certainly brought us much closer together. There were no more recriminations about what had gone wrong and there was a genuine affection between us, but whether there could ever again be anything more than friendship was a question that only time could answer.

When I got back to the inn, I barely had time to unpack my bag before I was fielding the first of a string of increasingly alarming phone calls, or being taken to one side by one of our dwindling band of regulars to be told about some of the things that had been going on while I was away. That was only the beginning. As the news spread around the Dale that I was back at the inn, more and more of our friends and locals kept contacting me to regale me with fresh horror stories of Gerry's reign at the pub. There had indeed been brawls with some customers, others had been banned by him in fits of drunken rage, and many more had simply voted with their feet and found other pubs to patronise. When not fighting with the customers, Gerry had been throwing open the till and inviting all and sundry to 'have a drink on Neil, he can afford it', or passing out, blind drunk, in a corner, and leaving the remaining customers to help themselves to beer, cash from the till, or anything else they fancied.

The owner of the garage where the Landrover had been repaired also called me. A few days earlier, having cadged a lift from a customer at the inn, Gerry had turned up at the garage, once more dead drunk, and tried to pick up the Landrover. When he was reminded that, as I had told both him and the garage, it had to stay where it was, he gave the garage owner a mouthful and stormed off. However, he stopped for a few more drinks in the village and that evening, after the garage had closed, he sneaked back, by then even more drunk, and broke in and stole the Landrover. He then set off up the dual carriageway that ran a few miles to the north of the inn.

Police patrolmen often sat in a lay-by near the summit of the dual carriageway and that evening a lorry driver pulled up when he reached the top, and told them about the eccentric driving of a man in a Landrover who had overtaken him three times as he crawled up the steep hill, swerving dangerously from side to side. Each time the Landrover had then bumped its way across the central reservation and disappeared back down the hill, only to reappear again a couple of minutes later, having re-crossed the central reservation again. 'He looked like he was both drunk and lost,' the lorry driver was saying, when he glanced back down the road. 'Blimey, look out!' he said. 'Here he is again.'

Sure enough, at that very moment, Gerry passed them at the wheel of the Landrover, still swerving all over the carriageway and evidently failing to register that there was a police car parked at the side of the road. He was about to complete yet another U-turn over the central reservation when the policemen turned on their blue light, pulled him over and arrested him. It turned out that Gerry was so drunk that he couldn't even find the turning on to the road that led to the inn and was driving up and down the dual carriageway trying to locate it, but that was now the least of his worries. When breathalysed, he proved to be three times over the alcohol limit, and police investigations then revealed that, contrary to his claims to me, he had never passed a driving test in his life and therefore not only was he driving without a licence, he was also doing so without any valid insurance. Faced with all that, the fact that he'd also broken into the garage and taken the vehicle without the owner's consent seemed neither here nor there. I never discovered whether he had also lied to me about the crash that had allegedly killed his parents, but by that time I was past caring.

As if all this was not enough, the landlord of a pub in the small town a few miles down the Dale then phoned me to say that a barman that Gerry had hired in my absence had been attempting to hawk barrels of beer around the pubs in the area, offering to sell them at half the wholesale price.

283

The barrels could only have come from the Inn at the Top, because we were the only pub in the whole area that sold that particular brand of beer. Faced with that catalogue of crimes, I confronted Gerry and sacked him on the spot. I felt particularly sad for his girlfriend, however, who had only recently arrived at the inn, having given up her own job to come and live and work with him. I had no idea whether she knew anything about the Mr Hyde side of Gerry's character. If she didn't, other than her unfortunate choice of partner, she was completely blameless, but nonetheless she obviously had to go with him.

Gerry's dismissal also lost me yet another customer, since he had befriended one of the very few regulars he hadn't already alienated: Richard, the world's tightest man, a farmer who – even among a community of farmers who were themselves never less than careful with their money – was legendary for his penny-pinching ways. Gerry turned up on Richard's doorstep later that day and told him such a sob-story about his brutal and unjustified dismissal that, without knowing any of the true circumstances but, perhaps remembering one of our free and frank exchange of views about his pathological meanness, which even extended to hanging surplus sheepdog puppies in his barn because 'they aren't worth the price of a shotgun cartridge', Richard not only never came to the pub again while I owned it, but also apparently spent his spare time bad-mouthing me to anyone else who would listen.

In the space of a few months I'd now lost a wife, a mother, a manager, most of my regular customers and any lingering affection I might have felt for the pub trade; once more Lady Bracknell sprang to mind. However, Sue and I were still the co-owners of the Inn at the Top, the tourist season was now beginning again and we couldn't just shut the doors and walk away from it. Even worse, the next production run of the *Good Beer Guide* was also starting, which meant that I had to be away from the inn for at least three days a week. Although our disenchantment with what had seemed like our dream just a couple of years before made the prospect pretty daunting, after discussing all the alternatives – most of them even more depressing – we decided to put the pub on the market and run it between us until a buyer could be found. Sue took sole charge for the three days I had to be in St Albans. It still wasn't the signal for a reconciliation, but we had at least buried the bitterness of the great split between us, and working together was the only solution we could see to the problem of the pub.

Her return was a help with the workload, but it put a serious dent in my social life since most of the unattached women in the district, hearing that Sue was back at the inn, made the natural, though inaccurate assumption that we had resumed living together as man and wife. In fact we occupied separate rooms at opposite ends of the landing, but my attempts to persuade potential girlfriends of that were met with sceptical looks that were usually followed by a blank refusal to even consider going out on a date.

Our friends and most of our old locals rallied round us and, strangely, as soon as we'd made the decision to sell the pub, everything changed. A great weight had been lifted from us and, although we now preserved a little of our sanity by shutting the bar at hours that were at least within sighting distance of the official closing time, we began to enjoy again the things that had drawn us to the inn in the first place, like the beauty of the surrounding landscape and the company of our friends and locals. We started to smile and laugh again – hell, sometimes we even looked forward to opening time! So much had our attitude changed that we even gave semi-serious thought to abandoning attempts to sell the pub and staying on there, but an inner, saner voice in our ears persuaded us that if we did, it would once more end in tears.

So we put the inn on the market. I contacted three different estate agencies that had licensed property divisions, one in London, one in Leeds and one with a branch in a Dales market town. Only the latter bothered to return the call, so we went with them, displaying once more an unerring ability to make the wrong decision under pressure. The agent who turned up to view the property was an alarmingly smug ex-public schoolboy, who displayed an absolute, unshakeable confidence in his ability to sell the place, so much so that actually listening to anything we had to say, or giving the property more than a cursory glance was clearly either unnecessary or beneath his dignity. However, we didn't have to like him in order for him to sell the pub for us, and his brash confidence was at least somewhat reassuring. He recommended an auction as the way to maximise the price and guarantee a purchaser, and a date was set for early

September. That left us to run the pub through the busiest part of the tourist season but we were once more relatively happy in our work and viewed that prospect without too much alarm.

Over five hundred people asked for the sale particulars from the agents, and over the course of the next few weeks, a succession of possible purchasers arrived at the inn to take a look round. They were a distinctly mixed bunch, ranging from an aristocratic couple who looked and sounded as if they'd taken a wrong turn while searching for a stately home to purchase, to a water board worker and part-time sheep breeder from another dale twenty miles to the south, who looked as if the price of a pint would have been a struggle, let alone the price of a pub.

Sue and I evaluated them all and came up with a short-list of those we thought might be serious bidders. At the head of the list was a couple who, judging by their clothes, jewellery and the top of the range car in which they arrived, wouldn't have any trouble in raising the money, and who seemed genuinely captivated by the place. They came back several times over the next few weeks, constantly saying how eager they were to buy it and begging us not to sell to anyone else before the date of the auction, without at least giving them the chance to match or beat the price.

Our only slight qualms about them were over the amount they both drank. We weren't exactly slow with a corkscrew or a bottle-opener ourselves, but we both knew that running a pub and drinking the contents of one was a guarantee of disaster, and neither of us drank at all when on duty behind the bar, whereas this couple could drink for Britain and every time they called in, they departed at least two, if not three sheets to the wind. Nonetheless, if they wanted to buy the pub as their own private watering hole, we certainly weren't going to discourage them, and we made them the odds on favourites to buy it.

On the day of the auction one of my friends and comrades from the *Good Beer Guide,* the legendary CAMRA Company Secretary, had come up dressed in his best suit – though, as he pointed out to me, 'the description "best suit" implies that the Company Secretary had more than one; truth will best be served by the deletion of the word "best"!' He was there to pose as a would-be purchaser to drive up the price in case there turned out to be only one genuine bidder in the room. I tried hard to avoid thinking about what might happen if there weren't any bidders at all, or if he got carried away with his role and wound up as the highest bidder. In the event his much-appreciated help wasn't needed, though it was a very close call. As the clock ticked round towards the scheduled time of the auction, prompt at twelve noon, virtually all of the people who'd come to view the inn and examine the books over the previous weeks and had then left swearing on their mothers' graves that they'd be back to bid at the auction, had failed to turn up. That included the hard-drinking couple we'd singled out as the most likely purchasers, even though they had been back to see it several times, and extracted a promise from us that we wouldn't sell it privately before the auction without telling them.

Almost the only couple we recognised were Alec and Margaret, the water board worker and part-time sheep breeder and his partner, a part-time barmaid in their local and 'not his wife', according to the inaccurate gossip started by one of our more sharp-tongued locals with a relative near the village where they lived, who still didn't look as if they had two pennies to rub together.

There was also a legendary former owner of the inn, Pat Lisle, who had shed a few stone and was now a shadow of his previous twenty-seven stone self and was clearly thinking of taking on the pub once more, if the price was right. One man who wrote to me after *The Inn at the Top* was published recalled Pat as 'a character if there ever was one. I had some quite shady business dealings with Pat in the early 1980's and he would visit me in an old and battered Rolls Royce; he always reminded me of Amos, the pub manager in Emmerdale Farm, when it first hit our television screens.'

During a highly eventful life, Pat had been by turns a railway porter, a signalman, a bookmaker, an artificial inseminator and a baker. He then became the owner of both a baby clothes shop and a racehorse, and went on to own a string of pubs; as well as the Inn at the Top, he ran the Rookhope Inn at the top of Weardale, and the Queens Head at Thornley, near Peterlee in County Durham. Even when just a humble railway porter – albeit acting as a bookie's runner on the side – he drove a 1949 Bentley. He set himself up as a bookie, much to the irritation of the established book-maker in the area. According to local lore, Pat's bookmaking came to an end when somebody put a very large bet on with him. In those days bookies routinely laid off large bets with one of the large racecourse bookmakers, but unfortunately for Pat, he only had one phone line and someone – presumably his rival – made a call to it and then left his phone off the hook, preventing Pat from dialling out and laying off the bet. The horse won, Pat lost a very large sum of money and that was the end of his bookmaking activities, as he disappeared over the hill, still driving his Bentley.

His continuing taste for the high life undoubtedly contributed to his bankruptcy in 1970, when he blamed that invariably fatal combination of 'drink, fast women, and slow horses'. He then claimed to have given up all three, before taking over a pub in Gloucestershire. When that burned down, he returned to the North-East, battled in vain to obtain planning permission to turn his farmhouse into a hotel and then successfully contested a parish council seat under the slogan 'Wear a smile, Vote for Lisle'. He then stood as the Labour candidate in Richmond, one of the safest Tory seats in the country, this time under a new slogan: 'Never fear, Patrick's here'. When he asked an old farmer from the Dale if he'd be getting his vote, the farmer said 'Will thou hellers like!' ('No' for those who don't speak Tyke) and bet him half a crown (12½p) that he'd lose his deposit. The farmer lost his bet. Pat won half a crown and over twenty per cent of the vote, though he expressed relief that he'd not been elected since 'The way they drink in Parliament, I'd be dead.' Were he to succeed in buying the inn for the second time in his life, one thing we could be certain of was that there would be very few dull moments up there.

A BBC television crew had also arrived that morning, come to film the last act in our drama, just as they had recorded the first one what seemed a different lifetime ago. They set up their cameras and then interviewed us and some of the assembled cast of characters while the clock ticked down to the starting time for the auction. Taking in the half-empty room as the auctioneer approached his temporary podium – an up-turned beer-crate – Sue and I exchanged a look that wasn't far from despair. Although we had paid off the bank loan, we still had the brewery loan and our silent partner to repay. After all this effort, toil and tears, were we now to be stuck with the pub for another year at least, or be forced to sell it for less than we had paid for it? The auctioneer's opening words did nothing to reassure us. No doubt he thought he was being clever – or perhaps, given his overwhelming hubris, he just didn't think at all – but starting off with 'Now, ladies and gentlemen, this isn't the best pub in the world by any means, but we're here to sell it today. We're looking for one of the great eccentrics...' was not exactly designed to inspire confidence in the bidders. If only my Uncle Olaf had been in the market for an inn, because they didn't come any more eccentric than him.

We'd bust a gut to get the trading figures for the previous six months from our accountant in time for the auction and they'd been delivered first thing that morning. They were highly impressive figures, or at least they would have been, had the auctioneer not then followed up his opening remarks by announcing the gross profit as if it were the turnover, thus instantly devaluing the figures by a good fifty per cent. To round off his disastrous preamble, he went on to list just about all of the pub's pitfalls and drawbacks without mentioning any of its attractions, which were not just its value as a tourist attraction and attendant high profitability, but also its location and its uniqueness. Surrounded by the National Park, no one would ever be permitted to build within miles of the place and even if it were to be shut down as an inn and used as a country retreat, let alone run as a thriving business, it should have been worth a fortune for that reason alone.

By now, I was ready to run across the bar, pull the auctioneer off his unstable perch and strangle him in front of a room full of witnesses, but the thought of the life sentence that I would have to serve, plus the faint, but fast-receding prospect that by a miracle someone might still be willing to buy the inn, despite the auctioneer, kept me rooted to the spot. He started the auction by asking for an opening bid of £50,000 but had to drop it to £10,000 before he got one. After that, with Pat Lisle one of those involved, the bidding limped slowly upwards without the need for interventions from my mate from CAMRA, until it stalled at £50,000. It was barely more than we'd paid for it almost two years before, and if it stayed at that price we'd have slaved for two years, invested thousands and knocked a few years off our lives for nothing. Then the lorry driver/part-time sheep farmer from down the Dales, Alec, raised his hand and put in a bid. When the other bidder raised him, he bid again and then again, and when the bidding finally came to a halt, the Inn at the Top had been knocked down to him for £82,500. It seems ludicrously cheap at today's prices – it's back on the market now for a mere £1.3 million, quite a step up from the £2,500 that the owner of the inn back in 1968, George Carter, had said he would take to be rid of it. Even the £82,500 we sold it for was probably only about half what it was actually worth, but the sheer relief that we wouldn't have to carry on slogging away at the pub for months and maybe years to come, lessened the sting of that a little … but only a little.

Predictably enough, the auctioneer was triumphant. 'I really had to sweat blood for that,' he said. 'We did well to get that much for this dump.'

Once more the temptation to grasp him warmly by the throat was almost overwhelming. 'Funnily enough,' I said, when I could finally trust my voice. 'I was just thinking the opposite. God knows what you've been saying to people who contacted you at the office, but perhaps if you hadn't spent the ten minutes before the auction cocking up the figures and denigrating everything about the place, we might have done rather better.' I was wasting my time, of course, for nothing would have punctured the armour of complacency and self-love that was wrapped around him like his camel-hair coat. He gave me a disdainful look and having completed the paperwork, he departed soon afterwards.

We shook hands with the new owners, Alec and Margaret, who seemed more dazed than delighted. 'I have never had a pub before, God knows what made me buy it,' was Alec's first reaction. 'We're eccentrics,' Margaret added, clutching his arm. 'As long as we're together, it doesn't matter.' I tried very hard not to reflect that it was almost exactly what Sue and I had said when we bought the pub less than two years before. 'I was that nervous,' Margaret said, 'that I had my hand in Alec's trouser-pocket! When the price reached £82,500 and he shouted "Aye", I thought "What have we done?"'

We left them to make a leisurely tour of inspection of their purchase, while we tidied up the bar and served a few customers. Among them, arriving hotfoot and slightly the worse for drink, were the couple who we'd been convinced would have been the new owners by now.

'Hello,' the man said. 'Not too late, are we?'

'Well, yes,' I said, pointing at the clock. 'The auction was at twelve noon, just like we told you, and just like it says on the sale particulars you've got in your hand. You are too late. It was sold about an hour ago.'

'Oh honestly,' his wife said. 'I knew we shouldn't have stopped for a drink on the way up here. What are we like?'

I could have told them but for once, words failed even me. While they, as usual, got drunk at one end of the bar, we talked through the process of handing over the pub with its new owners, and then settled in for our last three weeks at the inn.

Alec and Margaret could have sold the inn for a profit without even taking possession of it, because within minutes of them arriving home that afternoon, they said they had fielded a phone call from someone offering them £5,000 above the purchase price and a little later, some different would-be buyers – quite possibly the couple who'd stopped for yet another drink and missed the auction altogether  offered them 10,000 quid profit. However, by now they had got over the shock of having bought the inn and were unshakeable in their determination to take it over and they turned both offers down.

# CHAPTER 15

## Am I Heckers Like!

Three weeks later, all of our friends and regulars came up for a farewell party on our very last night. The farmers' wives brought a buffet with them so that Sue didn't have to cook, and since all the drinks were on us anyway, I didn't have to man the bar and we just let everyone help themselves; not since the discovery of 'continuity' during the filming of the Everest commercial had the farmers emptied their pints with such alacrity. Towards the end of the night – and it was a late one, even by the standards of the Inn at the Top – the farmers' choir serenaded us with a rendition of the local anthem 'Beautiful Dale'. Both of us had tears in our eyes as we listened to it and looked around the circle of faces of the people we'd come to know so well. There were more tears as we said our farewells to them all and exchanged promises to keep in touch and not be strangers. When the last one had disappeared into the night, we took a final starlit walk along the road and then went to bed for the very last time at the Inn at the Top.

As we left the inn the next morning, I at least was not travelling far. I had invested my share of the proceeds from the sale of the pub in a derelict farmhouse just a few miles away in a beautiful part of the upper Dale. Sue had bought a little cottage back near to the place we'd started from a dozen years before, but although we were living fifty miles apart, we kept in regular touch and neither of us was ruling out the possibility that we might get back together one day and build a new future together, though the one absolute certainty was that it wouldn't involve running an inn.

As for the Inn at the Top, unlike us, the couple who bought it proved to have both the necessary capital and the know-how to solve the problems that had bedevilled it for years. Working for the Water Board might have given Alec an 'in' with a company that drilled boreholes for farms and remote places like the Inn at the Top. According to local legend, a dowser was first of all employed and he marched up and down with his hazel wand before indicating the right place to drill, but that may just have been a bit of a rural myth because in fact, if you drill deep enough, you find water almost anywhere, and the first query of most drilling companies is usually 'Where do you want it?'

When they began drilling they found good quality drinking water at a depth of 168 feet. However, so extensive were the old coal workings from the days when the hill on which the Inn at the Top stood was riddled with working mine shafts, levels and galleries, that the borehole they sank had passed through at least two sets of old workings. As a result, a lining had to be fitted in the shaft before any water could be pumped up. For the first time ever, the Inn at the Top now had a reliable water supply. Alec and Margaret also bought a much more powerful generator, solving the inn's other perennial problem at a stroke and over the succeeding years, they re-modelled the bar, repositioning the staircase to the upper floors so that, for the first time ever, there was room to swing a cat behind the bar. Alec also rebuilt the west wall so it no longer turned black with damp every few weeks and eventually even built a large extension to serve as guest bedrooms and a 'bunkhouse' for hikers, complete with a drying room where they could hang their often sodden clothes to dry overnight.

Alec and Margaret's first winter at the inn, though not as savage as the first one we had endured, still saw them cut off by snowdrifts for a six week stretch. The beer froze in the pipes and they had ice 'four inches thick' on the inside of the windows, but such winters failed to put them off. They were clearly made of sterner stuff than me, for along with their three children, they stayed at the inn for the next twenty years. Margaret was the sort of feisty woman who has always thrived at the Inn at the Top – apart from the celebrated Susan Peacock, there was a nineteenth century, pipe-smoking landlady called Old Fanny who, when she ran out of tobacco, would smoke a pipe filled with tea-leaves instead. Margaret had a particular aversion to customers disturbing the peace of the inn by making or taking calls on their mobile phones. Most mobiles wouldn't work up on the hill anyway as they couldn't get a signal there, but those that did were banned. One ring was excused but if the offence was repeated, Margaret had been known to confiscate the phone and add it to the collection already festering in the pickled egg jar on the bar.

Alec and Margaret had to survive some tough years along the way, none more so than 2001 and 2002 when, because of the foot and mouth outbreak, visitor numbers collapsed and even the annual Sheep Show had to be cancelled. 240 Bed and Breakfast bookings were cancelled in 2001 alone, countless other bookings weren't even made in the first place, and casual visitors dried up as roads were closed and walkers told to stay off the moors. The normally bustling inn was deserted by nine every night and their plight was so desperate that they had to let three of the four staff go. Fortunately trade revived once the crisis was over and the inn was soon booming once more.

Although Alec and Margaret finally moved on a few years ago, their successors, Tracy and her partner, Mike, who took over the inn in 2005, have proved to be even better-equipped for the job, and certainly a lot more so than the pair of bungling amateurs who used to run it in the late 1970s and 1980s. In the ad hoc traditions of the Inn at the Top, Mike and Tracy only bought the inn after their plans to buy a place in Scotland fell through. 'We just searched for 'large properties' on the internet and the inn came up,' Tracy said. I immediately said to Mike 'Let's buy it',' and ten minutes later we'd made an appointment.'

Once installed they took delivery of a Hagglund BV206 – an ex-Swedish Army, amphibious tracked vehicle – that was supposed to be capable of 'floating' over the top of snowdrifts. Bought from an army surplus store, the £8,000 cost was more than offset by the avalanche of publicity that the shrewd landlady generated as a result. 'We got it because I'm a Southern wuss,' the Middlesex-born-and-raised Tracy said at the time. 'There was no way I was going to get snowed up in such an isolated place as this. The Met Office said it was going to be the worst winter since 1963 and we believed them. If it snows, we're ready for it.'

Mike and Tracy also have a barn at the rear of the inn as a place to stage music, weddings and other events, including regular live music, but even in their wildest dreams, they could not have imagined the line-up that would appear there as part of the 'Sing Ye From The Hillsides' festival, organised by Cumbrian band British Sea Power. Martin Noble, guitarist with the band, said they had 'stumbled across' the inn while touring. 'We were looking for unusual places to play and we were tipped off about the pub. It is just a magical place.' The festival was to be held outside the inn if the weather was fit but, given the unpredict-ability of the climate at the Inn at the Top, there were contingency plans to transfer to the barn if the wind got up and the weather turned ugly.

They put 200 tickets on sale for the Sing Ye From The Hillsides festival – the maximum number the barn could hold – and they were snapped up in minutes. The Arctic Monkeys' producer, James Ford, who had decided to hold his stag night at the inn, bought thirty tickets for his guests who included Mark Ronson, The Klaxons, and the Arctic Monkeys themselves. So a band that can fill the biggest stadia in the world found themselves playing to 200 people in the back room of an inn on the top of the Pennines!

A score of other bands played during the weekend and as well as the music there was a Yorkshire-style 'Olympics' with events ranging from cracker and doughnut eating contests, egg throwing, potato rolling, a tug-of-war, husky-racing, falconry, duck-herding, a pub quiz and an attempt to record the loudest ever human voice.

Quite what the audience that weekend would have made of the 'rock band' that appeared at the inn from time to time in the nineteenth-century is hard to say, either wild enthusiasm or total bemusement would have been equally possible. The founder of the band was a local farmer with the splendid name of Neddy Dick Alderson. His name showed that he was Neddy the son of Dick Alderson – there were so many Aldersons in the Dale that the only way to distinguish them from each other was by giving each one two names, or a nickname, based on some physical characteristic, like 'Gurt (Big) Bill', or, like 'Dick at Greenses', the name of the farm they occupied.

Things were even more confusing – and even more exotic – in the past. The Muster Roll for the local militia, 'The Loyal Dales Volunteers', at the time of the Napoleonic Wars included no less than eight Thomas Aldersons, who were distinguished from each other by the nicknames Grain Tom, Glouremour Tom, Screamer Tom, Poddish Tom, Tarry Tom, Tish Tom, Tripy Tom, and Trooper Tom. There was also a panoply of other remarkable nicknames including Assy Will Bill, Ayny Jack, Aygill Tom Bill, Becka Jack, Brag Tom, Bullet, Bullock, Jammie, Buck Reuben, Butter Geordie, Bowlaway, Brownsa, Jossy, Cis Will, Corry Joe, Codgy, Cwoaty Jack, Curly, Dickey Tom Johnny, Docken Jammie, Daut, Freestane Jack, Gudgeon Tom, Hed Jack, Awd John, Young John, Jams Jack, Mary Jack, King Jack, Katy Tom Alick, Kit Puke Jock, Kanah Bill, Knocky Gwordie, Lollock Ann Will, Marty Jwoan Ned, Mark Jammie Joss, Moor Close Gwordie, Nettlebed Anty, Peter Tom Willie, Peed Jack, Piper Ralph, Pullan Will, Roberty Will Peg Sam, Rive Rags, Skeb Symy, Slipe, Slodder, Swinny, Spletmeat, Strudgeon Will, Tash and Tazzy Will.

As Neddy Dick was picking his way among the rocks alongside a waterfall called Upper Kisdon Foss one day, he noticed that when one stone that he had dislodged struck another one, it emitted a musical note. Inspired by this, he collected various pieces of stone of assorted shapes and sizes and formed his 'rock band' which could produce a full scale of notes. He then stowed it in the back of his donkey cart and toured the district giving impromptu concerts with his 'band'. If a few rock tunes failed to excite his audiences sufficiently, he was also the proud owner of an American organ to which he had attached the bells collected from old clocks – they just don't make entertainment like that any more!

As well as hosting events by music superstars, since Tracy and Mike took over the inn, they have also persuaded Everest double-glazing to return and film a new commercial there, over twenty years after the first one. Before doing so they supplied the inn with another new set of windows which, come to think of it, puts something of a question mark over their famous slogan: 'You only fit double-glazing once, so fit the best, fit Everest.' However a spokesman for the company insisted that although the old windows had held up well over the years, they were being replaced with a more traditional, carbon-neutral design, aiming to make the pub more environmentally friendly. 'The owners wanted a more traditional look, and we have a wider range of designs on offer now than we did in 1985. The pub has taken quite a battering from the weather in recent years – there really is no better place to demonstrate our feather test.'

The path to the new commercial had not been quite as smooth as the Everest spokesman was suggesting, however. Soon after they took over, Tracy and Mike decided that the windows needed minor repairs and, believing that part of the original television deal I had struck with Everest was that the work had a lifetime guarantee, they contacted the company. A young man from Everest, describing himself as 'an engineer' though bearing a remarkable resemblance to a not very experienced salesman, duly arrived. He said he'd never heard of Ted Moult, knew nothing about a lifetime guarantee and insisted that Tracy and Mike would have to pay up front for any repairs or new windows they wanted.

'You could have knocked me down with the Everest feather when I heard that,' Tracy said.

'We were told that we weren't a priority call-out,' Mike added, 'and it appeared to us that we weren't important to them at all.' If that was indeed the company's attitude, Everest would soon be made to realise their mistake, for Tracy and Mike's collective stubbornness is matched only by their flair for generating publicity: good publicity for the inn and bad publicity for those who fail to live up to their high expectations of them. Everest was about to be conquered once more...

Not long afterwards, researchers on BBC's Watchdog began making some enquiries – 'I don't know how they got to hear about it,' Tracy said, the absolute picture of innocence, 'but they did and soon afterwards things began to happen.' After intensive negotiations a new agreement was reached, under which Tracy and Mike would get a full set of new windows and Everest would get a new advertisement. They even threw in some solar heating panels on the roof as well, and if they would work up there in that semi-arctic climate, they really would work anywhere!

The advertisement showed Ted Moult's successor, ITV sports presenter Craig Doyle, entering the inn, while workers were putting the finishing touches to the improvements. Tracy said that the original advert had 'really caught people's imaginations. About sixty per cent of our customers still ask about it. For example, they will want to know which window was used in the advert. It is great that it struck such a chord – everyone has a different memory of it, and it is an honour to be associated with something that has endured so long. We still have the feather – it takes pride of place in a frame above the bar.'

However, having hung there for twenty years, the famous feather and an accompanying photograph of Ted Moult in action with it disappeared after a stag night at the inn, either stolen by one of the revellers or by another customer using them as cover. Tracy described the photograph and feather as the inn's 'crown jewels' and said 'We are desperately saddened by their loss. Many customers ask about Ted Moult and the feather used in the draught test on the adverts and are always pleased to see the picture beside the window where it was filmed. While Everest has replaced and updated the double glazing, the picture and the feather are irreplaceable.' She promised that no further action would be taken against the thief, provided the feather and photograph were returned.

Sadly, the attempt to appeal to the thief's better nature or tweak his guilty conscience did not persuade him to return either the feather or the picture, both of which are still missing to this day, even though Tracy's partner Mike says he would still offer a reward if anyone ever knew of its whereabouts. However, it would be possible, football-style, to send on a substitute instead. After all, I remember seeing the director picking a feather out of a whole box of them when they were shooting the original Ted Moult commercial, so finding a replacement would not have been too arduous a task.

There was also an echo of the original 'War of the Windows' when, with the new advertisement in the can, it was revealed that, although home-owners do not need to apply for planning permission to install alternative energy equipment, commercial premises do. Since neither the inn's owners nor Everest had applied for planning permission for the alterations, they were now being told that the solar panels might have to be removed, unless retrospective planning consent could be obtained from the local District Council. Landlady Tracy was once more in combative mood as she declared, 'We thought all the paperwork would have been sorted out before Everest came in to do the work. It is unbelievable. I thought the council would have wanted us to do our bit for the climate, but it seems they are more interested in filling out the paperwork. We made sure the panels were put on the back of the building so they would not be intrusive. They came in February and spent five days here doing the work. It would be a shame if the panels do have to come down.'

A council spokesman then replied that: 'The rules that apply to installations like this are not simple, but it is our job to make sure they are followed. We hope to speak to the owners again and help them complete the paperwork.' As a result, following 'a number of discussions with the planning authorities to discuss the installation of solar panels at the inn', Everest were able to announce that though 'the appropriate documentation to seek formal permission was not lodged with the council, this oversight has now been corrected.'

Everest had one further hurdle to clear after one of their advertisements was banned by the Advertising Standards Authority (ASA) for potentially misleading viewers over how much hot water could be generated by their solar panels, but after a hasty amendment of the script, the advert was soon back on the air.

Soon afterwards Tracy, described in her own publicity as 'a little crazy', was firing from the hip again in a battle with what on the face of it was a far more powerful opponent: the multi-national fast food giant KFC, formerly known as Kentucky Fried Chicken. When the inn advertised a 'Family Feast' yuletide special – a traditional Christmas dinner with all the trimmings – on its website, Tracy received a threatening letter from a lawyer representing Kentucky Fried Chicken (Great Britain) Limited. The appropriately named Giles Pratt from the law firm of Freshfields Bruckhaus Deringer, claimed that 'Family Feast' was a registered trade mark of KFC, describing the company's fat, salt and sugar-laden cardboard 'bucket' of fried chicken and chips, with side orders and a large plastic bottle of cola – that's my description, not theirs, in case you hadn't guessed. The Pratt claimed that the inn was 'committing a grave infringement' of trademark law by using the term and threatened legal action if the words were not removed from the inn's website at once. 'In the circumstances,' he wrote, 'please confirm that you will adopt a different name to describe your meal deals.'

Tracy had been caught out by an April Fools'

Day prank earlier in the year when two of her locals sent her a letter, informing her that a new pub was to be built seventy yards further up the hill which would therefore be the new highest inn in England. At first she thought the letter from KFC's solicitors was another attempt to pull her leg, but she was then informed by the Pratt that it was 'no laughing matter' – you could have fooled me Giles. That her customers disagreed with his opinion was demonstrated when Tracy took another call from someone who claimed to be a lawyer representing Holiday Inn. He told her that the word 'inn' was a registered trademark of the company and that she was breaking the law by using it. Tracy replied with a two word expression that no one has ever been able to trademark and then put the phone down.

When she was asked whether she was planning to accede to the KFC lawyer's demands and change the website, Tracy responded in true Yorkshire fashion: 'Am I heckers like! I'm baffled and lost for words – and I'm never lost for words. We're out here in the middle of nowhere and we're being bullied by some big American company, but we don't back down easily.'

In fact, to someone with Tracy's gift for generating publicity for the inn, KFC's 'secret recipe' of threats and legal bluster was manna from heaven. An 'adrenaline-fuelled' few days followed, during which another firm of solicitors volunteered to fight her case free of charge and an article in *The Times* led to a snowstorm of other media coverage. Kentucky Fried Chicken found itself well and truly stuffed, and revealed as the ludicrous corporate bully it was in this case. Under the glare of negative publicity it was forced to back-down and drop the threat of legal action.

Struggling to rescue something from the train-wreck, a spokesman for KFC (GB) Limited said that 'KFC has to protect its trademarks against those who seek to trade off its brand. KFC has spoken to Mrs. Daly ... and confirmed that it will not take this case any further. This means that Mrs. Daly can continue to use the phrase 'Family Feast' on the pub's Christmas menu. It's an unusual situation that has been blown out of all proportion,' he added, failing to note that it was KFC themselves who had done the blowing out of all proportion. Magnanimous in victory, albeit with her tongue firmly in her cheek, Tracy told the media that she had 'Invited KFC to come here and have a meal and shake hands,' and then she sat back and counted the cash as torrents of customers, drawn by the media coverage, kept rolling up at the inn. Thanks to KFC, all her Christmases had truly come at once!

Although I'd left the inn, I was still living nearby, albeit in a rather less unforgiving environment, having bought one of Lordy's surplus farmhouses down in the Dale. Lest I be accused of hypocrisy in doing so, I have to point out that the house had been standing empty for five years before I bought it. However, although I was still in the area, I didn't go back to the inn for quite a few years, not so much because of the memories it held, though that was certainly a factor, but because I didn't want the new owners to feel I was looking over their shoulders all the time, or acting as a focus for any complaints about the way that they were running it, and, inevitably, there were a few, because if there's one thing that pub customers – and I speak as one – love more than a good pint, it's a good moan about something! Once the owners had become part of the furniture, I felt able to go back and I called in from time to time, had a drink with them, and went for a nostalgic walk around the moorland I knew so well. And every year, although work commitments often prevented it, I tried to get back for the sheep show, to see old friends, and sit up on the fellside listening to the Lofthouse and Middlesmoor silver band playing 'Beautiful Dale'.

Sue and I never did get back together. I've been very happily married to the second Mrs Hanson – a canny Geordie lass – for well over twenty years now and we have a grown up son and daughter of whom we're inordinately proud as well. Many years have now passed since I embarked on that great adventure at the Inn at the Top, but despite the failure of my own personal dreams and ambitions up there, my affection for the inn, the Dale and its inhabitants remains undiminished by the passing years.

Whatever else they might be, I hope that 'The Inn at the Top' and 'Pigs Might Fly' together make up a fitting celebration of a remarkable place, some extraordinary characters, a long-ago era, and a way of life that was disappearing even then and is now just a fast-fading memory. Despite the hardships and the traumas we faced along the way, we were fortunate – blessed even – to have known and owned the Inn at the Top in the last years of an era that has now vanished and will not return.

Thanks to the efforts of Alec and Margaret and, more recently, Mike and Tracy – though after she and Mike got married (finally!) in 2014, she now prefers to be known as Louise – the Inn at the Top is immeasurably improved from the ramshackle, belt and braces days when we ran it, but something has also been lost along the way. Much of the character, and many of the characters that made the pub so unique have faded and gone. Like Susan Peacock before them, Faith, Dick at Greenses, Clifford, Bill at Thorns, Jed, Reuben, Michael, Alwyn, Pat Jack, Gurt Bill Up T'Steps – whose nickname was changed to Bungalow Bill after he moved to single storey accommodation – Jimmy, Denis, Laurie, Bob, Jack, Willie, and many, many others, have gone to meet their maker and, perhaps inevitably, their successors tend to be cut from less colourful cloth.

For all our own naiveté, inexperience and occasional downright incompetence, we can also take pride in the fact that we rescued the pub from its decades-long downward spiral, began the work of restoration and rebuilding that our successors continued and completed, and in the process, helped to turn it into, not just a local, but a national and even international institution. The Inn at the Top is the highest pub in Britain – higher than the Cat & Fiddle, the Jamaica Inn, the Kirkstone Pass, the Isle of Skye and all the other false claimants to the title. It's one of the most famous pubs in the country, attracting visitors from all over Britain and the wider world beyond, and its name is ... well, you've worked that out by now, haven't you?

This Large Print Book for the partially sighted, who cannot read normal print, is published under the auspices of

## THE ULVERSCROFT FOUNDATION